Encountering Jesus Throughout the Bible

Encountering Jesus Throughout the Bible

by Sylvia Bambola

Heritage Publishing House

Copyright © 2021 by Sylvia Bambola. All rights reserved. No part of this book may be used or reproduced in any manner whatsoever without written permission of the publisher.

For information contact:
Heritage Publishing House
heritagepubhouse@gmail.com

ISBN: 978-09657389-3-4

Unless otherwise indicated, all Scriptures taken from Holy Bible, King James version, Cambridge, 1769.

Also by Sylvia Bambola

Non-Fiction
The Coming Deception
12 Questions New Christians Frequently Ask
Following the Blood Trail from Genesis to Revelation

Fiction:
Mercy at Midnight
The Babel Conspiracy
The Daughters of Jim Farrell
The Salt Covenants
Rebekah's Treasure
Return to Appleton
Waters of Marah
Tears in a Bottle
Refiner's Fire

To
My Children and Grandchildren
With Love

Table of Contents

Introduction 11
Creator 13
Light 25
Son of God 41
The Great I AM 63
Savior 77
Bread of Life 89
Warrior 95
Rock 103
Son of Man 125
Messiah 143
Shepherd 175
Healer 185
Bridegroom 197
Priest 211
Prince of Peace 229
King 239
Judge 277

Introduction

The Bible is an inexhaustible well of truth. I'm convinced that a lifetime isn't long enough to search out all its mysteries and treasure. Its depth and integrity are breathtaking. How can something, comprised of sixty-six books and penned over hundreds of years by forty different authors, be so cohesive and accurate, and validate each other? It can't. Not without the guidance of God Himself.

For me, it's a constant source of adventure, wonderment, and delight. But I think the most pleasant surprise was discovering how pervasive Jesus is throughout the Bible. He is literally everywhere, showing up as Creator, Bread, Savior, Bridegroom and more. And each appearance displays additional facets of His character and nature, His beauty, power, love, gentleness, and glory. He is altogether lovely and wonderful beyond words.

But how to convey this in a book? That was the question. Mentioning Jesus' appearance, chapter by chapter, would give snippets rather than a broad comprehensive picture of each facet of His identity. The best way forward seemed to be to take each encounter as they occurred in Scripture, then develop it by showing how these threads from the Old Testament carry into the New Testament, thereby providing a more cohesive picture.

As you take the journey with me and encounter Jesus' diverse aspects, I pray believers will fall deeper in love with Him and that non-believers will fall in love with Him for the first time. No one deserves it more.

Enjoy the adventure!

Creator

Jesus created everything.

In Genesis 1:1-29, as God created heaven and earth, the phrase *"And God said"* is found ten times, indicating God created everything by **speaking** it into existence, through the power of His creative Word. And the fact that God said it ten times is also significant. Numbers in the Bible have meaning. God used them to impart both practical and spiritual truths.

So, what does the number ten tells us? First, it is used worldwide in the "base ten" such as in our decimal system, providing universal mathematical balance. But the spiritual implications are also impressive, though too lengthy and unnecessary for this study. The important thing to understand is that the number ten indicates God's Divine order and government, as reflected in the Ten Commandments, as well as indicating perfect balance. It signifies His perfect order during creation, including the perfection of creation itself.

But how does Jesus figure into this? Amazingly, **He** was the Creator, and created everything in union with God the Father and Holy Spirit. John 1:1-3 states, *"In the beginning was the Word, and the Word was with God, and the Word was God. The same was in the beginning with God. **All*** *things were made by him; and without him was not any thing made that was made."*

John 1:14-17 clarifies this further. *"And the Word was made flesh, and dwelt among us (and we beheld his glory, the glory as of the only begotten of the Father) full of grace and truth. John bare witness to him, and cried, saying, This was he of whom I spake, He that cometh after me is preferred before me: for he was before me. And of his fulness have all received, and grace for grace. For the law was given by Moses, but grace and truth came by Jesus Christ."*

Here we see that the Word, this creative power, is none other than Jesus, the living, breathing **WORD** of God made flesh. That's why the Bible, God's Word, has the power to change lives. Hebrews 4:12 says, *"For the word of God is quick, and powerful, and sharper than any twoedged sword, piercing even to the dividing asunder of soul and spirit, and of the joints and marrow, and is a discerner of the thoughts and intents of the heart."* God's Word can reach those deep places in us that no other person or thing can. And by doing so, it can correct and change us.

But that's not all. Though Jesus did, indeed, make everything, Hebrews 1:3 tells us He also sustains everything while sitting at the right hand of God the Father. *"Who being the brightness of his glory, and the express image of his person, and* **upholding all things by the word of his power***, when he had by himself purged our sins, sat down on the right hand of the Majesty on high."*

In the above Scripture, "word" is *rhema* in Greek, and means "utterance." "Power" is *dunamis*, meaning, "force, miraculous power." From *dunamis* we get the word dynamite. It's a strong power word, a word rooted in and which proceeds from authority, muscle, dominance, force. *Dunamis* is the type of power that can do the impossible. In other words, the only reason our planet, indeed, the entire universe, remains intact is because Jesus is holding it together by the Word of His **power**. By His power He speaks things into existence. By His power He holds them together. If He should speak a different Word, everything would change.

Ephesians 3:9 also tells us that Jesus partnered with God to create everything. *"And to make all men see what is the fellowship of the mystery, which from the beginning of the world hath been hid in God, who **created** all things by Jesus Christ."*

Colossians 1:16 explains even further. *"For by him (Jesus) were all things **created**, that were in heaven, and that are in earth, visible and invisible, whether they be thrones, or dominions, or principalities, or powers: all things were **created** by him, and for him."* So, not only was everything created by Jesus, but everything was also actually created **for** Him.

After the apostle John was taken to heaven, he saw twenty-four elders and four beasts worshipping Jesus in Revelation 4:11 and heard them saying, *"Thou are worthy, O Lord, to receive glory and honour and power: for **thou hast created all things**, and for thy **pleasure** they are and were* *created."* John witnessed Jesus being acknowledged and praised as Creator of **all** things. This passage again confirms that all things were specifically created for Jesus' pleasure. Jesus delights in His creation and that means not only in the beautiful world around us but in each individual.

Moses, in his Deuteronomy 32 song, chided the Israelites for their past idolatry and predicted their future idolatry. In verse 18 he said, *"Of the Rock that begat thee thou art unmindful, and hast forgotten God that formed thee."* Jesus is the Rock, as we will see in a later chapter, and here Moses is referring to the Rock as Creator. Moses is saying that the Rock begat Israel. That word "begat" is *yalad* in Hebrew and means "to bear young, birth, to act as a midwife." This word tells us two things about Jesus. First, He is the Creator of mankind. Second, He served as "midwife" to Israel and birthed her as a nation.

Even as far back as Isaiah 43:15, we see Jesus claiming to be Creator. *"I am the LORD, your Holy One, the **Creator** of Israel, your **King**."* It is Jesus Who is King of Israel. It is Jesus Who will return after the seven-year Tribulation to claim the throne of David and rule for a thousand years. But in this verse, He also claimed to be Creator, specifically the Creator of the nation of Israel. Here that word "Creator" is *bara* in Hebrew and means, "to create, make, Creator, choose, dispatch." Like Deuteronomy 32:18, this verse tells us Jesus not only created mankind, but He also created Israel to be a special nation over which He Himself will rule as King during the millennial kingdom.

Jesus, Himself, in Revelation 3:14 acknowledged He is Creator by saying, "*These things sayith the Amen, the faithful and true witness,* **the beginning of the creation** *of God.*"

J.R. Church and Gary Stearman wrote a wonderful book entitled, *The Mystery of the Menorah*. In it they talked about the seven-branch candlestand like the golden menorah that once stood in the Jewish Temple, and how, in Revelation 1:13, John saw Jesus standing amid the seven candlesticks thus picturing Him as the middle or Servant Candle from which all other candles in the menorah were lit. In the same way, Jesus—The Word, The Creator—is the center of everything, as well as the Light of the world.

J.R. Church and Gary Stearman also talked about the different menorahs in the Bible. But here's the one that blows my mind. It's in Genesis 1:1 *"In the beginning God created the heavens and the earth."* In Hebrew, that sentence is made up of only seven words making it a word menorah. And in the very center of that sentence, in the position of the servant candle, is the first and last letter of the Hebrew alphabet, *aleph* and *tav*. Rabbis can't adequately explain why those two letters are there, but when translated into Greek it becomes abundantly clear. In Greek, they become *Alpha* and *Omega* which is what Jesus called Himself three different times in Revelation:

"*I am Alpha and Omega, the beginning and the ending.*"
Revelation 1:8

Encountering Jesus Throughout the Bible

"I am Alpha and Omega, the first and the last." Revelation 1:11

"I am Alpha and Omega, the beginning and the end, the first and the last." Revelation 22:13

Jesus, the Word, used the alphabet to describe Himself. He is the first and last, the beginning and the end, and everything in between. He is the author and finisher of all things. And He was in the very center of creation. What an amazing picture!

And oh, how wonderfully His creation reflects His generous nature. The world is full of diversity. Look at all the various plants, animals, and people. Even sunsets are different. Jesus has created incredible beauty, a reflection of His own beauty. And because He is Creator and we are made in His image (Genesis 1:26), we are also creative. First and foremost is the ability to create children. But our creative abilities don't end there. Think of art, music, photography, literature, movies—all creative works. But there are other ways to be creative, too, such as making interesting meals or desserts, decorating a home or sewing one's own clothes, creating beautiful flower gardens, creating jobs for others or creating organizational support for those jobs, etcetera. The list is endless because everyone has some creative ability. Even in this, God shows His kindness. He has not left us out of the creative process.

Additional references to God as Creator of heaven and earth:

Isaiah 40:26, *"Lift up your eyes on high, and behold* (God) *who hath **created** these things, that bringeth out their host by number; he called them all by names by the greatness of his might for that he is strong in power; not one faileth."*

Isaiah 42:5, *"Thus saith God the LORD, he that **created** the heavens, and stretched them out; he that spread forth the earth, and that which cometh out of it; he that giveth breath unto the people upon it, and spirit to them that walk therein."*

Isaiah 45:12, *"I have **made** the earth, and **created** man upon it: I even my hands, have stretched out the heavens, and all their host have I commanded."*

Additional references to God as Creator of mankind:

Aside from Isaiah 45:5,12, here are other references to God as Creator of man, leaving no doubt how we got here and refuting the idea we evolved from a primordial soup.

Psalm 100:3, *"Know ye that the LORD he is God: it is **he that hath made us**, and not we ourselves; we are this people, and the sheep of his pasture."*

Isaiah 44:24, *"Thus saith the LORD, thy redeemer, and **he that formed thee from the womb**, I am the LORD that maketh all things; that stretcheth forth the heavens alone; that spreadeth abroad the earth by myself."*

Jeremiah 1:5, *"**Before I** (God) **formed thee in the belly** I knew thee; and before thou camest forth out of the womb I sanctified thee, and I ordained thee a prophet unto the nations."* This specifically refers to Jeremiah but implies that God forms all of us in the womb and ordains us for individual and specific purposes. This is a strong indictment against abortion. Every child is precious to God and He has a unique purpose for each one. How many scientists destined to find cures for diseases; how many powerful, impactful teachers; how many brave, life-saving police; or nurturing, loving homemakers and the like were destroyed in the womb leaving our world poorer for it?

Other Scriptures regarding God's creative Word:

Jesus in Matthew 4:4 said, *"It is written man shall not live by bread alone but by every **word** that proceedeth out of the mouth of God."*

The phrase, *"done according to the **word** of the Lord,"* in both the Old and New Testament, is repeated over and over, because men of God knew that if God said it—it was reliable, powerful, and could be trusted. And it was done.

God said in Isaiah 55:11, *"My **word** . . . shall not return unto me void, but it shall accomplish that which I please and it shall prosper in the thing where to I sent it."*

Psalm 119:89 says, *"**Forever**, O Lord, thy **word** is settled in Heaven."* And forever means forever. God's Word will never change. It will never become obsolete. It will always be valid and powerful.

Jesus said in Matthew 24:35, *"Heaven and earth shall pass away, but my **words** shall not pass away."*

Though God's Word will stand forever, there will come a time after His one-thousand-year reign when Creator Jesus will say the word and create a new heaven and earth. *"And I (John) saw a new heaven and a new earth: for the first heaven and the first earth were passed away; and there was no more sea. And I John saw the holy city, new Jerusalem, coming down from God out of heaven, prepared as a bride adorned for her husband."* (Revelation 21:1-2)

Our words have power.

Because we are made in the image and likeness of God our words also have creative power. Even appropriating our salvation requires not only faith but words. Romans 10:9 says, *"if thou shalt confess with thy mouth the Lord Jesus and shalt believe in thine heart that God hath raised him from the dead, thou shalt be saved."*

Proverbs 18:21 says, *"death and life are in the power of the tongue and they that love it shall eat the fruit thereof."* Our words have consequences and will produce a harvest we will be forced to eat, whether good or bad. They have the power to steer the very course of our lives. Often, we get what we say. That expression about having to "eat our words" is true. If our words are full of doubt and fear, we will defeat ourselves.

Our words can also impact others, for good or bad. One example is Karen Carpenter, a famous singer during the late '60s to early '80s. Because someone called her, "Richard's chubby little sister," she began years of extreme dieting and ended up tragically dying in 1983 from heart failure caused by anorexia. Just that one little sentence changed her life and lead to her destruction.

Our words are so powerful that Jesus warned in Matthew 12:36 that *"every idle word that men shall speak, they shall give account thereof in the day of judgment."* That word "idle" means, "barren, without life, useless, lazy." So, if our words don't produce life, they are idle, barren, useless and can produce death. And we will be held accountable.

We need to understand that life and death truly are in the power of our words. Therefore, it's good to end the chapter by highlighting a few Bible verses regarding the power of our tongue.

What the Bible says regarding the tongue of death:

Psalm 10:7 pertains to the speech of the wicked, *"His mouth is full of cursing and deceit and fraud. Under his tongue is mischief and vanity."*

Psalm 52:2, also regarding evil speech, says, *"Thy tongue deviseth mischiefs; like a sharp razor, working deceitfully."* A sharp razor cuts, hurts, can destroy, and even kill. This applies to what we say about ourselves as well as others. Someone I knew repeatedly said that every December she always got sick. And that's exactly what happened. Her words became a self-fulling prophecy. They became a razor that allowed Satan to make her ill the end of every year. And razors can not only hurt, destroy, and kill health, they can also hurt, destroy, and kill marriages, incentive, love, fellowship, and the like.

We damage ourselves by confessing things like, "I'll never have anything," or "I'll never get a good job," or "No one likes me," etcetera. These are words that pull down rather than build up and can cause defeat in our life.

And what about our words spoken to, about, or over others? If a parent constantly tells his child, "You'll never amount to anything," or "You're lazy, stupid," etcetera, chances are that child will conform to the image of his parent's words.

What the Bible says regarding the tongue of life:

Proverbs 10:20, *"The tongue of the just is a choice silver."* Silver is a precious metal and has value. Therefore, speaking words of encouragement, words of life, is precious and valuable.

Proverbs 12:18 says that *"the tongue of the wise is health."* That word "health" in Hebrew means, "medicine, deliverance, cure, remedy." A wise person uses his tongue to speak God's Word over themselves, over others, and over situations, and is like medicine that can deliver, cure, or remedy a situation. It can also bring hope and healing to a person.

Proverbs 15:4, *"a wholesome tongue is a tree of life."* Wow! A tree of life! That means it sustains, nourishes, shelters and protects.

The above are just a few examples. But they should be enough to help us understand that words matter. The old saying, "sticks and stones may break my bones, but words will never hurt me," couldn't be more wrong.

May our Creator, who created everything by His Word, help us to use our own words for His glory and for the good of ourselves and others. May He help us guard our mouths and speak only those things that bring life.

Light

Seeing Jesus as Light in the Old Testament:

When it comes to Jesus, foreshadowing and symbolism often overlap. He is so richly and prolifically revealed in the Bible that it's difficult to separate it all. Jesus as Light of the world is a case in point. In the last chapter, we saw that Jesus was Creator and that He literally appeared in Genesis 1:1 as a word menorah, as the Servant Candle, the One not only in the center of creation, but the very light of the world and from which all spiritual illumination comes.

Genesis 1:3 tells us, *"And God said, Let there be **light**: and there was **light**."* This light does not refer to the sun, moon, or stars because they are created or recreated in Genesis 1:14-18. Rather, the light in Genesis 1:3 is the very light and power of God's Word spoken into the darkness. As we have seen, Jesus is the Word, and with that Word comes light and power. Here God is NOT creating Jesus but releasing Him, the eternal existent Light and Word, to begin creation/recreation.

John 1:6-9 clarified this, *"There was a man sent from God, whose name was John* (referring to John the Baptist). *The same came for a witness, to bear witness of the **Light**, that all men through him might believe. He was not the **Light**, but was* *sent to bear witness of that* **Light.** *That was the true* **Light,** *which lighteth every man that cometh into the world."*

It was John the Baptist's job to prepare the way and bear witness that Jesus was not only the Messiah but the light that entered this world to dispel the darkness and bring spiritual illumination to mankind.

And John in 1 John 1:5 boldly declared that, *"God is* **light."** James 1:17 declared that God is the *"Father of Lights."* And Ecclesiastes 2:13 tells us that *"light excelleth darkness,"* meaning that light is far superior to darkness.

John, in John 1:1-3, talked about the Word (Jesus) being the Creator, how all things were made by Him. In verse 4-5 John also talked about Jesus being the light. *"In him (Jesus, the Word) was life; and the life was the* **light** *of men. And the* **light** *shineth in darkness; and the darkness comprehended it not."* Jesus, the Creator, was the very light, power, and energy of creation.

In fact, God is compared to light throughout the Bible. Exodus 13:21 tells us, *"And the LORD went before them* (the Israelites) *by day in a pillar of a cloud, to lead them the way; and by night in a pillar of fire, to give them* **light***; to go by day and night."* It was Jesus, the light of the world, who guided the Israelites throughout their journey in the wilderness, the very light that went before them.

In the story of Job, we see how Satan killed Job's children, destroyed his possessions, then covered him with oozing sores, all to get him to turn from God. And Job's friends didn't help. They were full of unwanted advice, accusing Job of everything from unconfessed sins to hypocrisy. All the while, Job had difficulty understanding why this was happening to him. He thought about the sin in the world and how the wicked often seem to go unpunished. In chapter 24:13 he said, *"They (sinners) are of those that rebel against the **light**; they know not the ways thereof, nor abide in the paths thereof."* He implied that sinners walked in darkness, while light reflected the wisdom and holiness of God. So, Job equated God with light.

Further on, a self-pitying Job thought about how prosperous he had once been and said in Job 29:2-3, *"Oh that I were as in months past, as in the days when God preserved me; When his candle shined upon my head, and when by **his light** I walked through darkness."* Job acknowledged that it was God, Who in the past not only prospered him but preserved him from trouble and Whose light enabled him to walk through darkness and in spiritual illumination.

The Psalms also have a lot to say about God and light. I will only cover a few.

In Psalm 18:28 David declared, *"For thou wilt light my candle: the LORD my God will enlighten my darkness."* David was acknowledging that it's the light of God that gives us spiritual insight, that keeps us from walking in darkness.

David added to this theme in Psalm 27:1, *"The LORD is my **light** and my salvation; whom shall I fear? The LORD is* *the strength of my life; of whom shall I be afraid?"* Because of God's light, His illumination, we have nothing to fear. Not only will He guide us out of darkness, but He will enable us to live in that light by strengthening us. In short, God does it all.

Then in Psalm 36:9, David further declared, *"For with thee (God) is the fountain of life: in thy **light** shall we see light."* Only by God's light can we become enlightened and see light ourselves.

One of my favorite Scriptures is Psalm 119:105 and it couldn't be any clearer, *"Thy word is a lamp unto my feet, and a **light** unto my path."* Jesus, of course, is both the Word made flesh and the light. Everything we need is found in Him. It's through His Word, His light, that we can navigate this dark world successfully, and with integrity and holiness.

And here's more good news. Psalm 119:130 says, *"The entrance of thy words giveth **light**; it giveth understanding unto the **simple**."* That means we all qualify. We don't need ten degrees behind our name. No matter how simple we are, God can teach us and help us understand His Word. He can also help us apply it to our life, thereby enabling us to walk in light rather than in darkness. Truly, He is a merciful and wonderful God!

Moving on, we learn in Proverbs 4:18 that, *"the path of the **just** is as the shining **light**, that shineth more and more unto the perfect day."* If we follow God, the light of the world, and His ways, His light in us will begin to shine brighter and brighter. Why? Because we are being conformed into His likeness and since He is light, we reflect Him. Jesus, in Luke 16:8, called believers, *"children of **light**."* And in Matthew 5:14 He called the church (those true believers in Jesus), *"the **light** of the world."* That's only because we carry His light in us. Indeed, the Kingdom of God is a Kingdom of Light.

In Isaiah 2:4-5, Isaiah prophesied of the coming Messiah as King when men shall, *"beat their swords into plowshares,"* and exhorted Israel to, *"come ye, and let us walk in the **light** of the LORD."* Jesus is the Messiah that Isaiah talked about. And when Jesus rules and reigns for a thousand years on earth, His light will cover the earth.

Isaiah 60:19-20 confirmed this and spoke of Messiah's reign as King of kings and Lord of lords and what it would be like. *"The sun shall be no more thy light by day; neither for brightness shall the moon give light unto thee: but the LORD shall be unto thee an everlasting **light**, and thy God thy glory. Thy sun shall no more go down; neither shall thy moon withdraw itself: for the LORD shall be thine everlasting **light**, and the days of thy mourning shall be ended."* What an amazing time that will be! Jesus' light is so great there will be no need for any other.

But Isaiah also gave this warning, *"woe unto them that call evil good, and good evil; that put darkness for **light**, and **light** for darkness; that put bitter for sweet, and sweet for bitter!"* (Isaiah 5:20). Isn't that what we are seeing today? People proclaiming the very things God has called evil, as being good? One day they'll have a lot to answer for, especially since they have used their power and influence to lead many astray.

Isaiah 9:1-2 further prophesied that when Messiah came something wonderful would happen. *"The people that walked in darkness have seen a **great light**: they that dwell in the land of the shadow of death, upon them hath the **light** shined."* And that's just what happened when Jesus came and died for our sins. He was the great light. He was the one Who saved us from spiritual death. Because of Him we have a glorious future and the promise of everlasting life with Him.

Isaiah 42:6-7 also talks about the Messiah and says, *"I the LORD have called thee in righteousness, and will hold thine hand, and will keep thee, and give thee for a covenant of the people, for a **light of the Gentiles**. To open the blind eyes, to bring out the prisoners from the prison, and them that sit in darkness out of the prison house."* Jesus is that light. He also freed us captives from the prison and darkness of sin and brought us out into His marvelous light.

Isaiah repeated this in Isaiah 49:6, *"I will also give thee* (Messiah Jesus) *for a **light to the Gentiles**, that thou mayest be my salvation unto the end of the earth."*

And though Jesus has since ascended into heaven, how wonderful is God's promise that His light would reside in His church, in the body of Christ! *"Arise, shine; for thy **light** is come, and the glory of the LORD is risen upon thee. For, behold, the darkness shall cover the earth, and gross darkness the people: but the LORD shall arise upon thee, and* *his glory shall be seen upon thee. And the Gentiles shall come to thy **light**, and kings to the brightness of thy rising,"* (Isaiah 60:1-3). God has given the church a great calling—that of reflecting His light in a dark and dying world. But the church can't reflect His light if it compromises and tries to be like the world. Yet, that is the temptation in these last days. Oh, may the church remain faithful to the end!

Going on to the New Testament:

Sometime after Jesus returned from His forty-days in the wilderness He went to Capernaum and gave this reason for doing so, *"That it might be fulfilled which was spoken by Esaias the prophet, saying . . . The people which sat in darkness **saw great light**; and to them which sat in the region and shadow of death **light** is sprung up,"* (Matthew 4:14, 16). Jesus was speaking of Himself. The Scripture He fulfilled was Isaiah 9:1-2. He was that great light Who would light the way back to the Father.

In Luke 1:78-79, this is repeated in different words. *"Through the tender mercy of our God; whereby the dayspring from on high* (Jesus) *hath visited us. To give **light** to them that sit in darkness and in the shadow of death, to guide our feet into the way of peace."*

After Jesus took Peter, James, and John to the mountain of transfiguration, He was changed before their eyes. Matthew 17:2 described Him this way: *"his face did shine as the sun, and his raiment was white as the **light**."* What the apostles saw was Jesus not only engulfed in light, but light emanating from Him. What an amazing picture of

Jesus' glory, beauty, holiness, His very perfection! He is light itself.

Nicodemus, a Pharisee and ruler, was a man of high standing. He was also interested in the teachings of Jesus. This created a problem. How could he learn more about this unusual man without offending his peers and injuring his reputation or position in the community? But if he sought Jesus at night no one would know, no one would see, especially those in his crowd who opposed the Nazarene. Nicodemus must have thought if he were to support this man publicly, a man who many claimed was the Messiah, he first needed to know more about him.

Jesus knew Nicodemus' weakness as a people pleaser, just like He knows our weaknesses. But always gracious to sincere seekers of Truth, Jesus conferred with Nicodemus. Among the many things Jesus told him was this in John 3:19-21, *"And this is the condemnation, that **light** is come into the world, and men loved darkness rather than **light**, because their deeds were evil. For every one that doeth evil hateth the **light**, neither cometh to the **light**, lest his deeds should be reproved. But he that doeth truth cometh to the **light**, that his deeds may be made manifest, that they are wrought in God."*

There is irony here. Nicodemus had come to Jesus in the dark of night and now Jesus was telling him that **He** is light, and that Nicodemus's deeds would *"be made manifest."* That word "manifest" is *phaneroo* in Greek and means, "make public, to render apparent, declare, show." In other words, if Nicodemus wanted to follow The Light, it would become apparent. It would become illuminated. He wouldn't be able to hide it. The very people Nicodemus feared and tried to fool, would find out.

Jesus' statement is also illuminating in other ways. He's the light that has come into the world. His purpose: to dispel darkness. But here's the kicker. Jesus put His finger on why some people would reject Him. It's because they don't want the light to shine on them. They don't want their evil deeds exposed because they don't want to stop doing them. And they don't want to be held accountable for them, either.

In John 8:12, Jesus makes it even plainer by saying, *"I am the **light** of the world: he that followeth me shall not walk in darkness, but shall have the **light of life**."* Followers of Jesus must acknowledge and confess their sins. They can't cover them up or live a deceitful life. Jesus' light won't allow it.

Jesus also said in John 9:5, *"As long as I am in the world, I am the **light** of the world."* And then in John 12:35-36, *"Yet a little while is the **light** (Jesus) with you. Walk while ye have the **light**, lest darkness come upon you: for he that walketh in darkness knoweth not wither he goeth. While ye have **light**, believe in the **light**, that ye may be the children of **light**."* And in John 12:46 Jesus said, *"I am come a **light** into the world, that whosoever believeth on me should not abide in darkness."*

How rich is God's promise to us! And how wonderful to know that Jesus will, with His light, dispel every darkness in our life if we believe in Him.

I find the story of Saul of Tarsus interesting. He was no ordinary Jew. He was highly educated, having studied under the esteemed Rabbi Gamaliel (Acts 22:3). He was also zealous for God. That combination made him dangerous to the new followers of Christ. We first see him guarding the clothes of the executioners as he watched them stone Stephen (Acts 7:58). Persecution of Christians had already begun, and Saul was at the forefront. Acts 8:3 tells us, *"he* (Saul) *made havock of the church, entering into every house, and haling* (following, trailing) *men and women committed them to prison."* While Acts 9:1 says that Saul breathed *"out threatening and slaughter against the disciples of the Lord."* So, Saul not only put believers in prison, he killed them.

Saul did all this because he believed this new religion was blasphemous. I think it's fair to say Saul was not only zelous but arrogant. When it came to religious traditions and matters concerning God, Saul thought he knew it all and had it all together. This made him believe he was duty-bound to destroy everyone who disagreed with him. In other words, *he* would rid the nation of this blasphemy. Religious zeal and arrogance have been responsible for persecution throughout the ages. Saul's problem was that he was religious but not spiritual. He knew the law, the rules and regulations, he knew about God, but he didn't **know** God.

This was his condition as he traveled to Damascus carrying letters from the high priest giving him authority to round up and jail believers in Jesus. But something happened, *"as he journeyed, he came near Damascus: and suddenly there shined round about him a **light** from heaven: and he fell to the earth, and heard a voice saying unto him, Saul, Saul, why persecutes thou me? And he said, Who art thou, Lord? And the Lord said, I am Jesus whom thou persecutest."* (Acts 9:3-5)

In this Divine encounter, Jesus presented Himself as light. And after "seeing The Light," Saul was never the same. He became an ardent, fearless, and totally sold-out disciple. He also became the most prolific writer of the New Testament, showing that a real encounter with Jesus can change anyone.

Jesus commissioned Saul, who became known as Paul, to be an apostle to the Gentiles, and in Acts 26:18, spelled out exactly what He wanted him to do. *"To open their (Gentiles') eyes, and to turn them from darkness to **light** (to Jesus) and from the power of Satan unto God, that they may receive forgiveness of sins, and inheritance among them which are sanctified by faith that is in me* (Jesus).

Paul got it, and later in Romans 13:12 said, *"The night is far spent, the day is at hand: let us therefore cast off the works of darkness, and let us put on the armour of **light**."* He understood that Jesus, The Light, was the armor that wouldn't fail, the armor that keeps us on the right path and enlightens us, spiritually. He no longer counted on his impressive education. His experiences after

Damascus had shown him that all was nothing compared to the light and illumination of Christ.

In 2 Corinthians 4:4, Paul also understood that Satan blinded people's minds to keep them in darkness and from coming to Jesus. *"In whom the god (Satan) of this world hath blinded the minds of them which believe not, lest the **light of the glorious gospel of Christ**, who is the image of God, should shine unto them."* That's a powerful statement. We again see the connection of Jesus as The Word and Jesus as The Light, and the very *"image of God"* capable of bringing light and spiritual illumination to those in darkness.

Paul went on in 2 Corinthians 4:6 to say, *"For God who commanded the **light** to shine out of darkness, hath shined in our hearts, to give the **light** of the knowledge of the glory of God in the face of Jesus Christ."*

And here's good news. Paul, in Ephesians 5:8 tells us that, *"ye were sometimes darkness, but now are ye **light in the Lord: walk as children of light**."* In Colossians 1:12, believers are called *"saints in **light**."* So, those who believe in Jesus and follow Him become people of light. What a happy thought!

And here's another happy thought: Like Isaiah 60:19-20, Revelation 21:23 also makes clear that during Jesus' one-thousand-year reign, **He** will be the only light. *"And the city had no need of the sun, neither of the moon, to shine in it: for the glory of God did **lighten** it, and **the Lamb is the light thereof**."*

Now, Contrast that to darkness:

The Bible has a lot to say about darkness. Provers 4:19 says, *"The way of the wicked is as **darkness**."* And Ecclesiastes 2:14 says, *"the fool walketh in **darkness**."* So, we see that wicked and foolish people walk in darkness. And Ephesians 5:11 and 6:12 talk about the *"works of **darkness**"* and *"the rulers of **darkness**."*

Darkness is Satan's realm. And he desires to keep people there. He'll use everything in his power to do it. He'll blind their minds, use fear and pride, and even appear as an *"angel of light."* 2 Corinthians 11:14 says, *"for Satan himself is transformed into an angel of light."* That word "transformed" in Greek is *metaschematizo* and means, "to disguise." So, Satan, lord of darkness, will even disguise himself as an angel of light when he feels the need. He pretends to bring spiritual enlightenment when in reality he is bringing spiritual darkness. All bogus religions were birthed by this false "angel of light."

As mentioned previously, Isaiah 9:2 is a prophecy of the coming Messiah. Matthew 4:16 restates this Isaiah prophecy and applies it to Jesus. *"The people which sat in darkness saw great **light**; and to them which sat in the regions and shadow of death **light** is sprung up."* It would be Messiah Jesus Who would dispel the darkness, destroy its works, and defang Satan. Jesus, The Light, would do it all, and He did. There is nothing more to be done except to believe in Him.

Encountering Jesus Throughout the Bible

We owe God everything for not leaving us in darkness and at the mercy of Satan. *"Giving thanks unto the Father, which hath made us meet to be partakers of the inheritance of the saints in **light**: Who hath delivered us from the power of darkness, and hath translated us into the kingdom of his dear Son: In whom we have redemption through his blood, even the forgiveness of sins,"* Colossians 1:12-14. What a gift! And how sad for those who reject The Light.

Jesus, in Matthew 22, talked about the wedding of the King's son. It is a parable referring to Him. In the parable the invitation went out to everyone, but not everyone came. And those who tried to come without wearing the proper wedding garment were forbidden entrance. The wedding garment symbolizes the robe of righteousness one can gain only by believing in Jesus and allowing Him to become our righteousness. He is that very robe. There is no substitute.

So, here's what happened at the wedding: *"And he* (the king) *saith unto him, Friend, how camest thou in hither not having a wedding garment? And he was speechless. Then said the king to the servants, Bind him hand and foot, and take him away, and cast hm into outer darkness; there shall be weeping and gnashing of teeth."* (Matthew 22:12-13)

We will never be able to come to God based on our righteousness because, according to Isaiah 64:6, our righteousness is but filthy rags. Only those who come clothed in Jesus' righteousness (the wedding garment) will be allowed access to heaven and the wedding feast. Those who are not so clothed will be cast into *"outer darkness."* Darkness is the absence of light, the absence of Jesus. Where Jesus is, there is light. Where He is not, there is *"outer darkness."* Hell is a dark place. People who have rejected Him will finally get their wish—eternal existence without the Lord of Light. And this must surely break Jesus' heart, for He wants all to come into His marvelous light and be with Him for all eternity.

Son of God

As previously noted, Genesis revealed that Jesus was both Creator and Light. Also in Genesis 1:1-3 we learn there is a Godhead, a Trinity, and Jesus is part of it. We see how the Godhead moved together in Creation; how the Holy Spirit hovered over the earth while God the Father spoke forth His Word and called out Light. Then Jesus, God's Word and Light, was the creative force that made it all.

In Genesis 1:26 we see a more specific reference to the Trinity. *"And **God** said, Let **us** make man in **our** image, after **our** likeness."* The plural pronouns refer to the Godhead. In addition, that word "God" is *Elohiym*. *El* is the Hebrew and Semitic name for God. *Elohiym* is the plural of that name and occurs about two thousand times in the Old Testament. So, here in Genesis 1:26 we see God mentioned in the plural form, depicting the Trinity.

It's interesting that man, who was created in the image of God, is also triune according to 1 Thessalonians 5:23. *"I pray God your whole **spirit and soul and body** be preserved blameless unto the coming of our Lord Jesus Christ."* Notice man's three separate parts are listed in order of importance.

The Trinity also acted in consort when Nimrod built his tower and greatly displeased God. In Genesis 11:6-8 we see the Trinity's remedy. *"And the LORD said, Behold, the people is one, and they have all one language; and this they begin to do: and now nothing will be restrained from them which they have imagined to do. Go to, let **us*** (the Godhead) *go down, and there confound their language, that they may not understand one another's speech. So the LORD scattered them abroad from thence upon the face of all the earth: and they left off to build the city."*

Jesus, in Matthew 28:19, confirmed the makeup of the Godhead when He told His disciples to: *"Go ye therefore, and teach all nations, baptizing them in the name of the **Father**, and of the **Son**, and of the **Holy Ghost**."* This statement also reveals that, as the Son of God, Jesus is the second Person of the Trinity.

Romans 1:18-20 also mentions the Godhead. *"For the wrath of God is revealed from heaven against all ungodliness and unrighteousness of men, who hold the truth in unrighteousness; Because that which may be known of God is manifest in them; for God hath shewed it unto them. For the invisible things of him from the creation of the world are clearly seen, being understood by the things that are made, even his eternal power and **Godhead**, so that they are without excuse."* This says that God reveals Himself to every person through inner knowledge as well as through His creation. That means no one has an excuse or reason to deny His existence.

Sylvia Bambola

Other places where Jesus is revealed as the Son of God in the Old Testament:

Both foreshadowing and symbolism reveal Jesus as the Son of God throughout the Old Testament. One example is when Moses received the law three different times. Numbers are important in the Bible, and three is the number of the Trinity. In my book, *Following the Blood Trail from Genesis to Revelation*, I covered the importance of Moses receiving these commandments three separate times and restate some of it below.

Moses was first given the commandments verbally in Exodus 19-24. God spoke from the mountaintop and only Moses could approach Him. Then, after Moses sealed the covenant with a blood offering, God said in Exodus 24:1, *"Come up (Moses) unto the LORD, thou, and Aaron, Nadab, and Abihu, and seventy of the elders of Israel; and worship ye **afar off**.*" Now it was time to worship. And they were to do it **afar off**. But the average Israelite wasn't even allowed to touch the mountain. If he did, he would die. This speaks of God the Father, how, since the fall of Adam, His holiness caused Him to distance Himself from mankind, to keep them **afar off.** But the fact that Moses, Aaron—the soon-to-be High Priest—and his sons, Nadab and Abihu, and seventy elders could come closer reveals God's tender heart and His desire for man to be reconciled to Him so He could become our Father, Abba, Daddy. But until Jesus came it would have to be done through the law as represented by Moses, and a strict priesthood, represented by Aaron and his sons who would oversee the temple's blood sacrifices, and through prescribed laws which would be enforced by the Sanhedrin or Israel's tribunal of seventy elders representing perfect spiritual order.

The second time, in Exodus 31, the commandments were tangible, carved on tablets of stone, something that could be handled, touched. This spoke of Jesus who would come as a tangible man, to be handled and touched. He was the very WORD made flesh coming to fulfil the law. But before Moses even got off the mountain, the law was broken, showing man incapable of keeping God's laws and that the remedy is Jesus, the second Person of the Trinity, who, like the tables of stone, would also be broken at the cross.

The third time is in Exodus 34 where Moses received another set of tablets, which remained intact. When he came down the mountain, his face shone from being in the presence of God. This foreshadowed the Holy Spirit and the future covenant of grace and how only through the Holy Spirit are we capable of keeping the commandments. In these Exodus verses, the complete Godhead was revealed.

Another example of Jesus as Son of God is seen in Isaac which I also covered in *Following the Blood Trail*. In Genesis 22:1-19, God asked Abraham to sacrifice his son, Isaac. To some, it may seem inconceivable that God would ask such a thing, but what He was doing was symbolically revealing His plan of love and redemption through Jesus.

First, God told Abraham to take Isaac to a mountain that He would show him. The mountain turned out to be Mt. Moriah. Its significance is revealed in 2 Chronicles 3:1. *"Then Solomon began to build the house of the Lord at Jerusalem in mount **Moriah**."* Mt. Moriah would become the future site of the Temple and all the blood sacrifices made under Levitical Law. It was also the mount where Jesus would be sacrificed on the cross.

In Genesis 22:2, God called Isaac, "thine *only* son, Isaac, whom thou *lovest*." God called him this knowing Ishmael was Abraham's first born. But Ishmael was not the son of promise, while Isaac, a type of Jesus, was a foreshadowing of the *only* begotten Son Whom God *loved*. 1 John 4:9 says, *"In this was manifested the love of God toward us, because that God sent his **only** begotten Son into the world, that we might live through him."* Also, Matthew, Mark, Luke and 1 Peter all make mention that Jesus was God's **beloved** son.

Psalm 2 is a prophecy of Jesus, the coming King and Messiah. Psalm 2:7 says, *"I will declare the decree: the LORD that said unto me, Thou art my **Son**; this day have I begotten thee."* Here, God the Father declared that Jesus, Who is The Word, The Creator, The Light, would come to earth clothed in flesh. Why? So that Jesus could fulfill the Father's plan of salvation and die on the cross, then, at His second coming, reclaim the title deed to earth as its King.

Psalm 2:12 continues by saying, *"Kiss the **Son**, lest he be angry, and ye perish from the way, when his wrath is kindled* *but a little. Blessed are all they that put their trust in him."* This specifically refers to Jesus as the Son of God as well as the soon coming King of kings. In ancient times it was customary to kiss a king's foot to show him respect and to acknowledge his authority. This Psalm is saying we need to accept Jesus, the Son of God, now, while there is still time and bow to His authority. Those who don't will experience His wrath.

Returning to Isaac and his significance to Jesus as the Son of God, Genesis 22:6 says, *"And Abraham took the wood of the burnt offering, and laid it upon Isaac his son."* Picture Isaac carrying the bundle of wood for the sacrifice on his shoulder just as Jesus, in obedience to God the Father, carried the wooden cross or wood beam upon which he would be sacrificed. Scholars believe Isaac was a young man rather than a child when this occurred, yet he went along obediently, again foreshadowing Jesus' willingness to be obedient unto death.

It's interesting to note the prophetic nature of Abraham's response when Isaac asked, *"where is the lamb for a burnt offering?"* In Genesis 22:8 we read his answer, *"And Abraham said, My son, God will provide himself a lamb for a burnt offering."* But Abraham wasn't just talking about the ram he found caught in a thicket and killed in place of Isaac. What Abraham prophetically referred to was the fact that God would provide **Himself**, in the form of Jesus, as the Lamb without spot or blemish, to be slain for the sins of the world.

And then there's the story about the three Hebrew boys who were bound and thrown into the furnace because they refused to worship King Nebuchadnezzar's statue. These young men were among those captured after Nebuchadnezzar conquered Jerusalem, and they were carried to Babylon where they served at court. Though they had found favor there, Nebuchadnezzar was furious when they refused to bow before his statue. In response, he ordered the furnace to be heated seven times hotter than usual and had them thrown in. But to Nebuchadnezzar's amazement, nothing happened! And in Daniel 3:25 he said, *"Lo, I see four men loose, walking in the midst of the fire, and they have no hurt; and the form of the fourth is like the **Son of God**."*

Indeed, three were bound and thrown into the furnace but four walked among the flames. The fourth was none other than Jesus who protected the young men so completely that when they were finally allowed to come out, they were not singed, nor did they even smell of smoke.

The story shows Jesus as God and protector of those who believe in Him and how He will always be with us through our trials. But it also has great prophetic significance regarding the seven-year Tribulation and how God will protect His people when fiery trials ramp up seven times hotter. It's going to be a tough time but for those who come to Christ during the Tribulation, Jesus will be there to give them strength and courage, and He will walk in the midst of them.

Heavenly angels called Jesus the Son of God.

Beginning in the New Testament, God made Jesus' identity even plainer. First, in Luke 1:31-32, He sent the angel Gabriel to Mary in Nazareth to tell her that she had been chosen to give birth to a son whom she was to name Jesus. He would be no ordinary man, but the very Son of God. Gabriel told her, *"He shall be great, and shall be called the* **Son of the Highest***: and the Lord God shall give unto him the throne of his father David."* Gabriel went on to say in Luke 1:35, *"The Holy Ghost shall come upon thee* (Mary)*, and the power of the Highest shall overshadow thee: therefore also that holy thing which shall be born of thee shall be called the* **Son of God***."*

What an earth-shattering statement! I can't imagine what Mary, a simple teenage girl, must have felt and thought. Surely, she had to be frightened and overwhelmed. Yet, she was so utterly receptive and obedient one can readily understand why God had chosen her. Even so, there was to be no doubt of Jesus' identity. Before he was even born, God had an angel reveal it.

In the first chapter of Matthew, we learn that Mary and Joseph became engaged. But when Joseph found out Mary was pregnant, he was faced with a dilemma. If he exposed her, she would be stoned to death. Yet how could he marry such an unfaithful woman? It was best to divorce her privately. Before he could, an angel appeared to him in a dream and told him that Mary had conceived by the Holy Spirit and that this child would fulfill the prophecy that, *"a virgin shall be with child, and shall bring* *forth a son, and they shall call his name Emmanuel, which being interpreted is, **God with us**,"* Matthew 1:23.

Again, we are told that this child is God with us. Could God make it any plainer? Jesus was God Himself! And He was coming to be with us. How amazing and wonderful. It would be the fulfilment of the symbolism and foreshadowing peppered throughout the Old Testament.

God Himself called Jesus His Son.

When Jesus came out of the water after being baptized in the Jordan by John the Baptist, God the Father validated Him in Matthew 3:16-17. *"And Jesus, when he was baptized, went up straightway out of the water: and lo, the heavens were opened unto him, and he saw the Spirit of God descending like a dove, and lighting upon him: And lo a voice from heaven, saying, This is my **beloved Son**, in whom I am well pleased."* Mark 1:10-11 also described this incident.

God the Father again validated Jesus in Matthew 17:5 during Jesus' transfiguration on a mountaintop. When Peter, James and John saw Jesus talking with Moses and Elijah, Peter, ever impetuous, wanted to build three tabernacles, one for each of them. *"While he* (Peter) *yet spake* (regarding building the three tabernacles) *behold, a bright cloud overshadowed them: and behold a voice out of the cloud which said, This is my **beloved Son**, in whom I am well pleased; hear ye him."* This story was again told in Mark 9:7 and Luke 9:35.

Peter also mentioned how God called Jesus His son in 2 Peter 1:17. *"For he (Jesus) received from God the Father honour and glory, when there came such a voice to him from the excellent glory, This is my **beloved Son**, in whom I am well pleased."*

Hebrews 1:5 says this about Jesus: *"For unto which of the angels said he (God) at any time, Thou art my **Son**, this day have I begotten thee? And again, I will be to him a Father, and he shall be to me a **Son**?"*

God doesn't mince words. Through His angels He declared beforehand that He was about to come to earth in the form of man. Then He went out of His way to validate Jesus as His Son. But how could that be? How could God be on earth and in heaven at the same time? Because God is omnipresent. He is everywhere.

Jesus called Himself the Son of God.

In Matthew 11:27 Jesus talked about God His Father and Himself as the Son. Jesus also confirmed that God the Father had given Him all things. *"All things are delivered unto me (Jesus) of my Father: and no man knoweth the **Son**, but the Father; neither knoweth any man the Father, save the **Son**, and he to whosoever the **Son** will reveal him."*

John 3:35 tells us that, *"The Father loveth the **Son** and hath given **all** things into his hand."* So, John confirms that Jesus was given **all** things by the Father. And here's a wonderful thought: one day Jesus will return to claim what is rightfully His and rule over us as King.

In Matthew 26:64, when Jesus was taken to Caiaphas, the high priest's house, and forced to endure an illegal trial, the high priest asked Jesus if He was the Son of God. Jesus acknowledged He was by saying, *"**Thou hast said**: nevertheless I say unto you, Hereafter shall ye see the Son of man sitting on the right hand of power, and coming in the clouds of heaven."* The expression, "thou hast said" is an emphatic Hebrew expression meaning "yes!" or "indeed it is as you say!" or "you have said right!" Here, Jesus claimed to be the Son of God. That's why the high priest, in verse 65, tore his robes believing Jesus had blasphemed.

Mark 14:55-62 describes the same scene, but a bit clearer. Here, the high priest asked in verse 61, *"Art thou the Christ* (Messiah) *the **Son of the Blessed**? And Jesus said, I am: and ye shall see the Son of man sitting on the right hand of power, and coming in the clouds of heaven."*

Then Jesus said this about Himself in John 3:17-18: *"For God sent not his **Son** into the world to condemn the world; but that the world through him might be saved. He that believeth on him is not condemned: but he that believeth not is condemned already, because he hath not believed in the name of the **only begotten Son of God**."*

Jesus also said in John 5:25, *"Verily, verily, I say unto you, The hour is coming, and now is, when the dead shall hear the voice of the **Son of God**: and they that hear shall live."* The dead Jesus referred to are those spiritually dead through sin. Jesus, through His death and resurrection, made a way for us to escape eternal damnation and offered us eternal life instead. Since the Bible in multilayered, He could also have been referring to when, after his death, He would go to hell, reveal Himself, and preach to the dead in Abraham's Bosom, who were already declared righteous though their faith.

After Jesus healed a blind man in John 9, the Pharisees had a fit. It was the Sabbath and being religious rather than spiritual, they were greatly offended. To them, legalism trumped mercy. Immediately, they claimed Jesus couldn't be of God, otherwise He wouldn't heal on the Sabbath. Then, in their self-righteousness, the Pharisees expelled the former blind man from the Temple. When Jesus heard this and confronted the man in John 9:35, He said, *"Dost thou believe on the **Son of God**?"* The man responded, *"Who is he, Lord, that I might believe on him?"* Jesus' answer in verse 37 left no doubt. *"Thou hast both seen him, and it is he that talketh with thee."*

Throughout Jesus' ministry many Jews claimed He was demon possessed or mad, and often tried to trap Him. Finally, some came and said, *"How long dost thou make us to doubt? If thou be the Christ* (Messiah)*, tell us plainly,"* (John 10:24). Jesus answered them in John 10:36-38. You say of me, *"Thou blasphemest: because I said, **I am the Son of God**? If I do not the works of my Father, believe me not. But if I do, though ye believe not me, believe the works: that ye may know, and believe, that the Father is in me, and I in him."* At this point, Jesus was well known for all the miracles He had done. In fact, He had performed every miracle the rabbis claimed the Messiah would perform and those are the *"works"* Jesus told them to believe in. Yet they refused to believe. The proof was right in front of them and still they remained willfully ignorant.

Another time when Jesus was told Lazarus was sick, He said, *"This sickness is not unto death, but for the glory of God, that the **Son of God** might be glorified thereby."* Then, after Lazarus died, Jesus amazed everyone by raising him from the dead.

And finally, in Revelation 2:18, while Jesus dictated letters to the seven churches, He again called Himself the Son of God. *"And unto the angel of the church in Thyatira write; These things saith the **Son of God**, who hath his eyes like unto a flame of fire, and his feet are like fine brass."*

Even the Jews, while they may not have believed it themselves, acknowledged that Jesus believed He was the Son of God as evidenced in John 19:7. Jesus had been beaten and crowned with thorns and delivered to Pilate to be crucified. When Pilate told the priests to handle the matter themselves because he couldn't find any fault with Jesus, the Jews responded by saying, *"We have a law, and by our law he ought to die, because he made himself the **Son of God.**"*

Jesus also used parables to reveal Who He was. One example is the story in Matthew 21:33-41 (also repeated in Luke 20:9-18). In it, Jesus talked about the owner of a vineyard who left his estate in the care of farmers. When harvest time came, the owner sent his servants to collect the fruit from the vineyard. Instead of paying what was due, the farmers killed some, stoned and beat others.

Then the owner sent his **son**, thinking that surely the farmers would honor him. Instead, they killed the son believing they could steal his inheritance. Jesus was, of course, speaking of Himself, of His rejection by the Jews and His coming death. He was also speaking of the many prophets God had sent to Israel who had been abused or killed. In the next two verses, verse 42-43, Jesus said, *"Did ye never read in the scriptures, The stone which the builders rejected, the same is become the **head of the corner**: this is the Lord's doing, and it is marvelous in our eyes? Therefore say I unto you, The kingdom of God shall be taken from you, and given to a nation bringing forth the fruits thereof."* Jesus is not only the Son of God but the cornerstone. And this was a prophetic statement indicating that the Gentile nations, via His church, and He, as the cornerstone of that church, would be the ones who would bring forth the fruit He desired.

Demons called Jesus the Son of God.

When Jesus went to the *"country of the Gergesenes"* He encountered two demon possessed men who were not only violent but whose presence in the tombs made passage there impossible. I think it's safe to say the town's people were terrified of them. But as soon as those demon possessed men saw Jesus, **they** became terrified. And immediately the demons began to speak through the men in Matthew 8:29 (also found in Mark 5:7 and Luke 8:28). *"and behold, they* (the evil spirits) *cried out, saying, What have we to do with thee, Jesus, thou **Son of God**? art thou come hither to torment us before the time?"* This speaks volumes. Not only were the demons terrified and knew Jesus for Who He was, the Son of God, they also knew He had authority over them and that one day He would judge them.

In Mark 3 we are told that people came from all over to see Jesus after they heard of the mighty miracles He had done. Verse 11 says, *"And unclean spirits, when they saw him (Jesus) fell down before him, and cried, saying, Thou art the* **Son of God***."*

When Jesus went to Peter's house and found Peter's mother sick, He healed her by rebuking her fever. While He was there, many came to the house seeking healing, too. Luke 4:40-41 says, *"Now when the sun was setting, all they that had any sick with divers diseases brought them unto him (Jesus) and he laid his hands on every one of them, and healed them. And devils also came out of many, crying out, and saying, Thou art Christ the* **Son of God***. And he rebuking them suffered them not to speak: for they knew that he was Christ."*

It's interesting that Satan tried to make Jesus doubt He was the Son of God. Both Matthew 4:3-10 and Luke 4:3-12 tell us Jesus went into the desert for forty days to pray and fast in preparation for His ministry. He was hungry when Satan came to tempt Him. The first thing Satan said was, *"if thou be the* **Son of God***."* Satan then followed it with, *"command that these stones be made bread."* I've never fasted forty days, but I have fasted a few and at the end of them I could hardly wait to eat. Yes, the flesh is weak and even Jesus felt hunger. But though Jesus was greatly weakened, He knew Who He was, and that identity couldn't be shaken.

Satan's second temptation was also preceded with the statement, *"If thou be the **Son of God**."* Then he continued with (I paraphrase), "Just throw yourself off this high place and let the angels catch you." Oh, how desperate Satan must have been to get Jesus to question His identity! And Satan will try to get us to question our identity, too. Though the Bible calls us "sons and daughters" of God, "joint heirs with Christ," and "kings and priests," Satan will try to make us believe we are nothing and that God doesn't love us. We need to be firm in our knowledge of who we are in Jesus.

Finally, Satan gave up, and asked Jesus to worship him and if He would, he'd give Him all the kingdoms of the earth. This tells us that Satan oversaw those kingdoms otherwise Jesus would have corrected him. It also shows how much Satan wanted to be worshipped by the Son of God.

Disciples called Jesus the Son of God.

Jesus had just ministered to five thousand men plus women and children, and healed many. Think how tired He must have been. Yet, when He finished, He was concerned that these people were hungry, and this concern compelled Him to do another miracle by feeding them with five loaves of bread and two fish. Afterward, wanting to be alone and spend time with the Father and recharge His spiritual battery, He told His disciples to get into a boat and head to the other side. But a storm came and made it difficult for the disciples to navigate. What did Jesus do? He walked on the water to where they were. That's when Peter got the idea of walking out to meet Him. It went well until Peter noticed how treacherous the winds and waves were and began to sink, thus requiring Jesus to save him (Matthew 14:14-31). Then, after Jesus and Peter were safely in the boat, verse 32 tells us, *"they that were in the ship came and **worshipped** him (Jesus) saying, Of a truth thou art the **Son of God**."* According to Jewish law, only God could receive worship, and Jesus, being a good Jew, would never have allowed it if He were not God.

In Matthew 16:13-17 Jesus and His disciples went to Caesarea Philippi, a place of idol worship. The slopes of Mount Hermon were dotted with caves and niches filled with statues of pagan gods. It was also a chief location of Baal worship. It was here, in this setting, that Jesus asked His disciples who people said He was. They rattled off a few names until Jesus stopped them by asking, but who do **you** say I am? It's a question He will ask all of us. Peter's answer? *"Thou art the Christ, the **Son of the living God**."* Jesus was pleased and said it was His Father Who had revealed this to Peter. Then, in verse 18, Jesus began talking about His church and said, *"the gates of hell shall not prevail against it."* That statement was significant because there was (and still is) a cave in this area of Caesarea Philippi that people believed to be the very entrance to hell.

John, the apostle, recalled how Peter referred to Jesus as the Son of God after Jesus told the Jews that *"Verily, verily, I say unto you, Except ye eat the flesh of the Son of man, and drink his blood, ye have no life in you,"* (John 6:53). This statement was so shocking that many disciples stopped following Jesus. When Jesus asked his apostles, *"Will ye also go away?"* Peter answered, *"Lord, to whom shall we go? Thou hast the words of eternal life. And we believe and are sure that thou art that Christ, the **Son of the living God**,"* (John 6:67-68).

After Peter healed a lame man, people flocked to him in awe and he had to tell them that healing only came through Jesus, whom he called the **Son of God** twice in Acts 3: 1-26.

John, under the inspiration of the Holy Spirit, also called Jesus the Son of God in John 3:16, *"For God so loved the world that he gave **his only begotten Son**, that whosoever believeth in him should not perish, but have everlasting life."*

1 John 1:3, *"That which we have seen and heard declare we unto you, that ye also may have fellowship with us: and truly our fellowship is with the Father, and with his **Son**, Jesus Christ."* John goes on in 1 John 2:22-23 to say, *"Who is a liar but he that denieth that Jesus is the Christ? He is antichrist, that denieth the Father and the **Son**. Whosoever denieth the **Son**, the same hath not the Father: but he that acknowledgeth the **Son** hath the Father also."* He repeats this in 1 John 5:10-13. So, those who deny that Jesus is the promised Messiah and Son of God are both liars and

have the spirit of antichrist. What a powerful and sobering statement!

2 John 9 goes on to say, *"Whosoever transgresseth, and abideth not in the doctrine of Christ, hath not God. He that abideth in the doctrine of Christ, he hath both the Father and the **Son**."*

John also tells us in 1 John 4:15, *"Whosoever shall confess that Jesus is the **Son of God**, God dwelleth in him, and he in God."*

Believing that Jesus is the very Son of God is essential to having a relation with both Him and the Father. Again, why was it necessary for the Father to send the Son? Romans 8:3 makes it clear. *"For what the law could not do, in that it was weak through the flesh, God sending his own **Son** in the likeness of sinful flesh, and for sin, condemned sin in the flesh."* It's amazing, but God Himself bore all our sins in His flesh.

Then John made this statement in 1 John 5:20 leaving no room for doubt as to who he believed Jesus to be: *"And we know that the **Son of God** is come, and hath given us an understanding, that we may know him that is true, and we are in him that is true, even in his **Son** Jesus Christ. This is the true God, and eternal life."* Jesus is the Son of God, the true God and eternal life. Without Him there is no hope. We would be eternally lost. It's hard to wrap our finite mind around the fact that God came Himself, in the form of man, to pay the heavy penalty of sin and satisfy His pure and perfect sense of justice. Oh, how much He loves us!

And 1 John 3:8 goes further. *"He that committeth sin is of the devil; for the devil sinneth from the beginning. For this purpose the **Son of God** was manifested that he might destroy the works of the devil."*

John 20:31 sums it up this way, *"But these are written, that ye might believe that Jesus is the Christ, the **Son of God**; and that believing ye might have life through his name."*

The apostle Mark called Jesus the Son of God in Mark 1:1. *"The beginning of the gospel of Jesus Christ, the **Son of God**."*

Nathanael, in John 1:49, called Jesus the *"Son of God"* and the *"King of Israel,"* after Jesus told him he had seen him sitting under a fig tree (John 1:48).

The apostle Paul also declared that Jesus was the Son of God in Romans 1:3-4. In Acts 9:20, after his Damascus experience, Paul openly preached to the Jews in the synagogues telling them that Jesus was *"the Son of God."* And 2 Corinthians 1:19 tells us that not only Paul but Silvanus and Timotheus preached that Jesus was the **Son of God**.

Others who called Jesus the Son of God.

John the Baptist, who called himself, *"the voice of one crying in the wilderness,"* in order to *"Make straight the way of the Lord,"* also called Jesus the Son of God in John 1:34. *"And I* (John the Baptist) *saw, and bare record that this* (Jesus) *is the **Son of God**."*

Lazarus' sister, Martha, also called Jesus the Son of God. After her brother, Lazarus, died and was placed in a tomb, Jesus told her He was the resurrection and the life and asked if she believed in Him. Her answer: *"Yea, Lord: I believe that thou are the Christ, the **Son of God**, which should come into the world,"* John 11:27.

Then there is the story of the influential Ethiopian eunuch, a member of Queen Candace's court, who had come to Jerusalem to worship in the Temple. While the eunuch was returning home, an angel instructed Phillip to find him. When found, the Holy Spirit had Phillip join the man and explain the Bible passage he was reading. The passage was from Isaiah 53 regarding the Messiah who would come and die for our sins, *"as a lamb to the slaughter."* Phillip obeyed and explained that the passage referred to Jesus then told him about how Jesus had died and rose again and ascended into heaven. The eunuch believed and asked to be baptized. In Acts 8:37 Phillip responded by saying, *"If thou believest with all thine heart, thou mayest* (be baptized)." To that the eunuch answered: "*I believe that Jesus Christ is the **Son of God**."*

And finally, the Roman centurion and soldiers who watched, after Jesus died, how the sky darkened and the earth quaked, said He was the Son of God. *"Now when the centurion and they that were with him, watching Jesus, saw the earthquake, and those things that were done, they feared greatly, saying, Truly this was the **Son of God**,"* (Matthew 27:54, also in Mark 15:38-39).

It cannot be overstated what a miracle this was, that God Himself came down to earth and provided a remedy for us. Galatians 4:4-5 explains this. *"But when the fullness of the time was come, God sent forth his **Son**, made of a woman, made under the law, To redeem them that were under the law, that we might receive the adoption of sons."* Jesus did it all. He gave it all. All we need do is accept what He did and claim it for ourselves. If not, *"How shall we escape* (God's wrath and hell) *if we neglect so great salvation; which at the first began to be spoken by the Lord, and was confirmed unto us by them that heard him,"* Hebrews 2:3.

The Great I AM

Moses, a former prince of Egypt, had been tending his father-in-law's sheep for forty years. A strange occupation for a prince, but not for a fugitive who had killed a man then fled to Midian. What a different life from the hustle and bustle, the pomp and ceremony of the Egyptian court! Now, dust and the bleating of animals filled his day, and I imagine, loneliness, too, though he had married Zipporah and fathered two sons.

But isolation and solitude had their own rewards, for it was while he had taken the flock to Horeb, "the mountain of God," also called Mount Sinai, that something amazing happened. Amid the rugged terrain, Moses noticed a burning thorn bush. Hardly unusual since temperatures could soar into triple digits and sometimes things caught fire. Thorn bushes were quick burns that crackled loudly. But this one was different. This bush kept burning without being consumed. He had to investigate. And when he did, he heard God speak.

The first thing God told him was to remove his sandals because he was on *"holy ground."* Then He told him He was, *"the God of thy father, the God of Abraham, the God of Isaac, and the God of Jacob"* (Exodus 3:6). Why was God so specific? Because it was necessary to keep Moses from thinking that some strange god was talking to him. Moses knew he was an Israelite and surely knew his family's history, which included the God they worshipped. The familiar connection between God and his family seemed to put Moses at enough ease to enable God to instruct him to return to Egypt and lead the Israelites out of bondage.

But that's not what Moses wanted to hear. No longer a strong, proud, strutting prince, he was now a simple shepherd. His fighting days were over. He had no wish to return to a land that surely still held danger for him.

Oh, how patient and gracious God was! He assured Moses that He would come to Egypt with him. That's when Moses asked God His name. *"Behold, when I come unto the children of Israel, and shall say unto them, The God of your fathers hath sent me unto you; and they shall say to me, What is his name? what shall I say unto them?"* (Exodus 3:13).

God's answer: *"I AM THAT I AM . . . say unto the children of Israel, I AM hath sent me unto you,"* (Exodus 3:14).

But what does the name, I AM THAT I AM mean? It means that God is everything we need. Fill in the blank: "I AM HEALER" or "I AM PROTECTER," or "I AM PROVIDER," or "I AM SALVATION," etcetera. And the Jews understood this as evidenced by the various names they gave Jehovah God. Here are a few:

Jehovah-Jireh which means, "Jehovah will see or provide." We can trust Him to be our provider. Millions of people have experienced His supernatural provision and blessings.

Jehovah-Nissi, meaning, "Jehovah is my banner or standard." Standards or flags/banners were associated with warfare. It is God who gives us the victory in times of battle, those times when we face trials and difficulties.

Jehovah-Shalom means, "Yahweh is peace." If we want to experience inner peace or have peace in our lives, we need to submit to God, for it is only though Him that true peace comes.

Jehovah-Shammah means, "Yahweh is there." This indicates the presence of God and predicts His future presence during the Messianic kingdom when Jesus, the Second Person of the Trinity, will physically tabernacle with us in Jerusalem. But we don't have to wait that long. We can experience God's presence now, through His Holy Spirit who lives within every born-again believer.

Jehovah-Tsidkenu means, "Yahweh our righteousness," and speaks of the righteousness of Messiah, Jesus, Who imparts His righteousness to us when we come into the saving knowledge of Him.

But God is even more than all the above. God is willing and able to supply everything we need. When God called Himself, "I AM THAT I AM," He was telling Moses (and us) that not only was He all those things mentioned, He was also saying, "I AM courage, strength, wisdom, joy, and anything else you need." What a great God He is!

A side note: It's disturbing and sad that many in the New Age Movement claim divinity and when claiming it, refer to themselves as "I am." What, I wonder, will they say when they come face to face with the real I AM?

But did Jesus ever claim to be I AM?

Yes. Many times. First, let's look at the two most dramatic incidences.

The first one occurred in John 8. Jesus had been teaching in the Temple. As usual, the scribes and Pharisees tried to trap Him, this time by bringing Him a woman who had been caught in the act of adultery. They wanted to stone her but first they wanted to see what Jesus would say. They talked about Moses and the law, hoping Jesus would contradict them in some way. If He did, that would surely turn the people against Him. But that hope was dashed when He simply said, *"He that is without sin among you, let him first cast a stone at her,"* (John 8:7). And that put an end to that.

Still, they continued to bait Him. And when they tried playing the trump card about being Abraham's seed, Jesus had had it and told them, *"Verily, verily, I say unto you, Before Abraham was, **I am,**"* (John 8:58). Not only was He telling them that He existed before Abraham was even born, but that He was God Himself. By telling them, "I am," Jesus was referring to the burning bush when

God called Himself, I AM, and those scribes and Pharisees knew it. That's why in the next verse, verse 59, they *"took up stones to cast at him."* They wanted to stone Him for blasphemy.

The second dramatic event was in the garden of Gethsemane. Jesus had been in an agony of soul, praying and preparing for the terrible ordeal He knew lay ahead. He had sweated *"great drops of blood"* and wrestled with the devil. He had even asked His Father to let the cup of suffering pass from Him. But in the end, He bowed to the Father's will. He would stay the course. He would lay down His life for many. It was around this time that Judas came to the garden followed by a mob of soldiers carrying torches and swords. They had come at the order of the high priest and Pharisees. Their mission: to subdue Jesus and take Him to a mock trial that would be held secretly.

John 18 tells the story. In verse 4, Jesus asked them, *"Whom seek ye?"* They answered, *"Jesus of Nazareth."* Jesus responded, *"I am he."* That word "he" is italicized in the King James Bible, meaning it was not in the original text but added for clarity. So, Jesus simply said, **"I am."** And then something amazing happened in verse 6, *"As soon then as he had said unto them,* **I am** *(he), they went backward, and fell to the ground."* They couldn't stand in the face of the Great I AM. Simply by speaking a word, Jesus could have taken them all out. No man could have ever taken His life. It shows that He surrendered Himself willingly.

Other Bible references:

There are many places in the Bible where Jesus revealed Himself as the I AM. And they disclose not only Who He is, but also facets of His character and the wonderful things He can be to us, for us, and in us.

Statements by Jesus, the I AM, about Who He is:

Mark 14:62, *"I am"* the Son of God. This verse was already covered in the chapter, *The Son of God*. It pertains to the time when Jesus stood before the high priest during His illegal trial and the priest asked if He was the *"Son of the Blessed* (God),*"* and Jesus said, *"***I am**.*"* Jesus also confirmed this in John 10:36.

John 8:16, *"I am not alone."* Here, Jesus indicated He was part of the Trinity, the Godhead, and that God, the Father, was with Him. In John 10:30, He said that He and the Father were one.

John 14:10-11, *"I am in the Father."* Again, Jesus affirmed His Divinity and His place in the Godhead.

John 8:23, *"I am from above . . . I am not of this world,"* another confirmation of Jesus' Divinity. Also see John 17:14 and John 17:16 for more.

John 5:43, *"I am come in my Father's name."* Though Jesus is God and part of the Godhead, He acknowledged He was sent by Father God and came in His Father's name. Jesus further said in John 7:28-29, *"I am not come of myself, but he* (God the Father) *that sent me is true, whom ye know not. But I know him: for **I am** from him and he hath sent me."* Jesus was on a mission from the Father. His mission was to be born a man, die for our sins and then be raised from the dead and return to heaven. It was a mission born out of love. And only the deepest kind of love could have seen it through.

John 8:12, *"**I am** the light of the world."* We have already seen how Jesus was the very light in creation and here He is telling us He is the very light of the world. He is the very light that dispels the darkness. That's why in Revelation 21:23, the new heaven and earth will have no need for the sun or moon. *"And the city had no need of the sun, neither of the moon, to shine in it: for the glory of God did lighten it, and the Lamb* (Jesus) *is the light thereof."* Jesus will be the only light we need.

John 12:46, *"**I am** come a light into the world."* Here, Jesus again stated He is light, and His light has come into the world. How wonderful for this dark and evil world.

John 8:28, *"**I am** he* (the Son of Man)."* Why did Jesus call Himself the Son of Man? Because Leviticus established a legal precedent that only a relative could redeem that which was lost. Therefore, Jesus had to come in the flesh, to be one of us, to become our relative, before He could redeem us. More about this in the chapter entitled, *Son of Man*.

John 10:9, *"**I am** the door."* But a door to what? The very door to heaven! The door to salvation! To everlasting life!

He is the way back to the Father. He is the way of escape from our sins and wages thereof. He is our only hope. In John 10:1-9 Jesus said that anyone who doesn't come through Him (the door) is a *"thief and a robber."* In John 10:9, after Jesus said, *"**I am** the door,"* He said, *"by me if any man enter in, he shall be saved, and shall go in and out, and find pasture."* Then in Revelation 3:20 Jesus said, *"Behold I stand at the door* (the door of every person's heart*), and knock: if any man hear my voice, and open the door, I will come in to him, and will sup with him, and he with me."* How sad that so many people ignore Jesus' knock and keep their hearts closed to Him.

Matthew 20:23, *"**I am** baptized."* It would cost Jesus a great deal to become the "door." It would mean rejection, pain, suffering, and even death. And that's exactly what Jesus was talking about here. It was the baptism of suffering. He was referring to His coming suffering when He would be beaten and crucified for our sins. Oh, what He endured for us!

John 10:10, *"**I am** come that they may have life, and that they may have it more abundantly."* But this more abundant life can only come if we walk through the "door," through Jesus. Apart from Him only death and hell await.

John 8:24, *"If ye believe not that **I am** he, ye shall die in your sins."* Those who don't believe Jesus came from above, that He is the door, then walk through it, will surely die in their sins. But the sad part is they don't have to. If they just come to Jesus, they will be assured of eternal life. He did it all. He paid it all. People just need to believe and receive.

Matthew 9:13, *"I am not come to call the righteous, but sinners to repentance."* Jesus was saying, *"I am come for sinners."* Romans 3:23 tells us that *"For all have sinned, and come short of the glory of God."* All means all. No exceptions. That means we all need a Savior, and Jesus is it.

Matthew 5:17, *"I am not come to destroy but to fulfill* (the law and prophets). In other words, Jesus was saying, *"I am come to fulfil the law."* Jesus did the necessary work of perfectly fulfilling the law and prophecy (God's promises made through the prophets) in order to satisfy the Father's perfect sense of justice. Someone had to pay, to atone for the sins so repulsive to God, and that Someone was Jesus. If Jesus had changed His mind in the garden of Gethsemane and refused to go the distance, we would all be without hope.

Matthew 10:35, *"I am come to set a man at variance against his father . . . daughter against her mother, the daughter in law against her mother in law."* Jesus knew some would believe, others not, and that believers and unbelievers would frequently be part of the same family. Accepting Jesus often requires courage. In numerous countries, Muslims can kill family members who have converted to Christianity. Even in Christian countries, family relationships can become strained when one member accepts Jesus, and the others don't. But Jesus will give all those who come to Him the courage to turn their backs on the world and turn to Him, even when it means conflict and strife, even when it makes them at odds with the people they love.

Luke 12:49, "*I am come to send fire on the earth.*" When we come to Jesus, He will set us on fire by His Holy Spirit so we can burn with zeal for Him. And life will never be the same.

John 9:39, "*For judgment I am come into this world.*" God the Father placed all the penalty of sin on Jesus. Sin was indeed judged. That also means since Jesus' first coming, the world is without excuse. If people reject Him after what He did, then there is no recourse but to let them carry the judgment for their own sins which means to live all eternity in hell.

John 11: 25, "*I am the resurrection and the life.*" Again, it is only Jesus who can resurrect us from our spiritual deadness and sin-life, and give us His life, His joy, His peace, His everything that makes life worth living. And after we die physically, we will be resurrected with new life and be with Him forever.

John 14:6, "*I am the way, the truth, and the life,*" And Matthew 7:14 tells us that way is "*narrow*" because it is only through Jesus. I don't know how many more ways Jesus could have said it. Here again, He affirmed that He is the only way, the only truth and the only means for an abundant life here on earth, then eternal life after we die physically.

John 13:19, "*I am he* (the Messiah whom the scriptures spoke of)." The Scriptures, both in the Old and New Testament, are full of references to Jesus' first and second coming, of what would happen to Him, how He would be betrayed and then killed for us, and how someday He will return as king. It is there, spelled out for anyone who cares to see.

John 13:13, "*I am* (Master)." Yes, Jesus is Master over us. Whether we yield to Him in this life or not, according to Philippians 2:10, one day every knee will bow at the mention of His name.

John 10:11 and 14, "*I am the good shepherd.*" Jesus went on to describe what kind of "good shepherd" He was: "*the good shepherd that giveth his life for the sheep.*" Sheep are incredibly defenseless. They need constant tending and watching. They are easy prey for predators such as wolfs, bears, and lions. And dare I say it? They are also clueless. Maybe "obtuse" is the better word. They would graze a pasture bare then remain there and starve if the shepherd didn't drive them to another field. They would plunge headlong into a river and drown if the shepherd didn't steady them. Shepherding is a fulltime job. It requires a gentle but steady hand like the hand Jesus uses when dealing with us, His sheep. He watches over us, protects us, guides us, and tenderly cares for our every need. And, yes, He actually gave His life for us. He is, indeed, the good shepherd in every way.

John 15:1, "*I am the true vine.*" Jesus repeated this in John 15:5 and added that we are the branches and if we abide in Him, we will produce much fruit. But here's the kicker, *"for without me ye can do nothing."* We can do all things through Christ who strengthens us, but we can't do one thing for the Kingdom of God without Him. As long as we are attached to Him, the Vine, we will be fine and do fine. But as soon as we get separated things go downhill. Just like a branch separated from its source, we will wither and become barren.

John 6:35 (and John 6:48), *"I am the bread of life."* John 6:51 goes on to say, *"I am the living bread which came down from heaven."* It is no coincidence that Jesus was born in Bethlehem, which means, "house of bread." He is the bread that nourishes and sustains us. He is the very manna from heaven and was prophetically symbolized by the manna given to the Israelites during their forty-years of wandering in the desert. After Jesus ascended to heaven, He did not leave us to fend for ourselves. He sent His Holy Spirit to shepherd us just like a good shepherd would. But He also left us His Word. And when we ingest it, we partake of Him as the Bread of Life. And it's no ordinary bread, either, but bread that came straight from heaven and this bread, His Word, will sustain us, fill us, satisfy us, and strengthen us.

Mark 14:28, *"I am risen."* Here, Jesus predicted His death but also that He'd rise again. And He did just that after three days. Death and hell couldn't hold Him. He conquered them both. And because He did, He will also raise those who become His, and they will never experience hell.

John 18:37, "*I am a king.*" Jesus also said right before this in John 18:36, "*My kingdom is not of this world.*" When Jesus first came, it was not to set up His kingdom, much to His disciples' disappointment. They had hoped He would be the new king of Israel, deposing the cruel Roman rulers. But it was not to be. He came to suffer, to die, to atone. But that was then. The next time He comes it WILL be as King. Jesus will return to earth and rule for a thousand years on the throne of David. And He will rule with a rod of iron. But what a kingdom it will be! Wolves will dwell with lambs and there will be no more wars. In the face of that, one can only say, "Come quickly, Lord Jesus!"

Statements by Jesus, the I AM, about His character and abilities:

Matthew 11:29, "*I am meek and lowly in heart.*" How tender, patient and kind Jesus is! And He is so meek and gentle. It's hard to imagine the enormity of the glory, power, wealth and splendor He gave up in order to come to earth as a lowly human, born in a smelly stable and grow up as a man Who labored with His hands, then traveled around the country as a homeless preacher. In addition, He was often misunderstood, maligned, hated, plotted against, and finally murdered. Yet, He did all this without pride or arrogance, so unlike kings and rulers who often bludgeon and abuse others with their power and position. Though Jesus is meek, make no mistake, He is not weak. He is not to be trifled with and when He returns, He WILL return in power and majesty, and all the world will tremble in His presence.

Encountering Jesus Throughout the Bible

Luke 22:27, *"I am among you as he that serveth."* Jesus came as a servant. He even washed His disciples' feet to illustrate a servant's heart, and what should be the heart of every believer. He also said that he who wants to be great should be the servant of all. In this age of selfies and narcissism, being a servant, for many, is unappealing. But that's exactly what we must become if we want to follow Jesus.

Matthew 9:28, *"I am able."* Jesus had just healed the woman with an issue of blood, as well as raised Jairus' dead daughter when He was confronted by two blind men. They cried out, *"Thou son of David, have mercy on us."* That's when Jesus asked, *"Believe ye that I am able to do this?"* Their answer: *"Yes, Lord."* We, too, need to say "yes" to that question. We need to believe that Jesus is able to do all the Bible says, and not only that, but that He wants to do it for us.

That goes along with Luke 9:18 when Jesus asked His disciples who people said He was. After mentioning a few names, Jesus stopped them and asked, *"But whom say ye that I am?"* We will need to answer that question, too. Do we believe the Bible or the world? The answer will have far reaching consequences.

And finally, John 13:33 says, *"I am with you."* How amazing is that? The Great I AM is with us! And He promises to never leave us or forsake us. Now that's a promise we can hang our hat on.

Savior

Of all the typology and symbolism depicting Jesus, this one has the most impact on us. Indeed, if Jesus had not become the Lamb of Sacrifice, our Savior, all of us would remain lost in our sins and our future would be hopeless. No one would be able to escape God's wrath and the punishment of eternal hell.

But why exactly was this sacrifice necessary? The reason is detailed in my book, *Following the Blood Trail from Genesis to Revelation*, but I will repeat some of it here.

In Genesis 3:1-24, we see the fall of Adam and Eve. Our first parents foolishly bought Satan's lie that if they ate of the forbidden fruit they would become "as gods." Instead of becoming "gods" their act produced a spiral-down scenario that has caused nothing but heartache and pain from that time to this.

After they realized the evil they had done, they attempted a "cover-up" by clothing themselves with wilting fig leaves sewn into aprons (Genesis 3:7). Since then, man continues trying to cover up his sins by means of his own handiwork, his own solutions, his own good works. Every religion, except Christianity, tries to show men how to work their way back to God; how to sew aprons. Only Christianity shows how God worked His way back to man.

Unfortunately for Adam and Eve, God would have none of it. Fig leaves were hardly sufficient to cover their gross sin of disobedience. Though angry and heartbroken, God took matters into His own hands and covered them Himself by killing an innocent animal and establishing the criteria for covering sin: innocent blood. Thus, the killing of an innocent animal in the Garden of Eden foreshadowed what was to come.

But the blood of innocent animals was only a temporary solution, until the Perfect Solution could be realized — nothing less than the blood of God Himself. It was a solution that had been on the planning board before the earth was created. Revelation 13:8 talks about the *"Lamb slain from the foundation of the world."* And John the Baptist (John 1:29) called Jesus, *"the Lamb of God which taketh away the sin of the world."* Adam and Eve's sin did not take God by surprise. Right from Genesis we see the foreshadowing of the future Lamb of God, the future Savior Who would come thousands of years later.

More Old Testament Foreshadowing:

In Genesis 22:1-19 God asked Abraham to take his son, Isaac, to a mountain He would show him in order to offer Isaac as a sacrifice. The mountain was Mt. Moriah, which 2 Chronicles 3:1 tells us is where Solomon built the Temple in Jerusalem, the site of Levitical blood sacrifices, as well as the place where Jesus, Himself, would be sacrificed.

As previously mentioned, God called Isaac, *"thine **only** son, Isaac, whom thou **lovest**,"* knowing that Ishmael was also Abraham's son. But Isaac, not Ishmael, was the son of promise, a foreshadowing of Jesus, the *only* begotten Son Whom God *loved*. 1 John 4:9 tells us, *"God sent his **only** begotten Son (Jesus) into the world,"* and Matthew, Mark, Luke and 1 Peter all say that Jesus was God's **beloved Son**.

And recall how, *"Abraham took the wood of the burnt offering and laid it upon Isaac his son,"* Genesis 22:6. Like Isaac who carried the bundle of wood on his shoulder, the wood upon which he was to be sacrificed, so Jesus carried the wooden cross upon which He would be sacrificed. Isaac, a young man at the time, could easily have thwarted his aging father's attempt to kill him, yet he went along obediently, again, a foreshadow of Jesus' willingness to be obedient unto death.

We can only imagine Abraham's grief at the thought of having to kill his beloved son; paralleling God the Father's grief as He allowed His perfect, holy, spotless Son to become the blood sacrifice of the New Covenant.

Again, note the prophetic nature of Abraham's response when Isaac asked, *"where is the lamb for a burnt offering? And Abraham said, My son, God will provide himself a lamb for a burnt offering,"* (Genesis 22:7-8). This didn't refer to the ram caught in a thicket and killed in place of Isaac.

Rather, it referred to the fact that God was going to provide **Himself**, in the form of Jesus, as the Lamb without spot or blemish, to be slain for the sins of the world.

Another Old Testament foreshadowing of Jesus as the Lamb is the Passover described in Exodus 12:1-13. Moses had been sent by God to deliver his people out of four-hundred years of Egyptian bondage. Nine plagues had fallen and still Pharaoh refused to free the Israelites. The tenth and final plague would see all first-born males, both man and animal, die.

To protect His people from the angel of death, God instructed Moses to have each household take a male lamb, without spot or blemish, in other words, perfect, and put the blood of that lamb on the doorposts and doorframe of their house. In Exodus 12:12 God told Moses, *"I will pass through the land of Egypt this night, and will smite all the firstborn in the land of Egypt, both man and beast."*

Notice God didn't say He was only going to kill all first-born Egyptians. Instead, He said *"**all the first born in the land** both man and beast."* What protected the Israelites? Exodus 12:13 tells us: *"And the blood shall be to you for a token upon the houses where ye are: and when I see the blood, I will pass over you, and the plague shall not be upon you to destroy you, when I smite the land of Egypt."*

Being Israelites didn't save them. Only the blood of an innocent lamb, applied to their doorposts, caused the angel of death to "pass over" them. It speaks of the already established Kingdom principle that only blood could save. It was a beautiful foreshadowing of Jesus, the perfect Lamb of God and of His blood applied to the doorposts of our hearts when we accept Him, causing us to pass from spiritual death into eternal life.

The Day of Atonement (Exodus 30:10) also carries great significance. God commanded that, *"Aaron shall make an atonement upon the horns of it* (the ark of the covenant) *once in a year with the blood of the sin offering of atonements; once in the year shall he make atonement upon it throughout your generations: it is most holy unto the Lord."*

So, once a year, according to Leviticus 16, to atone for the sins of the nation of Israel, the high priest went into the Holy of Holies before the ark of the covenant and poured blood over the mercy seat. The ark was a wooden box covered in gold, topped by a golden lid and two angels on each end. The space between the angels was the mercy seat.

Only a high priest could enter the Holy of Holies, and only after he had ritually purified himself. Fear always came with the job. If one didn't purify properly or the sacrifice was not acceptable, it meant instant death. That presented a problem. If the priest died, how was his body to be removed? The solution, small bells sewn around the hem of his garment and a rope tied around his ankle. If the jingle of bells could be heard, those outside knew he was still alive. But if the bells stopped for long, indicating the priest had died, he could be pulled out by the rope.

Leviticus details numerous other types of animal sacrifices for individual sins, showing the cleansing of sin to be a very bloody and violent act. It shows how serious sin is to God. It was also a prelude to the brutal, violent, bloody act of crucifixion where sin would be, once and for all, dealt with, not as a sin covering, like putting a clean shirt over a dirty garment and covering it up as in the Old Testament, but a total forgiveness and cleansing of sin under the New Covenant.

The New Covenant makes Jesus' identity clear.

It's no accident that Jesus, the Lamb of God, was born in Bethlehem near the Tower of the Flock, or *Midgal Edar* in Hebrew, also called Shepherd's Field. It was where lambs were raised for temple sacrifices. God had orchestrated this carefully. He was signifying that His Lamb, the perfect Lamb of Sacrifice, had arrived. And who were the first to hear the announcement of this great event? The shepherds tending the flocks in Shepherd's Field!

Zechariah 13:1 says, *"In that day there shall be a fountain opened to the house of David and to the inhabitants of Jerusalem for sin and for uncleanness."* David's birthplace was Bethlehem, another reason Jesus was born there. This Zechariah prophecy refers to both Jesus' blood sacrifice and where the fountain for the cleansing of sin would spring.

When Jesus celebrated the Passover with His disciples, Matthew 26:26-28 says, *"And as they were eating, Jesus took bread, and blessed it, and brake it, and gave it to the disciples and said, Take, eat, this is my body. And he took the cup and gave thanks, and gave it to them saying, Drink ye all of it, For this is my blood of the new testament, which is shed for many for the remission of sins."*

Here, Jesus told them to eat his body and *drink* his blood. We must understand how radical a statement this was and how horrifying it was to a Jew. Ingesting blood was forbidden in the Hebrew religion. It was reserved for God alone, and according to Leviticus 17:11 God declared it the only means of covering sin and receiving forgiveness *"For the life of the flesh is in the blood and* **I have given it** *(blood)* **to you upon the altar to make an atonement for your souls: for it is the blood that maketh an atonement for the soul.***"*

In John 6:53-54, Jesus had already told His disciples that *"Except ye eat the flesh of the Son of man and drink his blood, ye have no life in you. Whoso eateth my flesh and drinketh my blood, hath eternal life; and I will raise him up at the last day."* Because of that, many stopped following Him. This statement was just too radical. And according to Jewish law, blasphemy. That's because they didn't understand what Jesus really meant.

And what Jesus said was radical.

In the Garden of Eden, God had already established that His requirement for the remission of sins was the shedding of innocent blood. And that requirement was clearly understood in both the Old and New Testament. Remember, Leviticus 17:11 said, *"the life of the flesh is in the blood,"* and that it was *"the blood that maketh an atonement for the soul,"* while Hebrews 9:22 says, *"almost all things are by the law purged with blood; and without shedding of blood is no remission* (of sins).*"*

But what no one could imagine was that God Himself would provide that innocent blood; that it would be **His** blood. And God wasn't just going to sprinkle that blood on us or anoint parts of our body as He had done in Exodus 24:8 and Leviticus 13. Instead, He was offering to share His very life with us.

Leviticus, as well as the Old Testament story of Ruth, set the standard that only a relative could redeem that which was lost. That's why Jesus had to come in the flesh, to become our kinsman, our relative. And at the last supper, when Jesus offered the bread and wine, He was offering His very life, the life of God Himself, to live in us by the indwelling of the Holy Spirit.

Romans 8:1, written after Jesus' death and resurrection, says, *"There is therefore now no condemnation to them which are in Christ Jesus."* Why? Because Jesus' blood sacrifice was a once-and-for-all perfect sacrifice. It covered all our sins and became the basis for the new contract between God and man.

Sylvia Bambola

After the Passover feast, Jesus became the Passover lamb.

The Temple priests offered two lambs daily: one in the morning accompanied by trumpets to announce the first sacrifice as well as the opening of the doors of the Temple; and one in the afternoon, indicating the last sacrifice of the day. During the six hours in between, the priests would oversee the sacrifices made by the people for their individual sins.

Exactly at the third hour or 9 a.m., when the priests offered the first lamb of the day, Jesus was crucified. And He hung on the cross for six hours, the very six hours when people brought their personal sacrifices to the temple. During this time, He became sin for us, taking on all our shame, guilt, and emotional anguish. Then, at the ninth hour or 3 p.m., as the priests offered their second and last lamb of the day, Jesus died.

And just as the high priest, according to Leviticus 16, went into the Holy of Holies once a year and sprinkled the blood of the sacrifice on the altar and mercy seat seven times, so Jesus also shed His blood seven times. In the Bible, seven is the number of perfection and completion, such as seven days of creation, seven golden lampstands, the seven churches, the seven seals, seven trumpets, etcetera.

The first time Jesus shed His blood was during the agony in the garden where He sweated *"great drops of blood,"* (Luke 22:44). Second: when they tore off His beard and struck Him in the face (Isaiah 50:6; Luke 22:63-65). Third: the whipping post when He received thirty-nine lashes that split open his back. Fourth: when Jesus was crowned with thorns and the soldiers beat Him over the head with a reed, driving the thorns deeper (Matthew 27:29-30). Fifth: when they nailed His hands to the cross; hands that had healed so many. Sixth: when they nailed His feet to the cross; feet that had walked the dust of the earth as He went about showing us how to live. And Seventh: when the soldier pierced His side, and blood and water came out (John 19:33-34).

The empty tomb:

When Mary Magdalene went to the tomb in John 20:1-12, it was empty. The rock slab where Jesus' body had laid was covered in blood, the blood that had seeped through the linen cloth that had wrapped Him. And there, sitting at the head of the slab and another at the foot, were two angels in white, symbolizing the ark of the covenant with the two angels on each end and the bloody mercy seat in between. How rich the Bible is! And how much God wants us to understand what He did for us!

Jesus gave it all.

There was nothing left for Him to give. And just before He died, He said, "IT IS FINISHED." That word "finished" in Greek is *teleo/telos* and means, "completed, **paid in full.**" Jesus paid the penalty for all our sins in full. He completely satisfied God's requirements, God's holiness, and God's justice. And it wasn't a cover up of sin like in the Old Testament, but a complete cleansing and forgiveness.

It gives Jesus the right to say, *"I am **the** way, **the** truth and **the** life, no man comes to the Father but through me,"* (John 14:6). And that's why Jesus can also call Himself the "door" through which all must come if they want to come to the Father. Jesus also said, *"all that ever came before me (Jesus) are thieves and robbers,"* (John 10:8). There are not many ways to God. There is only One. And that way is Jesus, and that door is Jesus. In Matthew 7:14 Jesus said it best: *"Because strait is the gate, and narrow is **the way**, which leadeth unto life, and few there be that find it."*

One final thought: This blood requirement and Jesus' blood payment is vastly different from the concept of earning our salvation. The Bible clearly states salvation cannot be earned. Ephesians 2:8-9 says, *"For by grace are ye saved through faith; and that not of yourselves: it is a gift of God not of works, lest any man should boast."*

We do good works because we love God, not because we are trying to work our way to heaven or get God to love us. He already does! He already loves us completely and totally!

Encountering Jesus Throughout the Bible

Bread of Life

As previously mentioned, Bethlehem means House of Bread. It wasn't by chance that Jesus was born there, the very place where the Bread or Manna from heaven came down as flesh. But long before that, the Bible alluded to it through symbolism and foreshadowing.

The first is in Genesis 14:18-19.

"And Melchizedek king of Salem brought forth **bread** *and wine: and he was the priest of the most high God. And he blessed him* (Abraham) *and said, Blessed be Abram of the most high God, possessor of heaven and earth."* So, we have this king of peace, for that is what Salem means, coming to Abraham with **bread** and wine, and blessing him. And in verse 20 we see Abraham giving him tithes. It infers that a covenant was made here between Abraham and Melchizedek. It also foreshadows a future covenant of bread and wine.

But who exactly was Melchizedek, this king and priest of the most high God? Psalm 76:2 tells us that, *"In Salem also is his* (God's) *tabernacle, and his dwelling place in Zion."* So, we see that Salem is God's tabernacle and Melchizedek was both the king and priest of God's tabernacle. Hebrews 7:1-3 gives us even greater insight. *"For this Melchisedec, king of Salem, priest of the most high God, who met Abraham returning from the slaughter of the kings, and blessed him; To whom also Abraham gave a tenth part of all; first being by interpretation King of righteousness, and after that also King of Salem, which is King of peace;* **Without father, without mother, without descent, having neither beginning of days, nor end of life; but made like unto the Son of God; abideth a priest continually."**

There is only one person who fits this bill, and that One is Jesus. Only Jesus could be called King of Righteousness and King or Prince of Peace. Only Jesus had no beginning nor has an end. Therefore, we must conclude that Abraham was met by the preincarnate Jesus who presented him with bread and wine as a foreshadowing of His future covenant of bread and wine when He, as the Son of God without beginning or end, would, as Righteousness itself, lay down His life and spill His blood in a new covenant with mankind, symbolized by bread, which refers to His body, and wine, which refers to His blood.

Next, is the foreshadowing of unleavened bread.

In Exodus 12 God instituted the Passover. As part of His instructions, God, in verse 15, commanded the Hebrews to eat unleavened bread for seven days. *"Seven days shall ye eat unleavened bread; even the first day ye shall put away leaven out of your houses: for whosoever eateth leavened bread from the first day until the seventh day, that soul shall be cut off from Israel."* Why? Because leaven was symbolic of sin, of impurities, and this further foreshadowed Jesus as the future bread from heaven, the bread without sin or impurities. And just as Jesus is without leaven, without sin, if we believe in Him, we, too, can have a life free from the bondage of sin.

Both Matthew 26 and Luke 22 talk about Jesus celebrating Passover and the feast of unleavened bread at the last supper thus indicating He was not only the Passover lamb but also the pure unleavened bread from heaven.

Then in Exodus 16,

God began raining down bread from heaven which the Israelites called manna. It was freely given. The people did not have to work to produce it, but only gather it. And they could gather as much as they wanted for that day, but only for that day, for the manna had to be freshly collected each day or it would spoil. The manna itself was life sustaining and more than sufficient to provide the strength they needed for their strenuous march across the desert. All this was a type of Jesus as bread, symbolic of His Word. We don't have to toil for it, either, just gather it up daily. Like the Israelites, we need fresh manna each day, a fresh word from the Lord found in the Scriptures. And that Word, His bread, is life sustaining and more than enough to give us the needed strength to maneuver our own deserts.

Other Breads:

Though Jesus is the Bread of Life which came down from heaven there are other breads, too. Proverbs 4:17, referring to the wicked, says, *"For they eat the **bread** of wickedness, and drink the wine of violence."* If we don't accept the bread and wine Jesus offers, what is left? Only the bread of wickedness and the wine of violence. How sad that people would prefer that to the awesome offerings of Jesus.

What Jesus said about Himself regarding being bread:

Matthew 15 recounts how Jesus spoke about God's commandments, sin, and what defiles a man just before a Canaanite woman came to Him whose daughter was *"vexed with a devil."* Jesus ignored her and told His disciples in verse 26, *"It is not meet to take the children's* (those from the house of Israel) ***bread**, and to cast it to dogs."* Here, Jesus equated His Word, His teachings, with bread. This same story is repeated in Mark 7. In the end, Jesus granted the woman's request because she exhibited great faith. But it's clear in these passages that Jesus considered His Word, bread.

Mark 14:22, Luke 22:19 and Luke 24:30 all describe the last supper where Jesus took bread, broke it, and declared it to be His body that was to be broken for us.

In John 6:31-33, Jesus was even more specific when He said, *"Our fathers* (the Israelites) *did eat manna in the desert; as it is written, He gave them bread from heaven to eat. Then Jesus said unto them, Verily, verily, I say unto you, Moses gave you not that **bread** from heaven; but my Father giveth you the true **bread** from heaven. For the **bread** of God is he which cometh down from heaven, and giveth life unto the* *world."* Jesus went on to say in verse 35, *"I am the **bread** of life; he that cometh to me shall never hunger."* So, Jesus is the very bread that gives life. He repeated it again in John 6:48, and added this in verses 50-51, *"This is the **bread** which cometh down from heaven, that a man may eat thereof, and not die. I am the living **bread** which came down from heaven: if any man eat of this **bread**, he shall live for ever: and the **bread** that I will give is my flesh, which I will give for the life of the world."* And in verse 58 Jesus said, *"This is that **bread** which came down from heaven: not as your fathers did eat manna, and are dead: he that eateth of this **bread** shall live fore ever."*

Eating Jesus' bread (His Word, believing what He said and what He accomplished by His death and resurrection) gives us life not only here on earth via freedom from sin and by entering the fullness of what God has, but eternal life as well. Conversely, if we don't eat of His bread, if we, instead, eat of the bread of wickedness as mentioned in Proverbs 4:17, we will not have fullness of life here on earth nor eternal life in heaven.

The disciples carried this theme throughout the New Testament such as in 1 Corinthians 10:16-17 which says, *"The cup of blessing which we bless, is it not the communion of the blood of Christ? The bread which we break, is it not the communion of the body of Christ? For we being many are one bread, and one body: for we are all partakers of that one **bread**."* That one bread, of course, is Jesus. Because of Him, believers are all one body, one in Him. Oh, how wonderful to be part of the body of Christ!

Warrior

Jesus is a mighty warrior. He is Captain of the Host of heaven and commands a vast army. How do we know?

First, we'll look at the Old Testament.

In Joshua 5:13-15, Joshua was preparing to enter the Promised Land. His first target: Jericho. But before the battle even began, he met the Captain of the heavenly host and asked him in verse 13, *"Art thou for us, or for our adversaries?"* The Captain responded, *"Nay* (I'm not for you or your adversaries); *but as captain of the host of the LORD am I now come."* Then look what happened. *"**And Joshua fell on his face to the earth, and did worship**, and said unto him, What saith my lord unto his servant? And the captain of the LORD'S host said unto Joshua, **Loose thy shoe from off thy foot; for the place whereon thou standest is holy**, and Joshua did so."*

Notice that Jesus, the Captain, first told Joshua He was here on the Lord's business. God has His own agenda and Jesus, the second Person of the Godhead, was there to see it realized. Next, Joshua fell to the ground and worshipped Him. For a Hebrew to worship anyone or anything but God was blasphemy. Joshua would never do it. He saw what happened to all those who had worshipped the golden calf—how three thousand men were slain at God's command. Therefore, for Joshua to prostrate himself and worship the Captain meant he knew that he was in the presence of God. To confirm this, Jesus, the Captain, told Joshua to remove his shoes because he was standing on holy ground. We've seen this before when Moses approached the burning bush and was told by I AM to remove his shoes because he was on holy ground. By the Captain telling Joshua to remove his sandals because he, too, was *"on holy ground,"* He was proclaiming Himself to be the very same I AM.

Next, we see Abijah, king of Judah (the two southern tribes) warring against Jeroboam, king over Israel (the ten northern tribes). But Abijah didn't want to fight Israel. Before this battle, he stood on Mount Ephraim and proclaimed that Jeroboam, and Israel with him, had forsaken God. Then Abijah, in 2 Chronicles 13:12 said, *"And, behold, **God himself is with us for our captain**, and his priests with sounding trumpets to cry alarm against you. O children of Israel, fight ye not against the LORD God of your fathers; for ye shall not prosper."* But Jeroboam refused to heed the warning. Apparently, he was overconfident in his strategically placed army that now surrounded Abijah's. But victory was not to be Jeroboam's. God, as Captain, indeed intervened and Abijah ruled the day. This verse in 2 Chronicles clearly shows that Jews believed and acknowledged that God was not only a warrior, but the Captain of the angelic hosts that could either fight for or against them.

The battle is the Lord's.

Both 1 Samuel 17:47 and 2 Chronicles 20:15 tell us the battle is the Lord's. Though these words were spoken to God's people, Israel, we, too, as His people, can apply it. That means we can rest confidently in God whenever we go through tough times. He is there with us, fighting for us, working behind the scenes. We just need to trust and obey Him.

Psalm 24 talks about the citizens of God's kingdom. It extols His greatness and calls Him the *"King of glory."* Then verse 8 says, *"Who is this King of glory? The LORD strong and mighty, **the LORD mighty in battle**."* It's God Himself who is this King, who fights for us, the citizens of His kingdom. After all, it's a king's primary duty to protect His kingdom and subjects. And God has all the resources He needs to do it. He is never caught off guard, out flanked, or out maneuvered. What a comfort to know we are part of a kingdom ruled by such a great and powerful King!

Exodus 14:14 says, *"The Lord shall fight for you."* So does Deuteronomy 1:30, 3:22, 20:4, Nehemiah 4:20, Exodus 14:25, and Joshua 23:10. When something is repeated that many times we need to sit up and take notice. God is not a man that He should lie. He means what He says and says what He means. And what God has said over and over is that we can trust Him to fight for us. And doesn't Romans 8:31 say, *"If God be for us who can be against us?"* NO ONE!

Isaiah prophesied the downfall of Babylon by the Medes. Regarding this, he said in Isaiah 13:4, *"The noise of a multitude in the mountains, like as of a great people; a tumultuous noise of the kingdoms of nations gathered together: the LORD of hosts mustereth the host of the battle."* Here Isaiah is prophesying that the LORD of hosts (in other words, the Captain of the Lord's hosts) will muster the Medes to do battle against the Babylonians. It is Jesus, the Captain of the Host, who will orchestrate this battle through human vessels.

Amos 4:13 says, *"For, lo, he that **formeth the mountains, and createth the wind**, and declareth unto man what is his thought, that maketh the morning darkness, and treadeth upon the high places of the earth, The LORD, The God of **hosts** is his name."* Amos is saying that God, the creator of all things, is also the God of hosts. We have already seen that the creator is none other than Jesus, so Amos is confirming that Jesus is also the God of hosts. That word, "hosts" is *tsbaah* in Hebrew and means an army. Jesus has a powerful heavenly army, an army that He leads, which means He is a great warrior.

God, the *mighty* warrior!

In Psalm 18:34 David said, referring to God, *"He teacheth my hands to war."* David repeated this in Psalm 144:1, *"Blessed be the LORD my strength, which teacheth my hands to **war**, and my fingers to **fight**."* If God taught David to fight that means God is a warrior. Indeed, Exodus 15:3 comes right out and says it. *"The LORD is a man of **war**: the LORD is his name."*

Numerous Scriptures call God our shield and buckler. Both are defensive weapons in war. 2 Samuel 22:31 says, *"He* (God) *is a **buckler** to all them that trust in him."* Psalm 18:30 repeats this. Then David, in Psalm 35:2 asks God to, *"Take hold of **shield** and **buckler**, and stand up for my help."* In other words, David was asking God to do battle for him. Proverbs 2:7 tells us that God is, *"a **buckler** to them that walk uprightly."*

In Genesis 15:1 God tells Abraham, *"fear not Abram: I am thy **shield**."* While Deuteronomy 33:29 says, *"Happy art thou, O Israel: who is like unto thee, O people saved by the LORD, the **shield** of thy help, and who is the **sword** of thy excellency! and thine enemies shall be found liars unto thee; and thou shalt tread upon their high places."* In both Scriptures that word "shield" is *peripateo* and means, "to tread all around, to trample." God is our protection, and He will trample our enemies. Notice He also wields a sword, His Word, which is sharper than any two-edged sword (Hebrews 4:12). He is indeed a mighty warrior. And He wars on our behalf.

The New Testament also shows Jesus as a warrior.

Much of the New Testament reveals Jesus as the Lamb of God who was slain; the Lamb who came to earth to die in order to pay for our sins. But in Revelation 1:14, 2:18, 19:12 we see a different Jesus. Here, lightning shoots from His eyes of fire. It is impossible to exaggerate Jesus' awesome power, His strength, His ability, His fierce warrior-like countenance. While the apostle John was on the Isle of Patmos, he saw Jesus this way and said in

Encountering Jesus Throughout the Bible

Revelation 1:17, *"When I saw him* (Jesus) *I fell at his feet as dead."* The sight of Jesus in His glorified body completely overwhelmed John. I think that will be everyone's reaction when first seeing Jesus as He truly is. No longer the meek and mild Lamb led to the slaughter, Jesus will return as a mighty warrior to claim what is rightfully His, and He means business.

Revelation 19:13-15 gives us a picture of this mighty warrior, *"he* (Jesus) *was clothed with a vesture dipped in **blood**: and his name is called The Word of God. And the **armies** which were in heaven followed him upon white horses, clothed in fine linen, white and clean. And out of his mouth goeth a sharp **sword** that with it he should **smite** the nations."* At the end of the Tribulation, Jesus' garments will be covered with the blood of His enemies. Notice He will also carry a sword. Though He is the Prince of Peace, at this juncture He will not bring peace but will *"smite the nations."* Revelation 19:11 says that Jesus' purpose at this time will be to *"judge and **make war**."* All those who do not belong to Him will fall.

First, He will go to Bozrah to rescue the Jewish remnant hiding in the mountains of Moab and Edom. Then He will go to Jerusalem and stand on the Mount of Olives, splitting it in two. Then on to Armageddon where He will destroy the entire army of antichrist with His sword. Revelation 19:21 says, *"And the remnant* (of antichrist followers) *were **slain** with the **sword** of him* (Jesus) *that sat upon the horse, which **sword** proceeded out of his mouth: and all the fowls were filled with their flesh."* While 2

Thessalonians 2:8 says Jesus will destroy the Wicked one, the antichrist himself, *"with the brightness of his coming."*

Imagine that! Jesus will vanquish the antichrist's entire army just by opening His mouth! That is power beyond comprehension. What a terrifying day that will be for unbelievers. But what a wonderful day it will be for those who belong to Him.

But for now, our battle continues.

2 Corinthians 10:3-4 says, *"For though we walk in the flesh, we do not **war** after the flesh: For the **weapons** of our **warfare** are not carnal, but mighty through God to the pulling down of **strong holds**."* All the words in bold are fighting words, words of warfare. And that Greek word here for "war" is *strateuomai* and means "a soldier, to serve in a military campaign." Yes, we are in a war. We are soldiers. But God is with us, helping us pull down strongholds in our minds and lives, and helping us achieve victory.

But just who are we fighting? Ephesians 6:12 tells us. *"For we **wrestle** not against flesh and blood, but against principalities, against powers, against the rulers of the darkness of this world, against spiritual wickedness in high places."* Our fight is not with people but with the demonic realm. That's why Ephesians 6:13 goes on to tell us to put on the *"whole armour of God."* In addition to helping us fight our battles, God has provided all we need to protect ourselves.

In 1 Timothy 1:18, Paul exhorted Timothy by saying, *"This charge I commit unto thee, son Timothy, according to the prophecies which went before on thee, that thou by them mightest **war** a good **warfare**."* Timothy had come from a godly family. He had been given much, in the spiritual sense, and Paul was reminding him of that, as well as the warfare he would encounter, warfare common to all believers. Paul went on to tell Timothy in 1 Timothy 6:12 to, *"**fight** the good **fight** of faith."* Again, in 2 Timothy 4:7, Paul, who knew his life was soon to end, tells Timothy, *"I have **fought** a good **fight**, I have finished my course, I have kept the faith."*

As Christians we are engaged in spiritual warfare and sometimes the battle can be fierce. But we have not been left defenseless. Hebrews 2:10 tells us that Jesus is the "captain" of our salvation. That word "captain" is *archegos* in Greek and means "chief leader, author." So, Jesus not only provided the means of our salvation, but through His Word and Holy Spirit provided the means to win every battle. How great is our God! May we, like Paul, be able to say, when our time is up, *"I have **fought** a good **fight**, I have finished my course, I have kept the faith."*

Rock

The Rock of living water:

The rule of first mention states that the first time a word is mentioned in Scripture, pay attention, because it usually carries great meaning not only in that instance but throughout the rest of the Bible. The first time "rock" is mentioned is in Exodus 17:6. The Israelites had been wandering in the dusty wilderness and were thirsty. Water was scarce and difficult to find. Frightened, angry, and desperate, they apparently forgot how God had brought them out of Egypt, then protected and provided for them. All they could see was their problem.

Panicking, they murmured against Moses so heatedly that he feared for his life. His recourse was to consult God, Who told him in Exodus 17:6, *"Behold, I will stand before thee there upon **the rock** in Horeb; and thou shalt smite **the rock**, and there shall come water out if it, that the people may drink. And Moses did so in the sight of the elders of Israel."*

That word "rock" is *sur* in Hebrew and means, "a cliff, rock, boulder, refuge." It can also mean, "reliability and strength." At that time, the gods of various nations were called "rocks," implying they were strong and reliable.

But water out of a rock? Who would believe such a thing possible? Obviously, Moses. God had promised He would stand before Moses on *the* rock, not just any rock, but *the* rock in Horeb. Horeb in Hebrew means, "desolate" and is the name for the Sinaitic mountains. The Israelites, indeed, found themselves in a desolate place. Moses had already seen God do amazing miracles, so getting water out of a rock might have seemed unorthodox but not impossible. So, Moses obediently searched out the rock in question and when found, struck it with his rod. And lo and behold, so much water came gushing out it was enough to satisfy both the vast number of people and their flocks.

Two things are important to note. First, God is the one who would *"stand"* before Moses *"upon the rock."* That word "stand" is *amad* in Hebrew and means, "to stand, remain, endure, appoint, arise, confirm, establish."

It was God the Father who picked the Rock and stood on or confirmed it as a foreshadowing of how God would stand upon or confirm another Rock, Jesus, when Jesus, at age thirty, was baptized by John in the Jordan. Thirty was the age when a Hebrew male, destined for the Aaronic priesthood, ritually purified himself and entered the ministry. That's what Jesus was doing in the Jordan, ritually purifying Himself in accordance with the law before beginning His own ministry. And when He emerged from the water here's what God said in Luke 3:22 (and also in Matthew 3:17 and Mark 1:11), *"And the Holy Ghost descended in a bodily shape like a dove upon him* (Jesus) *and a voice came from heaven, which said,* **Thou art** *my beloved Son; in thee I am well pleased."* In that statement, God confirmed His Son, the Rock.

In their desolation, God directed the Israelites to the remedy, to a specific rock. In like manner, Jesus, The Rock, God's beloved Son, was to be the remedy to a desolate and desperate world mired in sin. The Rock, Jesus, was also to be struck as God approved and watched with a broken heart. And who was to smite the rock? In Horeb it was the man, Moses. At Calvary it would also be by man's hand. And that word "smite" is *nakah/naka* and means, "to give wounds, punish, beat, slay, slaughter, kill." And this is what happened to Jesus as He became the sin offering so that, like the rock at Horeb, rivers of living water could flow from Him, too.

Isaiah 53:5 says, *"But he was **wounded** for our transgressions, he was **bruised** for our iniquities: the **chastisement** of our peace was upon him; and with his **stripes** we are healed."* That word "wounded" (*challah*) means, "wound, break, slay, afflicted." The word "bruised" (*daka*) means, "to crumble, beat to pieces, destroy, humble, crush, broken." And "stripes" (*chaburah)* mean, "bound, black and blue, hurt, wound." While "chastisement" (*mocrowth*) means, "correction". All four words give an accurate picture of what was done to Jesus and what He endured.

In Deuteronomy 8:15 God makes it clear that though it was Moses who struck the Rock, it was God Who caused the water to flow out of it. In this same way, through the will of God the Father, man would be allowed to strike

Jesus so that through His death and resurrection living waters could come forth and save many.

In Psalm 78:15, 20, Psalm 105:41 and Psalm 114:8 the psalmist also acknowledged that releasing the water from the rock was God's doing. And Isaiah 48:21 again specifically stated that it was God who caused *"the waters to flow"* and adds that God *"clave the rock."* That word "clave" is *baqa* in Hebrew and means, "to rend, break, rip open, rip up, tear." It is a word associated with violence and warfare. *The Theological Wordbook of the Old Testament* adds that, "as a result of this tearing and ripping open, the contents may 'burst forth.'" And lastly, that word "clave" also means "win." What a rich picture of how God, in order to satisfy His holiness and justice, poured out the full force of His wrath, not on mankind who deserved it, but on His precious Son, Jesus, the innocent and spotless Lamb. That meant Jesus had to be ripped and opened so the contents of His love, His living water could "burst forth." It was also an act of war against the devil, a war Jesus won by his death and resurrection.

And the benefits to man were, oh, so amazing. Jesus said in John 7:38, *"He that believeth on me, as the scripture hath said, out of his belly shall flow rivers of living water."* And in John 4:7-15, He told the Samarian women at the well that He could give her *"living water,"* and *"whosoever drank of the water that I (Jesus) shall give him shall never thirst; but the water that I shall give him shall be in him a well of water springing up into **everlasting** life."* Jesus' living water would not only satisfy our spiritual thirst but carried with it the promise of eternal life.

If any doubt remains as to who the Rock is, 1 Corinthians 10:1-4 should lay it to rest. This Scripture also talks about the Israelites' and their encounter at Horeb and says that, *"all our fathers were under the cloud, and all passed through the sea; . . . And did all drink the same spiritual drink: for they drank of that spiritual **Rock** that followed them: and that **Rock** was Christ."*

Ephesians 5:26 tells us that we are sanctified and cleansed *"with the washing of water by the word."* Jesus is both the Word and the living, cleansing water.

So, from the very beginning, in first mention, we see Jesus as The Rock. As previously stated, the ancients called their gods, "rocks," too. But unlike those gods, here was a Rock Who could really be counted on. Here was a Rock that was truly strong and reliable, One who could and would provide for their needs and sustain them, and One Who could provide for and sustain all mankind.

Years later, the Israelites again found themselves thirsty, this time in the desert of Zin. Again, they blamed Moses and Aaron. I paraphrase, "We should never have left Egypt to die in the wilderness." Again, Moses sought God. Numbers 20:7-8 says, *"And the LORD spake unto Moses, saying, Take the rod, and gather thou the assembly together, thou, and Aaron thy brother, and **speak** ye unto the **rock** before their eyes; and it shall give forth his water, and thou shalt bring forth to them water out of the rock: so thou shalt give the congregation and their beasts drink."* God was prepared to do what He did in Horeb and bring water out of a rock. But this time, Moses was to speak to the rock rather than strike it.

One can only imagine the frustration Moses felt after so many years of leading this murmuring and complaining horde. He was old now, and his sister, Miriam, had died in Zin. Perhaps he was still grieving her death or simply tired of dealing with these stiff-necked people because Moses called them *"rebels."* But his frustration would cost him dearly. Here's what happened: *"Moses and Aaron gathered the congregation together before the **rock**, and he said unto them. Hear now, ye **rebels**: must we fetch you water out of the rock? And Moses lifted up his hand, and with his rod he **smote** the **rock** twice: and the water came out abundantly, and the congregation drank, and their beasts, also,"* (Numbers 20:10-11).

Though Moses had disobeyed by smiting the rock instead of speaking to it, God was gracious and made water come forth in order to satisfy the need of the people and the animals. But Moses' punishment would be great. God would not allow him to enter the Promised Land, and he died on Mount Nebo just overlooking it.

This illustrates the importance of Moses **not** striking the rock. God was setting up the prophetic picture of Jesus as The Rock Who was to be smitten only once, as indicated in the Scriptures below. And through his disobedience, Moses corrupted this foreshadowing.

Romans 6:10, *"For in that he (Jesus) died, he died unto sin **once**: but in that he liveth, he liveth unto God."*

Hebrews 9:28, *"So Christ was **once** offered to bear the sins of many; and unto them that look for him shall he appear the second time without sin unto salvation."*

Before Moses died, he composed a song about God in Deuteronomy 32:4: *"He is **the Rock**, his work is perfect: for all his ways are judgment: a God of truth and without iniquity, just and right is he."* Like the surrounding nations, Moses, too, declared his God was not only a rock, but **the Rock**, indicating He was the only true Rock and above or superior to all other "rocks". In Deuteronomy 32:15 Moses again called God the Rock of Jeshurun's salvation. Jeshurun is the symbolic name for Israel and that word "salvation" is *Yeshua*, which is Jesus' Hebrew name.

The Rock of safety/salvation:

Sometime after Moses struck the rock at Horeb, he asked God to allow him to see His glory. God responded by telling Moses no man could see His face and live. But because God greatly loved Moses and because they had a special relationship, God agreed to allow Moses to see His goodness. But he could only do so after following specific instructions. *"And the LORD said, Behold, there is a place by me, and thou shalt **stand** upon a **rock**: And it shall come to pass, while my glory passeth by, that I will put thee in a **clift** of the **rock**, and will cover thee with my hand while I pass by: and I will take away mine hand, and thou shalt see my back parts: but my face shall not be seen,"* Exodus 33:21-23.

How rich and revealing this is! First, that word "rock" is the same one used in Exodus 17:6, *sur*, the very rock that foreshadows Jesus. But this time, Moses was told to **stand** upon it. That word stand (*natsab/netsib*) means, "to station, appoint, erect, present." It also implies a military position. So, Moses was to take his position on the rock and when God passed by, He would place Moses in its **clift** or cleft. That word "clift" is *neqarah/naqar* and means, "to bore, pierce, thrust out, hole." Only by being placed in this thrusted out, pierced place, would Moses be able to see the goodness of God. And that word "goodness" (*tuwb/towb*) means, "welfare, good things, beneficial, pleasant, happy, favorable, right."

What does this tell us? It says that in this same way we are safe when we stand on Jesus, The Rock, and are hidden in His pierced work at Calvary. Only by standing on The Rock and hidden in Him can we see the goodness of God, His favor in our lives, His benefits. How wonderful God is! How greatly He loves us and wants to have a special relationship with us. But this can only be achieved through The Rock.

The Song of Solomon is a love story between King Solomon and a Shulamite woman. Interestingly, that word "Shulamite" means, "bride, peaceful or peace, be in a covenant of peace." It's a perfect picture of the love between Jesus and His bride, the church, who is in a covenant of peace with Him. In chapter 2:14, the king tells his beloved, *"O my dove, that art in the **clefts of the rock**, in the secret places of the stairs, let me see thy countenance, let me hear thy voice, for sweet is thy voice and thy countenance is comely."* Notice, his beloved, his bride, is in the clefts of the rock, safe and hidden, a place where they can speak to each other in secret. What a beautiful picture of Jesus' love and desire for intimacy with us. And it's only in that cleft where this intimacy can occur.

On the other hand, Isaiah 2:21, Jeramiah 49:16 and Obadiah 3 all carry a warning from God to those who dwell in the wrong **clefts of the rock** or try to create their own clefts. Though they think they are safe, they are deceived. It is a false security. *"The pride of thine heart hath deceived thee, thou that dwellest in **the clefts of the rock**, whose habitation is high: that saith in his heart, Who shall bring me down to the ground?"* (Obadiah 3). Although the above verse was addressed to Edom, it holds a lesson and warning for all. There is no safety in any rock but Jesus.

David understood this and declared it in many of his writings by saying things like, *"For in the time of trouble he* (God) *shall hide me in his pavilion: in the secret of his tabernacle shall he hide me; he shall set me up upon a **rock**,"* (Psalm 27:5). David, after asking God to keep him safe and deliver him from his enemies said in Psalm 28:1, *"Unto thee will I cry. O LORD my **rock**."* And again, in Psalm 31:2-3, *"Bow down thine ear to me; deliver me speedily: be thou my strong **rock**, for an house of defense to save me. For thou art my **rock** and my fortress; therefore for thy name's sake lead me, and guide me."* In fact, the Psalms are full of David's petitions to God, his Rock. Psalm 40:2, 42:9 and 61:2 are just a few more.

After God delivered David from Saul and his enemies, David said in 2 Samuel 22:2-3, *"The LORD is my **rock**, and* *my fortress, and my deliverer; The God of my **rock**; in him will I trust: he is my shield and the horn of my salvation, my high tower, and my refuge, my savior; thou savest me from violence."* David repeated this in Psalm 18:2 and continued this theme in both 2 Samuel 22:32 and Psalm 18:31, *"For who is God, save the LORD? and who is a **rock**, save our God?"* He also said, *"The LORD liveth; and blessed be my **rock**; and let the God of my salvation be exalted,"* (2 Samuel 22:47, Psalm 18:46). And in 2 Samuel 23:3, David called God, *"the **Rock** of Israel."*

But Moses also prophesied that in the future, Israel would abandon God causing Him to judge His people. At that time, God would say to them, *"Where are their gods, their rock in whom they trusted,"* (Deuteronomy 32:37). And because this future Israel would trust in other rocks, other gods, they would have no strength, and calamity would come upon them.

Jesus said in Matthew 7:24-25, *"whosoever heareth these sayings of mine, and doeth them, I will liken him unto a wise man, which built his house upon a **rock**: And the rain descended, and the floods came, and the winds blew, and beat upon that house; and it fell not: for it was founded upon a **rock**."* Jesus spoke in terms easy to understand. Here, He gave His listeners a picture of a house that because it was built on a firm foundation, was able to withstand the adverse effects of nature. It's easy to see how this also applies to the spiritual. Jesus never promised there wouldn't be storms in our life. But the promise is that if we believe and obey His words, we will be able to withstand them. What a comfort! Life is full of trials and tribulations, and if it's not built on a firm foundation, sooner or later those storms can destroy it.

The Rock of the impossible:

Moses, in his song, extoled God for His greatness in achieving the many victories on behalf of the Israelites and said, *"How should one chase a thousand, and two put ten thousand to flight, except their Rock had sold them and the LORD has shut them up. For their rock is not as our **Rock**, even our enemies themselves being judges,"* (Deuteronomy 32:30-31).

Here, Moses acknowledged that if God, The Rock of Israel, had not intervened, there would be no victory, and though other nations called their god a "rock" there was no Rock like Israel's Rock and even the surrounding nations knew and acknowledged it.

Then there was barren Hannah, beloved wife of Elkanah. Peninnah, Elkanah's other wife, wasn't as loved as Hannah and vented her resentment by using Hannah's barrenness to hurt and humiliate her. In those days, barrenness carried a stigma because it was believed the barren woman was under God's curse. It was a source of great shame.

After trying for years to get pregnant, Hannah, devastated and desperate, went to the Temple to plead her case before God. When Eli, the priest, saw her praying and weeping, he believed she was intoxicated (1 Samuel 1:1-28). After she assured him she was seeking

God out of grief and with a sincere heart, he told her, *"and the God of Israel grant thee thy petition that thou has asked of him,"* (1 Samuel 1:17).

And God did just that. She bore the prophet Samuel and dedicated him to the Lord. As she rejoiced over God's faithfulness, she said, *"There is none holy as the LORD: for there is none beside thee: neither is there any **rock** like our God."* Samuel would become great in Israel. Hannah's God, her Rock, had proven to be the God of the impossible, able to do above and beyond what anyone could imagine.

Luke 1:37 tells us, *"For with God nothing shall be impossible."* And Ephesians 3:20 says, *"Now unto him that is able to do exceeding abundantly above all that we ask or think, according to the power that worketh in us."*

Nothing, absolutely nothing, is impossible for God, our Rock.

The Rock of the narrow way:

The Bible continually surprises me with its depth and hidden meanings. One example is found in 1 Samuel 14:1-14 when King Saul's son, Jonathan, and Jonathan's armor bearer head for a Philistine garrison with the intention of doing battle. Because God was with Jonathan, he and his bearer ended up slaughtering the garrison of about twenty men. Though it's a historical event, it also has great symbolic meaning. 1 Samuel 14:4 says, *"And between the passages, by which Jonathan sought to go over unto the Philistines' garrison, there was a sharp* **rock** *on the one side, and a sharp* **rock** *on the other side: and the name of the one was* **Bozez***, and the name of the other* **Seneh***."*

The Philistines were Israel's principal adversary from 1200-1000 B.C. Now, Jonathan, on his way to do battle with them, had to pass through a narrow gorge flanked by large rocky masses. But why would Scripture bother to name those rocks? Let's dig deeper.

Bozez means, "shining, to bleach, to be white." It also refers to the costly cloth used by the royal court in their priestly garments as well as in the veil of the Jewish Temple. *Seneh* means, "thorn, prick." So, we see here two representations of Jesus, The Rock.

The first, *Bozez*, refers to Jesus' royalty as King of kings and Lord of lords (Revelation 19:15), and as high priest after the order of Melchisedec (Hebrews 5:10), shiny and white (Revelation 1:13-16). It also alludes to Jesus' bride and army as described in Revelation 19:14, who He has bleached or made white through His righteousness and who He has made a kingdom of kings and priests. Notice, the references to "white" and "fine linen." *"And the armies which were in heaven followed him* (Jesus) *upon white horses,* **clothed in fine linen, white and clean.***"*

The other, *Seneh*, depicts Jesus, The Rock, who was pricked and is associated with thorns (the crown of thorns). Between the two, the path was narrow, confined, but it led to the vanquishing of Israel's age-old enemy.

We, too, have age-old enemies, the devil, as well as death and hell. And the only way to overcome or vanquish them is by walking the narrow path guarded by Jesus, our Savior, and Jesus our King and High Priest.

Jesus said in John 14:6, *"I am **the way**, the truth, and the life: no man cometh unto the Father, but by me."* And in Matthew 7:14 He said, *"strait is the gate, and **narrow is the way**, which leadeth unto life, and few there be that find it."* It's not rocket science. Walking that narrow path is the only way to live if we want a victorious life. And just as Jonathan, who walked the narrow path, overcame great odds, and vanquished a garrison, so if we walk the narrow path, **the way** of God, we, too, can overcome great odds (sickness, poverty, strife, etcetera). And death no longer has a sting but was overcome by Jesus, as was hell. So, we, too, overcome them because of the blood of the Lamb and because we are now hidden in Christ.

Rock of Offense:

Isaiah 8:14 says that God will be, *"a stone of stumbling and for a **rock** of offence."* And that's just what Jesus, the Messiah, was to the Jewish nation when He came as Immanuel from the tribe of Judah. Many religious Jews of that day rejected Him. They just couldn't believe that God would physically dwell among them.

Jesus Himself acknowledged this when He said in Luke 20:17-18 (and also in Matthew 21:42) *"What is this then that is written, The **stone** which the builders rejected, the same is become the head of the corner? Whosoever shall fall upon* *that **stone** shall be **broken**; but on whomsoever it shall fall, it will grind hm to **powder**."*

Roman 9:31-33 explains it further. *"But Israel which followed after the law of righteousness, hath not attained to the law of righteousness. Wherefore? Because they sought it not by faith, but as it were by the works of the law. For they stumbled at that stumblingstone; As it is written, Behold, I lay in Sion a stumblingstone and **rock of offence:** and whosoever believeth on him, shall not be ashamed."* Salvation and righteousness were not to come by works, but by the stumbling stone, the very stone the builders rejected.

Jesus did, indeed, become the cornerstone of the Kingdom of God on earth. And those who fell upon Him, those who acknowledged Him and accepted Him as Savior and Lord, would be broken. They would be called to die to self. They would be broken from old habits and old ways of thinking, and would acknowledge their nothingness before God. They would be changed, from glory to glory, though sometimes through a painful process because hardship is a good teacher. But those who did not come to The Rock would be the ones it would fall upon and turn to powder. That word "powder" (*iuo* in Greek) means, "to destroy." In other words, those who reject Jesus, The Rock, will be destroyed. Their future in hell will accomplish that. Jesus warned of this very thing in Matthew 10:28, *"fear not them which kill the body, but are not able to kill the soul: but rather fear him which is able to **destroy** both soul and body in hell."* That word "destroy" here means, "to destroy fully." In other words, total destruction.

1 Peter 2:7-8 adds, *"Unto you therefore which believe he (Jesus) is precious: but unto them which be disobedient, the **stone** which the builders disallowed, the same is made the head of the corner. And a **stone** of stumbling, and a **rock** of offence, even to them which stumble at the word, being disobedient; whereunto also they were appointed."*

Jesus is still a Rock of offense. Many reject Him, mock Him, deny His accomplished work. Even so, He is here for everyone who cares to come to Him. His arms are wide open, revealing nail-scarred hands. He laid it all down for us so we can be with Him forever. And for those who do come, He will be their strong and reliable God. But those who reject Him will have a terrifying future in hell and be destroyed in both soul and body.

Rock as Creator:

In Deuteronomy 32:18 Moses chided his people for their idolatry and said, *"Of the **Rock** that begat thee thou art unmindful, and hast forgotten God that formed thee."* Here, Moses equated The Rock with the Creator. We have already seen in the first chapter that Jesus is indeed the Creator of all. This description in Deuteronomy refers not only to The Rock being Creator but as the One who birthed Israel as a nation. In the same way, Jesus can make those who come to Him, new creations.

Isaiah 51:1 says, *"Hearken to me, ye that follow after righteousness, ye that seek the LORD: look unto the **rock** whence ye are **hewn**, and to the **hole** of the **pit** whence ye were* *digged."* That phrase *"the rock whence ye are hewn"* also alludes to the creative nature of Jesus.

Just a brief word study is revealing. "Pit" (*bowr/bor*) means, "a pit, cistern, well, dungeon." "Hewn" is *chatseb* in Hebrew and means, "to carve, make, hew." The "hole" (*maqqebeth*) means, "a hammer, puncture, bore, curse, pierce." And "digged" (*noqeph/naqar*) means, "bore, pick, dig."

Both the Israelites and mankind were in a **pit** of destruction, a dungeon, before Jesus came along and rescued us all. The Israelites were saved from the slave pits of Egypt and we, those individuals who believe in Him, are saved from the pit of sin and hell where we were separated from God. But Jesus, like a **hammer**, created an opening, a **hole**, by becoming a **curse** for us and by being **pierced** on the cross, thereby **digging** us out of our pit and enabling us to leave our old life behind and embrace our new life in Christ.

In addition, God, in Jeremiah 23:29, likened His word to a hammer. Through Jeremiah, God chastised Israel for Baal worship and their false prophets. *"Is not my word like as a fire? saith the LORD; and like a **hammer** that breaketh the **rock** in pieces"* The Bible often has layers of meanings. Because "rock" can refer to a false god, God may be saying He could break the false god, Baal, into pieces. But it could also refer to the breaking of The Rock, as foretold in His Word, such as in Isaiah 53:2-5, which talks of the suffering Messiah and how the Messiah must be broken in order to pay for our sins.

Encountering Jesus Throughout the Bible

The Rock of Christianity:

This has been a matter of debate for centuries. Who is the Rock upon which Jesus built His church? Some say Peter, others disagree. Let's look at what Jesus actually said in Matthew 16:18, *"And I say also unto thee, That thou art Peter and upon this **rock** I will build my church; and the gates of hell shall not prevail against it."* Both Peter (*petros*) and that word "rock" in this Scripture, which is *petra,* are similar yet imply different things. Peter (*petros*) indicates a piece of rock, while rock (*petra*) implies a mass of rock.

So, is the church to be built upon Peter, the piece of rock or The Rock? The answer lies in the few verses above this one when Jesus asked His disciples who people said He was. They cited a litany of names: John the Baptist, Elias, Jeremias or one of the prophets. That wasn't the answer Jesus had been looking for, so He pressed the point. *"But whom say **ye** that I am?* And when Peter answered in Matthew 16:16, *"Thou art the Christ, the Son of the living God,"* Jesus told him that this was a Divine revelation from God the Father, Himself. Then in the following verse, Jesus made the statement about building His church. But the rock upon which His church was to be built was not Peter, but upon Peter's revelation that Jesus was the Son of God, The Rock. Peter, the little rock, was to become a new creature after Christ's death, reflecting his Master in order to become "a chip off the old block." Peter understood this because as mentioned, he said in I Peter 2:6-7 that Jesus was the corner stone, the head of the corner. A chief or head corner stone is the first stone placed in the corner of a foundation and affected the placement of all other stones. By calling Jesus the head of the corner, Peter acknowledged that Jesus was the foundation of the church, that it was Jesus upon which the church and its entire foundation was to be built, not him.

The Rock of judgment:

Now, we come to the last Rock and perhaps the most exciting as well as frightening. In Daniel 2:14-45, Daniel was asked to interpret King Nebuchadnezzar's dream. The king had dreamed of a giant statue with a gold head, silver chest and arms, belly and thighs of brass, legs of iron, and lastly, feet of an iron and clay mixture. What did it mean?

Daniel, faithful servant of God, was given understanding through Divine revelation that the statue represented the current and future world empires that would influence or impact the nation of Israel. The head of gold was Babylon. The silver chest and arms symbolized the Mede and Persian empire which would, in one night, conquer Babylon. The belly and thighs of brass represented the empire that followed the Medes and Persians. It was Alexander the Great's Greek empire and the subsequent splitting up of that empire by Alexander's top four generals after Alexander's death. The legs of iron represented the strong and oppressive Roman Empire. The feet of clay and iron symbolized the revived Roman Empire or One World Government yet to come in the last days just prior to Jesus' return. And that empire would be mingled with an inferior element making it weaker than the original Roman Empire.

During his description, Daniel inserted this prophecy: *"Thou sawest till that a* **stone** *was cut out without hands, which smote the image upon his feet that were of iron and clay, and brake them to pieces. Then was the iron, the clay, the brass, the silver, and the gold broken to pieces together, and became like the chaff of the summer threshing floors; and the wind carried them away that no place was found for them: and the* **stone** *that smote the image became a great mountain, and filled the whole earth,"* Daniel 2:34-35.

The stone, of course, is Jesus the Rock, who will come after the seven-year-Tribulation and judge the earth. At that time, all earthly empires will be done away with, and Jesus, Himself, will rule for a thousand years.

It's interesting to note what the reaction of the rulers and those rejectors of God will be as the end nears. Revelation 6:15-17 gives a pathetic picture of them cowering in fear. *"And the kings of the earth, and the great men, and the rich men, and the chief captains, and the mighty men, and every bondman, and every free man, hid themselves in the dens and in the* **rocks** *of the mountains; And said to the mountains and* **rocks***, Fall on us, and hide us from the face of him that sitteth on the throne, and from the wrath of the Lamb: for the great day of his wrath is come; and who shall be able to stand?"*

Amazingly, these people will know and understand what is about to happen, that Jesus is about to return to earth, and instead of repenting and crying out for mercy, they ask the rocks to fall on them and hide them. In the natural, we see an image of frightened humanity hiding in caves and hoping the rocks and mountains will provide a covering or barrier between them and Jesus, and insulate them from His wrath. It could also indicate a desire to die, hoping that death would enable them to escape this coming wrath, because in biblical times, stones were instruments of death. They were used to kill those who broke Levitical laws covering blasphemy, idolatry, and adultery, all of which could be spiritually leveled against those who reject the One True God.

Stones or rocks were also used for building altars where one worshiped his god/s. In the same way, these people in Revelation 6, who have rejected the true Rock, may be, spiritually speaking, calling upon their rocks—their idols, their gods, their resources, their power, their name, their position, or anything else they have worshiped and relied on—to protect them now. It seems they will hide in caves, hoping that all their old safety mechanisms will help them, rather than turn to God. It's beyond sad.

But, unfortunately for them, nothing will help them now. All their position, wealth, and power won't save them when the rightful King of the earth comes to claim His throne. And it will be an awesome sight. *"And I saw heaven opened, and behold a white horse; and he that sat upon him was called Faithful and True, and in righteousness he doth judge and make war. His eyes were as a flame of fire, and on his head were many crowns; and he had a name written, that no man knew, but he himself. And he was clothed with a vesture dipped in blood: and his name is called The Word of*

God. And the armies which were in heaven followed him upon white horses, clothed in fine linen, white and clean. And out of his mouth goeth a sharp sword, that with it he should smite the nations: and he shall rule them with a rod of iron: and he treadeth the winepress of the fierceness and wrath of Almighty God. And he had on his vesture and on his thigh a name written, KING OF KINGS, AND LORD OF LORDS," Revelation 19:11-16.

Son of Man

Jesus called Himself the Son of man. So did others. Nearly eighty-five times in the New Testament He references Himself or is referenced this way. Why? It had to do with the law of redemption laid out in Leviticus. The law states that if one who sold his land or possessions could not redeem them at a later time, a relative could. Leviticus 25:25 says, *"If thy brother be waxen poor, and hath sold away some of his possessions, and if any of his **kin** come to **redeem** it, then shall he **redeem** that which his brother sold."* Leviticus 25:48 goes on to say that if a person sells himself, *"After that he is sold he may be **redeemed** again; one of his **brethren** may **redeem** him."* So, it wasn't just anyone who could act as redeemer. By law it had to be the person himself or a kinsman, thus establishing the prerequisite that only a relative could redeem that which was previously sold if the seller was unable to do so.

Webster defines redeemer as someone who redeems or "buys back, recovers as by paying a fee, to set free, ransom, rescue." And isn't that just what mankind needed? Adam and Eve sold themselves into sin's bondage for the promise of becoming "gods." And that followed mankind down through the ages. Unable to buy himself back from his bondage, man needed a kinsman to do it. And that Kinsman Redeemer was Jesus, who redeemed and purchased us with His blood.

Prior to Jesus' death and resurrection, salvation came through faith in God and His Word. Genesis 15:6 says that because Abraham believed in the Lord, in other words had faith in Him, God *"counted it to him for righteousness."* But this faith didn't gain Abraham, or anyone else living in Old Testament times, entrance into heaven. Because of Adam and Eve's sin, heaven was barred to all mankind. Those in the Old Testament whose faith was counted "for righteousness" entered Paradise after death. According to Luke 16:22-26, there was a pleasant place located near a horrific chamber of hell but separated by a *"great gulf fixed."* Even so, those in this seeming paradise could still see the people consigned to fiery torment. But after Jesus' resurrection everything changed. Heaven's doors were opened to all who were counted "righteous." Paradise itself and those in it were transported there. Then going forward, heaven and Paradise became the destination of all who had faith in Jesus, who believed in Him and His Word, and what He accomplished.

But how do we know that Paradise, once in the bowels of the earth or hades, is now in heaven? First, as previously mentioned, Scripture tells us that though Abraham and Lazarus were in hades, it was a pleasant place separated, by a gulf, from the torment and fires of hell. That pleasant place had to be Paradise. Secondly, Jesus promised the man on the cross next to Him, the man the King James Bible called a "malefactor," meaning criminal, that he would be with Jesus that very day **in Paradise** (Luke 23:43). And since we know from Ephesians 4:9 and Acts 2:31 that Jesus descended to hell and was there for three days, the only way that criminal could be with Jesus the same day in Paradise was if Paradise was located in the underworld.

While in hell, Jesus *"preached unto the spirits in prison,"* (1 Peter 3:19). These "spirits" were the dead in hades. Then Jesus, *"When he ascended up on high,* **he led captivity captive and gave gifts unto men**,*"* (Ephesians 4:8-10). That word "gifts" in Greek means, "present." But it also means, "bring forth, deliver, receive." This is referring to Jesus' ascension when He took Paradise and those in it, to heaven. Jesus was "bringing forth" those righteous once confined to the underworld. He had conquered captivity itself—sin, death, and hell—and they were now His captives. His blood was the remedy for sin. While Revelation 1:18 tells us that Jesus secured the keys of death and hell. Heaven's doors were now wide open, and Paradise had become part of heaven. That's why Paul, in 2 Corinthians 12:2-4, could say that he was caught up to the third heaven into *"**paradise**"* and why Revelation 2:7 tells us that overcomers, believers in Jesus, will *"eat of the tree of life, which is in the midst of the **paradise** of God."*

Symbolism and foreshadowing in the Book of Ruth.

The Book of Ruth is all about the kinsman redeemer. It's also a love story. It reveals the depth of God's love and illustrates the role of the kinsman. It is a beautiful foreshadowing of Jesus as our Kinsman Redeemer.

Let's take a brief look.

A famine had hit Bethlehem-Ephratah as well as the neighboring area. Thinking the best course of action was to move, Elimelech took his wife, Naomi, and their two sons to Moab. There, disaster struck. Elimelech died. Fortunately, the sons were old enough to support the family and they eventually took Moabite wives. But after several years, both sons died leaving their widows, Orpah and Ruth, to live with Naomi who had no means of support. Things looked bleak until good news arrived: the famine was over in Israel. Time to go home. In Bethlehem, Naomi would be in her hometown surrounded by people she knew and with whom she had much in common.

When her daughters-in-law learned of her plans, they wanted to go, too, but Naomi tried talking them out of it. *"Turn again, my daughters: why will ye go with me? Are there yet any more sons in my womb, that they may be your husbands?"* (Ruth 1:11).

In those days, Jewish levirate law required a childless widow to marry one of her husband's single brothers so he could raise up seed for his dead brother. Neither Orpah nor Ruth had children. That's why Naomi tried to discourage them by saying she had no more sons for them to marry, then tried clinching it by claiming she was too old to remarry and bear children. If that wasn't enough, she added, *"If I should say, I have hope, if I should have an husband also to night, and should also bear sons; Would ye tarry for them till they were grown? Would ye stay for them from having husbands?"* (Ruth 1:12-13). Naomi was saying that even if she got married that night and got pregnant right away and had sons, why should they wait for those sons to reach marriageable age when they could marry someone else sooner?

It made sense to Orpah who tearfully returned to her family. But Ruth refused to go, saying in Ruth 1:16-17, *"for whither thou goest, I will go; and where thou lodgest, I will lodge: thy people shall be my people, and thy God my God: Where thou diest, will I die, and there will I be buried: the LORD do so to me, and more also, if ought but death part thee and me."* So, it was settled. Ruth would return to the land of Judah with Naomi.

Although the famine was over, the women hardly faced a life of luxury. Neither had an income nor any means of support. Fortunately, it was the time of the barley harvest when the poor could glean the corners of the fields. By gleaning, Naomi and Ruth could keep from starving.

Enter the hero:

Naomi happened to have a wealthy relative, Elimelech's brother, Boaz. Without knowing Boaz was Naomi's kinsman, Ruth began gleaning his field. She did this faithfully then something wonderful happened. Boaz noticed her. Her lack of complaining, her devotion and care for the aging Naomi, piqued his interest. He told her to glean only in his field where he could protect her, and then he instructed his men to leave extra sheaves, *"handfuls of purpose,"* for her to gather. He even invited her to eat the food that had been provided for his reapers.

When Naomi realized Ruth had been gleaning in Boaz's field, she saw the hand of God at work and instructed Ruth to continue only gleaning there. And for nearly fifty days, Ruth did, gathering first barley, then wheat. It was during this period that Naomi saw the possibility of Boaz acting as kinsman redeemer on their behalf. When it came time to thresh the harvest, Naomi hatched a plan. She instructed Ruth to wash, anoint herself, and dress, then go to the threshing floor. In Ruth 3:4 she told her daughter-in-law, *"And it shall be, when he* (Boaz) *lieth down, that thou shalt mark the place where he shall lie, and thou shalt go in, and uncover his feet, and lay thee down; and he will tell thee what thou shalt do."*

Why did Naomi tell Ruth to do this? Because, by laying at Boaz's feet, Ruth was asking him, as Naomi's kinsman, to become her protector. When Boaz saw a woman lying near him in the dark, he became startled and asked who she was. *"And she answered, I am Ruth, thine handmaid: spread therefore thy skirt over thine handmaid: for thou art a near kinsman."* He did, and by doing so pledged to be her kinsman-redeemer. He was promising not only to protect her but to redeem Elimelech's property for Naomi. Boaz did, indeed, do all this and more. He married Ruth and they became the great-grandparents of

King David. And even more wonderful, they are of the bloodline of Messiah, Jesus, Himself.

As previously mentioned, the Book of Ruth illustrates the spiritual truth that only a kinsman can redeem. Boaz, as a type of Christ, revealed the need for Jesus to come in the flesh as our relative, to redeem us and spread His cloak, His mantle of protection over us. Thus, He left His abode in heaven and became a man. And that's why Jesus constantly referred to Himself as Son of man.

What an amazing thing Jesus did! He willingly left the majesty of heaven and His exalted position to be born in a humble stable, to work with His hands as a carpenter, and walk the dusty footpaths of Israel. And then He endured the agony of betrayal, abuse, scorn, a fake trial, and finally an excruciating death just so He could redeem us. Oh, how much God loves us! How can such a sacrifice be ignored?

Other references to God as Redeemer in the Old Testament:

There were many, but I'll only highlight a few.

The concept of God as redeemer was established early in Scripture. In Exodus 6:6, God declared Himself redeemer. *"Wherefore say unto the children of Israel, I am the LORD, and I will bring you out from under the burdens of the Egyptians, and I will rid you out of their bondage, and I will* **redeem** *you with a stretched out arm, and with great judgments."*

Then Moses, in Exodus 15:13, also declared God, Israel's redeemer. *"Thou (God) in thy mercy hast led forth the people which thou hast **redeemed** (from Egyptian bondage): thou hast guided them in thy strength unto thy **holy habitation**."* After God redeemed Israel, He brought them to Mount Sinai in order to meet with them and give them His laws. In other words, He brought them to his "holy habitation."

King David acknowledged God as His redeemer in Psalm 19:14. *"Let the words of my mouth, and the meditation of my heart, be acceptable in thy sight, O LORD, my strength, and my **redeemer**."*

Proverbs 23:10-11 says, *"Remove not the old landmark; and enter not into the fields of the fatherless: For their **redeemer** is mighty; he shall plead their case with thee."* Of course, the redeemer mentioned here is God. He already proclaimed Himself as protector of orphans. In Exodus 22:22-24 God commanded, *"Ye shall not afflict any widow, or fatherless child. If thou afflict them in any wise, and they cry at all unto me, I will surely hear their cry; and my wrath shall wax hot."* And Psalm 68:5 says, *"A father of the fatherless, and a judge of the widows, is God in his holy habitation."* One can't abuse or defraud a widow or orphan without incurring God's judgment. He truly is their redeemer.

God Himself, in Isaiah 43:14, again acknowledged He is the redeemer. *"Thus saith the LORD, your **redeemer**, the Holy One of Israel."*

Other Scriptures revealing God as redeemer:

Psalm 34:22, *"The LORD **redeemeth** the soul of his servants: and none of them that trust in him shall be desolate."*

Psalm 111:9, *"He (God) sent **redemption** unto his people: he hath commanded his covenant for ever: holy and reverend is his name."*

Psalm 130:7, *"Let Israel hope in the LORD: for with the LORD there is mercy, and with him is plenteous **redemption**."*

Psalm 49:15, *"But God will **redeem** my soul from the power of the grave: for he shall receive me."*

Jeremiah 15:21, *"And I (God) will deliver thee out of the hand of the wicked, and I will **redeem** thee out of the hand of the terrible."*

Nehemiah 1:10, *"Now these are thy (God's) servants and thy people (Israel) whom thou hast **redeemed** by thy great power, and by thy strong hand."*

Isaiah 43:1, *"But now thus saith the LORD that created thee, O Jacob, and he that formed thee, O Israel, Fear not: for I have **redeemed** thee, I have called thee by thy name; thou art mine."* And just like Israel, after Jesus redeemed us, we, too, became His.

God declared Himself redeemer throughout the Old Testament, and repeatedly redeemed His people, Israel.

God changes not. He is the same yesterday, today and forever. The fact that God is redeemer was clearly established in the Old Testament, and fully realized in Jesus, the Second Person of the Trinity, in the New Testament.

Jesus as Redeemer in the Old Testament:

Deuteronomy 15:15 (and repeated in Deuteronomy 24:18) says, *"And thou shalt remember that thou wast a bondman in the land of Egypt, and the LORD thy God redeemed thee."* Though the rescuing of Israel from Egyptian bondage was an actual event, it was also prophetic, pointing to a time when God, through Jesus, would redeem mankind.

In Scripture, Egypt is a type of the evil world system. The Israelites had been its slaves, just as we were enslaved by Satan and this corrupt world. But God brought His people out of bondage by His mighty hand, a foreshadowing of how Jesus would bring us out of bondage by His mighty hand. And it would be mighty indeed. It took nothing less than His precious blood to do it. Jesus also led us to His holy habitation by enabling us to have a personal relationship with Him and indwelling us by His Holy Spirit.

In Psalm 78, the psalmist worried that future generations in Israel would forget God so he recounted, as a record to these generations, the amazing story of their exodus from Egyptian bondage. He told of all the sins his people committed in the wilderness, then said this in verse 35,

*"And they remembered that God was their rock, and the high God (or Most High) their **redeemer**."* We already learned that Jesus is the Rock. And here He is also called, Redeemer.

Then, in the Book of Ruth, we saw how wealthy Boaz, a type of Christ, became the kinsman redeemer and took a Gentile bride. It's the perfect illustration of Jesus, the wealthy King of Glory, who came to earth to act as our Kinsman Redeemer, then took a Gentile bride, the Church.

Job is also an interesting Biblical figure. He endured much, both at the hands of Satan and his friends who constantly criticized him. Yet, in Job 19:25-26 he said, *"For I know that my **redeemer** liveth, and that he shall **stand at the latter day upon the earth**: And though after my skin worms destroy this body, yet in my flesh shall I see God."*

Despite all his suffering, Job clung to the belief that God would redeem him, that even if his body were destroyed, he would see God in the end. He also made a prophetic statement that in the last days his redeemer would stand upon the earth. He was speaking about Jesus, about the time when Jesus would come to earth to redeem mankind as the Lamb without spot or blemish. But I think it can also prophetically include Jesus' second coming when He will once again return to earth, splitting the Mount of Olives, then ridding the planet of evil before establishing His Kingdom of Peace.

Isaiah 44:6 says, *"Thus saith the LORD the King of Israel, and his **redeemer** the LORD of hosts; I am the first, and I am the last; and beside me there is no God."* What a powerful statement! It reveals so much. As we will see in a later chapter, Jesus is the King of Israel. We have already seen He is the Captain of the heavenly hosts or the Lord of Hosts. And He is also the first and last as revealed in Revelation 1:8 where Jesus said, *"I am Alpha and Omega, the beginning and the ending."* And in Revelation 1:11 He said, *"I am Alpha and Omega, **the first and the last**."* So, here in Isaiah 44:6, Jesus revealed Himself in four ways: as King, Redeemer, Captain of the Host, and as the First and the Last.

Then, in Isaiah 44:24, Jesus revealed Himself again. *"Thus saith the LORD, thy **redeemer**, and he that formed thee from the womb, I am the LORD that maketh all things: that stretcheth forth the heavens alone; that spreadeth abroad the earth by myself."* We have already learned that Jesus is the Creator of everything. Therefore, it is Jesus, the Second Person of the Trinity, here acknowledging that He is Creator while at the same time claiming to be Redeemer.

Isaiah 47:4 goes on to say, *"As for our **redeemer**, the LORD of hosts is his name, the Holy One of Israel."* Again, we see Jesus as both Captain of the Host and Redeemer.

Isaiah 49:26b adds this: *"I the LORD am thy Saviour and thy **Redeemer**, the mighty One of Jacob."* Here, in addition to Redeemer, God also called Himself, "Saviour." He repeats this in Isaiah 60:16b. And of course, we know the Savior is Jesus.

Isaiah 54:5 adds even more. *"For thy Maker is thine husband; the LORD of host is his name; and thy **Redeemer** the Holy One of Israel; The God of the whole earth shall he be called."* So, our Redeemer is also our husband. God called Israel, His wife, and Jesus called us, the church, His bride. He is our Redeemer, but as these few Scriptures reveal, He is so much more.

Isaiah 51:11, *"Therefore the **redeemed** of the LORD shall return, and come with singing unto Zion; and **everlasting** joy shall be upon their head: they shall obtain gladness and joy; and sorrow and mourning shall flee away."* This is a prophetic statement. All those redeemed by the Lord will surely *"come with singing unto Zion"* because Zion is the place where Jesus will set up His millennial kingdom. It will be a time of great joy, a joy that will last all eternity.

And Isaiah 59:20 says, *"And the **Redeemer** shall come to Zion, and unto them that turn from transgression in Jacob saith the LORD."* We know that Jesus came to Zion to lay down His life and redeem us. And He will come to Zion again to rule and reign for a thousand years. And He is Redeemer for those who *"turn from transgression"* and turn to Him.

Isaiah 62:12 says we shall be called, *"the holy people, The **redeemed** of the LORD: and thou shall be called, Sought out, A city not forsaken."* What a wonderful future we, as believers in Jesus, have!

Encountering Jesus Throughout the Bible

Jesus as Redeemer in the New Testament:

Galatians 4:3-5 lays it out well: *"Even so we, when we were children, were in bondage under the elements of the world: But when the fulness of the time was come, God sent forth his Son, made of a woman, made under the law, To **redeem** them that were under the law, that we might receive the adoption of sons."* No longer slaves and in bondage, we who believe in Jesus are now sons. How wonderful is that?

Galatians 3:13 says, *"Christ hath **redeemed** us from the curse of the law, being made a curse for us: for it is written, Cursed is every one that hangeth on a tree."*

Titus 2:14 tells us why Jesus did this: *"that he might **redeem** us from all iniquity, and purify unto himself a peculiar people, zealous of good works."* So, believers are His peculiar people, and we do good works because we love Him and are grateful for everything He has done for us.

1 Peter 1:18-19 says, *"Forasmuch as ye know that ye were not **redeemed** with corruptible things, as silver and gold from your vain conversation received by tradition from your fathers; But with the precious blood of Christ, as of a lamb without blemish and without spot."*

Nothing in all of creation could have redeemed us except the blood of Jesus. Why and how this blood criteria came to be is covered in my book, *Following the Blood Trail from Genesis to Revelation.*

Romans 3:24 also tells us that our redemption is in Christ Jesus. And Ephesians 1:7 says, *"In whom (Jesus) we have **redemption** through his blood, the forgiveness of sins, according to the riches of his grace."* Colossians 1:14 repeats this.

Jesus, our Kinsman Redeemer, paid for us with His blood. Hebrews 9:12 says, *"Neither by the blood of goats and calves, but by his (Jesus') own blood he entered in once into the holy place, having obtained **eternal redemption** for us."* Don't miss that word, "eternal." That means our redemption is forever. We don't have to be redeemed over and over again. Jesus paid for us once and that's the end of it.

Hebrews 9:15 is even more detailed: *"And for this cause he (Jesus) is the mediator of the new testament, that by means of death, for the **redemption** of the transgressions that were under the first testament, they which are called might receive the promise of **eternal** inheritance."* When Jesus said on the cross, "it is finished," He meant it.

1 Corinthians 1:30 goes on to say, *"But of him are ye in Christ Jesus, who of God is made unto us wisdom, and righteousness and sanctification, and **redemption**."* Oh, how precious Jesus is! He is not only our redemption but our wisdom, righteousness, and sanctification.

In Revelation, when Jesus, the Lamb in heaven, takes the scroll with the seven seals, all heaven rejoices. Revelation 5:9 says, *"And they* (the saints in heaven) *sung a new song, saying, Thou* (Jesus) *art worthy to take the book, and to open* *the seals thereof: for thou wast slain, and hast **redeemed** us to God by thy blood out of every kindred, and tongue, and people, and nation."* What Jesus did for us is so enormous and wonderful that we will be praising Him throughout all eternity.

The Son of Man:

Though Jesus was the Son of God, He called Himself or was called by others the Son of man many many times. This was to accentuate the fact that He was our Kinsman Redeemer, that He had come to earth as a man, that he was one of us, a relative who could and would rescue us.

But hundreds of years before Jesus made His appearance on earth as a baby in Bethlehem, Daniel, in a vision, saw Him as the Son of man. *"I (Daniel) saw in the night visions, and, behold, one like the **Son of man** came with the clouds of heaven, and came to the Ancient of days, and they brought him near before him. And there was given him* (the Son of man) *dominion, and glory, and a kingdom, that all people, nations and languages, should serve him: his dominion is an everlasting dominion, which shall not pass away, and his kingdom that which shall not be destroyed."*

Daniel saw Jesus as the Son of man, our Kinsman Redeemer, returning to earth as King of Kings, the One who would reign for a thousand years and be worshiped by the whole world. And this to be followed by the creation of a new heaven and earth over which Jesus will rule eternally.

In Acts 7:56, when the disciple, Stephen, was being stoned to death he saw Jesus. *"Behold, I (Stephen) see the heavens opened, and the **Son of man** standing on the right hand of God."*

John the apostle was on the Isle of Patmos when he saw Jesus, *"in the midst of the seven candlesticks one like unto the **Son of man**, clothed with a garment down to the foot, and girt about the paps with a golden girdle,"* Revelation 1:13.

How fortunate that Jesus came as the Son of man. If He hadn't there would be no hope for us. He redeemed us out of the pit of sin and made us sons, kings, and priests. What a blessed Redeemer!

Psalm 107:2 says, *"Let the **redeemed** of the LORD say so, whom he hath **redeemed** from the hand of the enemy."* Jesus has indeed redeemed us from the hand of our enemy, Satan, and given us an incredible future. And like the psalmist said, we should be honored, eager, and ready to "say so."

Encountering Jesus Throughout the Bible

Messiah

The Jews had been waiting for their Messiah for centuries, and tragically, when He arrived, many didn't recognize Him.

First, let's see what they expected.

Rabbis of old believed two different Messiahs would come: first, Messiah ben Joseph, the suffering servant, and secondly, Messiah ben David, the one who would rule over Israel. What they didn't understand was that there would only be one Messiah, but that he would come twice. Jesus indeed came the first time as Messiah ben Joseph, the suffering Messiah who was brutalized and died for our sins. But He will soon return as Messiah ben David, the King of kings and Lord of lords. And what a glorious day that will be!

The only two times the word "Messiah," which means, "anointed one," appears in the Old Testament are both in Daniel 9:25-26. *"Know therefore and understand, that from the going forth of the commandment to **restore** and to build Jerusalem unto the **Messiah the Prince** shall be seven weeks, and threescore and two weeks: the street shall be built again, and the wall, even in troublous times. **And after threescore and two weeks shall Messiah be cut off, but not for himself**: and the people of the prince that shall come* *shall destroy the city and the sanctuary; and the end thereof shall be with a flood, and unto the end of the war desolations are determined."*

What amazing passages! Daniel was prophesying the coming of Jesus as Messiah. Notice, he said that the Messiah would be cut off, **but not for himself,** meaning He was to die for the sake of others. Also, Daniel so accurately pinpointed the timing of Messiah's coming that none, but God, could have revealed this to him.

Let's dissect what he said.

First, Daniel wasn't talking about literal weeks. That word "weeks" here is *shabuwa* and means, "weeks of years." A week of years is seven years. Therefore, according to the angel Gabriel, who gave Daniel this prophecy, the scenario would cover seventy weeks of years or 490 years (70 weeks of years x 7 years). These are further broken down into two distinct time frames. First, 7 plus 62 weeks of years or 483 years (69 weeks of years x 7 years) from the time Jerusalem is restored and rebuild to the time when Messiah would be cut off **but not for himself.**

Did that happen? Yes! Cyrus decreed that the Temple in Jerusalem should be rebuilt in 538/7 B.C. Darius confirmed Cyrus' decree in 520 B.C. But it wasn't until 457 B.C. that Artaxerxes granted autonomy to Judah, then confirmed it by a second decree in 445/4 B.C. It is this date that is significant because that word "restore" in Daniel 9:25 means, "return ownership," not just rebuild. And that didn't happen until 445/4 B.C. when ownership of Jerusalem was fully restored to the Jews. Using 444 B.C. as a springboard, Julius Africanus, an early church father, calculated the time when Messiah would be cut off, *"but not for himself,"* by converting the Jewish calendar, which is based on the phases of the moon, to the Gregorian/Roman calendar, based on the solar year. When he did, he came up with the date, April 6, 32 A.D., the very year many Bible scholars believe Jesus was crucified.

But that leaves one more week of years or 7 years before, according to Daniel, the Messiah would reign in His kingdom. It's been almost 2000 years since Jesus left this earth. What happened? The Church Age! For nearly 2000 years we have experienced the age of grace, but that will soon end. Sometime after it does, the final week of Daniel's prophecy will be fulfilled. And it has everything to do with the nation of Israel. After believers are raptured and taken to heaven, the final week of Daniel's prophecy will be realized in the seven-year Tribulation often called Jacob's Trouble. It's the final seven years before Jesus returns during which time Israel will be judged as well as prepared to accept her Messiah and become the head of nations. It will also be the time when the earth and those Gentile unbelievers still living, will be judged through the various seal, trumpet, and bowl judgments mentioned in the book of Revelation. During that time, the antichrist will appear. I won't go into detail other than what is included in Daniel's prophecy regarding *the people of the prince that shall come"* and who *"shall destroy the city and the sanctuary."*

Just who are the people of the prince, the ones who already destroyed Jerusalem and the Temple in 70 A.D.? It was the Romans headed by Titus and Vespasian. Therefore, the prince or antichrist to come will be from their lineage. Prior to the destruction of the Second Temple, Israel's Jewish ruling class began mingling their bloodline with both Greek and Roman rulers so it's possible that the antichrist could be a Gentile but also have Jewish blood. J.R. Church believed this Jewish bloodline would be connected to the tribe of Dan, and cites as a clue, that the tribe of Dan is not among the 144,000 Jewish evangelists mentioned in Revelation. For more insight, I recommend his book, *Daniel Reveals the Blood Line of the Antichrist*.

Going back to Daniel: in his day, Nebuchadnezzar was a prophetic picture of the antichrist. When the three Hebrew boys refused to bow to his stature, Nebuchadnezzar commanded the furnace to be made seven times hotter before throwing them in, foreshadowing the seven-year Tribulation when things are going to heat up and when there will also be a ruler who commands his statue to be worshipped. In addition, after God judged Nebuchadnezzar for his pride, the king went insane and lived like a wild beast for seven years, an insightful parallel to the insanity of the antichrist which Revelation 13:1-8 refers to as a "beast".

Because Daniel gave such impressive and accurate details, it means that Messiah had to come before the destruction of Jerusalem and the Temple. Ancient rabbis understood this. Even their Talmud claims this. But sad to say, modern rabbis teach that Daniel 9:25-26 does not speak of their Messiah, and they have assigned various other meanings to these Scriptures.

Why? What happened?

Some olden-day rabbis, who understood and believed Daniel's prophecy, didn't like it and sought to blur its understanding. One way they did this was to change their dating. According to J.R. Church, the Jewish calendar is off by 243 years. If we were to add that to the current Jewish year of 5781 (as of September 2020), it would bring us to the year 6024, which means 6024 years from the creation of Adam. That puts us well into the "after 6 days" reference in Matthew 17:1 and Mark 9:2 which prophetically refer to the return of Jesus in His glory after sixth thousand years of human history, followed by the seventh thousand-year-period, a Sabbath of rest, when Jesus reigns as King on the earth. In these chapters, Jesus is transfigured, a typology of His return as King of kings and Lord of lords. He is also seen talking with Moses and Elijah who many Bible scholars believe are the two witnesses that will return to earth during the Tribulation. Though I favor Elijah and Enoch in this role because neither one died but were translated or raptured to heaven alive, nevertheless, the transfiguration is a foreshadowing of Jesus' glorious return and clearly indicates we are in the "last days," meaning the time is short. We need to redeem it.

Encountering Jesus Throughout the Bible

How the early rabbis created the discrepancy.

The current Jewish calendar claims to date history from creation or AM (*Anno Mundi*) which is Latin for, "from the creation of the world." In his book, *Daniel Reveals the Blood Line of the Antichrist* page 240, J.R. Church detailed several mistakes that throw off the calendar. Church said, "The Jews have always known that their calendar was flawed. Though the rabbis will argue for the authenticity of their calendar, which is based upon the *Seder Olam Rabbah*, they know that their dates are wrong. Furthermore, some of them know the reason why."

Jews began their system of dating in 312 B.C. because of Simon the high priest's promise to Alexander the Great that they would use the year of his conquest of the empire as the beginning year in their legal documents and this was called the *Minyan Shtarot*. This system was used by most of the Jewish population until A.D. 1517 when Egypt was conquered by the Turks and *Anno Mundi*, which had only been used by a few Jewish communities since the 9th century, then become the official system. They based this calendar on the *Seder Olam Rabbah* (The Book of the Order of the World) which Yose ben Halafta composed in the middle of the second century A.D. Halafta studied under the father of the *Mishnah*, Rabbi Akiva ben Joseph, the same Rabbi Akiva who approved of the Bar Kokhba revolution and declared the rebel leader, Bar Kokhba, to be the Messiah. In 135 A.D. Bar Kokhba was killed and the revolution ended.

But Yose ben Halafta's work continued. According to J.R. Church's same book, page 242, "Over the next 20 years, Yose ben Halafta and his colleagues compiled the *Seder Olam Rabbah* for one primary purpose—to make Daniel's 70 weeks point to Bar Kokhba as the Jewish Messiah." How did they accomplish it? By not following Scripture when calculating the age of the patriarchs such as Terah's ages (Abram's father) or improperly stating Abram's age when receiving the Abrahamic Covenant or miscalculating the reign of kings such as removing fourteen years from Amaziah's reign and others.

But a whopping 164 years alone were removed by listing and calculating the reign of five Medo/Persian kings instead of the thirteen that actually reigned. And Halafta used the book of Daniel to justify this as it mentions only five. The total of all these errors adds up to 243 years.

Some Jewish rabbis admit there's a problem in their calendar. One who did is Rabbi Simon Schwab who said in his book, *Comparative Jewish Chronology*, (page 188):

"It should have been possible that our Sages—for some unknown reason—had covered up a certain historic period and purposely eliminated and suppressed all records and other material pertaining thereto. If so, what might have been their compelling reason for so unusual a procedure? Nothing short of Divine command could have prompted . . . those saintly 'men of truth' to leave out completely from our annals a period of 165 years and to correct all data and historic tables in such a fashion that the subsequent chronological gap could escape being noticed by countless generations, known to a few initiates only who were duty-bound to keep the secret to themselves."

Rabbi Schwab and others eventually admitted that these dates might have been falsified to keep people from believing that the Daniel prophecies referred to Jesus as the Messiah. What a tragedy! What a disservice these men did to generations of their people by concealing their Messiah. How many countless Jews have died without coming to salvation in Jesus because of this gross coverup?

The current or prevailing theory among Jews is that Messiah will come after the building of the third Temple in Jerusalem. Indeed, the Temple Institute has been planning it for years. They've already replicated Temple furniture, including the golden menorah, as well as priestly garments. In addition, stones have been cut for the Temple itself. Also, in 2004, the Sanhedrin was reinstituted by a conglomerate of over 100 rabbis. But it has yet to gain national recognition or acceptance. Nevertheless, all systems are GO. All that is missing is their Messiah.

But Scripture tells us Israel will be fooled. When they covenant with the antichrist, who many will believe is their Messiah, they will be making a covenant with "death and hell," (Isaiah 28:15) and their "Messiah" will end up desecrating their Temple, and this *"abomination of desolation"* (Matthew 24:15) will lead to their mass persecution.

Sylvia Bambola

Foreshadowing of Messiah in the Old Testament:

There are many references to the Messiah throughout the Old Testament. Most of them are under the heading of either "the anointed one" or "God's anointed" or "son of David."

Let's look at a few.

Psalm 2:2, *"The kings of the earth set themselves, and the rulers take counsel together, against the Lord, and against his anointed."* This is a prophecy of how Jesus, the Messiah, would be rejected, and rulers would rebel against Him. But then God said this in Psalm 2:4-7: *"He that sitteth in the heavens shall laugh: the Lord shall have them in derision. Then shall he speak unto them in his wrath, and vex them in his sore displeasure. Yet have I set my king upon my holy hill of Zion. I will declare the decree: the LORD hath said unto me, Thou art my Son; this day have I begotten thee."* No matter how many try to prevent Messiah, Jesus's reign, there will come a day when God will put down all rebellion and install Jesus as King of kings and Lord of lords on the throne of David in Jerusalem.

Psalm 45 also speaks of the Messiah. Verses 2-7 say, *"Thou are fairer than the children of men: grace is poured into thy lips: therefore God hath blessed thee for ever. Gird thy sword upon thy thigh, O most mighty, with thy glory and thy majesty. And in thy majesty ride prosperously because of truth and meekness and righteousness; and thy right hand shall teach thee terrible things. Thine arrows are sharp in the heart of the king's enemies; whereby the people fall under thee. Thy* *throne, O God, is for ever and ever: the sceptre of thy kingdom is a right sceptre. Thou lovest righteousness, and hatest wickedness: therefore God, thy God, hath **anointed** thee with the oil of gladness above thy fellows."* What an amazing picture of Jesus, the Messiah, returning to rule. How similar this is to Revelation describing Jesus returning as King on a white horse with a sword on his thigh, followed by His army, and ready to vanquish His enemies.

And of course, there is this well-known passage in Isaiah 61:1-2, *"The Spirit of the Lord GOD is upon me; because the LORD hath **anointed me** to preach good tidings unto the meek; he hath sent me to bind up the brokenhearted, to proclaim liberty to the captives, and the opening of the prison to them that are bound: To proclaim the acceptable year of the LORD."* It's the same Scripture Jesus quoted in the synagogue when announcing His ministry (Luke 4:18).

Old Testament Scriptures concerning the son of David:

In Psalm 132, God promised that David's seed would sit upon the throne and rule forever. It was a Messianic prophecy that the Messiah would come from the line of David and that Messiah's rule would be an everlasting one. Verses 11, 13, 17-18 give us a good picture. *"The LORD hath sworn in truth unto **David**; he will not turn from it; of the **fruit of thy body** will I (God) set upon thy throne . . . For the LORD hath chosen Zion; he that desired it for his habitation . . . There will I make the **horn of David** to bud: I have ordained a lamp for **mine anointed**. His enemies will I clothe with shame: but upon himself shall his crown flourish."*

Because of this, Messiah was often referred to as the son of David.

In Psalm 89:2-4 God restated His promise to David. *"For I (God) have said, Mercy shall be built up for ever: thy faithfulness shalt thou establish in the very heavens. I have made a covenant with my chosen, I have sworn unto **David** my servant, **Thy seed** will I establish for ever, and build up thy throne to all generations. Selah."* And Psalm 89:35-37 continues the theme, *"Once have I (God) sworn by my holiness that I will not lie unto **David**. **His seed** shall endure for ever, and his throne as the sun before me. It shall be established for ever as the moon, and as a faithful witness in heaven. Selah."* The "forever" throne, of course, is the throne of Jesus.

Isiah 9:1-7 talks about the coming Messiah who will bring light into the world. Verses 6-7 describe Him. *"For unto us a child is born, unto us a son is given: and the government shall be upon his shoulder: and his name shall be called Wonderful, Counsellor, the mighty God, the everlasting Father, The Prince of Peace. Of the increase of his government and peace there shall be no end, upon the **throne of David**, and upon his kingdom, to order it, and to establish it with judgment and with justice from henceforth even for ever. The zeal of the LORD of hosts will perform this."*

What a revealing Scripture! Not only will Messiah sit upon the throne of David, but He will be God, Himself, as well as Wonderful, Counsellor, and Prince of Peace. What a loving, merciful, and faithful God we serve! He has already kept part of this promise by sending Jesus as our kinsman redeemer. And He will keep the rest by having Jesus return to claim His kingdom and take His rightful place on David's throne.

In Jeremiah 23:5-6, God said this about the One who shall come out of the line of David. *"Behold, the days come, saith the LORD, that I will raise unto* **David a righteous Branch***, and a King shall reign and prosper, and shall execute judgment and justice in the earth. In his days Judah shall be saved, and Israel shall dwell safely: and this is his name whereby he shall be called THE LORD OUR RIGHTEOUSNESS."* Jesus is that righteous branch, but He is so much more. He is not only our Lord, but our righteousness.

And here's another prophecy concerning Messiah in Jeremiah 33:14-15, *"Behold, the days come, saith the LORD, that I will perform that good thing which I have promised unto the house of Israel and to the house of Judah.* **In those days***, and at that time, will* **I cause the Branch of righteousness to grow up unto David;** *and he shall execute judgment and righteousness in the land."* Here, God spoke through the prophet Jeremiah and gave him insight into the future, a time referred to as *"in those days,"* when Jesus will return to rule as the Righteous Judge.

In Ezekiel 34, God rebuked the leaders of Israel for their corruption and failure to lead the nation in righteousness. He called these wicked leaders, shepherds, and the people of Israel, sheep. But then in verses 22-24, God promised that a new Shepherd from the house of David, a future Messiah, would come and protect Israel. *"Therefore will I* (God) *save my flock* (Israel), *and they shall* *no more be a prey; and I will judge between cattle and cattle. And I will set up one **shepherd** over them, and he shall feed them, even **my servant David;** he shall feed them, and he shall be their **shepherd**. And I the LORD will be their God, and **my servant David** a prince among them; I the LORD have spoken it."*

Who was God referring to when He spoke about *"my servant David"*? Bible scholars acknowledge that David ruled for 40 years and most believe that David's reign was from 1007 B.C. to 967 B.C. But Ezekiel wrote this during the Babylonian captivity which occurred about 373 years after David's reign. So, obviously God wasn't talking about David. Rather, He was referring to David's seed, Messiah Jesus, who would someday sit on David's throne in Jerusalem and rule the world.

Then Ezekiel was given the vision of dry bones and asked by God if these bones could live again. That was a tough one. As mentioned, Israel was in Babylonian captivity. The future looked bleak. Would the nation ever rise again? Only God knew, which was Ezekiel's response to the question. God then told Ezekiel to prophesy and breathe on the bones, after which they came to life. Then here's what God said would happen in Ezekiel 37:22 and 24: *"And I (God) will make them one nation in the land upon the mountains of Israel; and one king shall be king to them all: and they shall be no more two nations, neither shall they be divided into two kingdoms any more at all . . . **And David my servant shall be king over them;** and they all shall have one shepherd: they shall also walk in my judgments, and observe my statutes, and do them."*

Again, this prophecy was given long after David's death. It was a futuristic prophecy for when Israel would no longer be divided into north and south but become one. That happened on May 14, 1948 when David Ben-Gurion proclaimed the establishment of the State of Israel. Now, Israel is an undivided nation, no longer separated into a Northern Kingdom (10 tribes) and Southern Kingdom (Judah and Benjamin). But the prophecy has only been partially fulfilled. Messiah Jesus has yet to take His rightful throne and rule over the millennial kingdom.

Did anyone ever call Jesus the son of David?

Yes, too numerous to mention. I'll only reference a few.

But first we need to understand that the Jews no longer awaited Messiah ben Joseph, but were looking for a king, Messiah ben David, who would overthrow the harsh stranglehold of Rome and establish a new Jewish kingdom. When Jesus asked the Pharisees in Matthew 22:42, *"What think ye of the Christ?* (the anointed one, the Messiah) *whose son is he? They say unto him, The **son of David**."* This confirms that the Jews were still waiting for and believing the anointed one, the Messiah, would come from the lineage of David. In that respect, nothing had changed. And when they spoke of the coming Messiah, he was referred to as the "son of David."

But they were no longer looking for the Messiah described in Isaiah 53:2-10: *"For he* (Messiah*) shall grow up before him as a tender plant, and as a root out of a dry ground: he hath no form nor comeliness; and when we shall see* him, there is no beauty that we should desire him. He is despised and rejected of men; a man of sorrows, acquainted with grief: and we hid as it were our faces from him; he was despised, and we esteemed him not. Surely he hath borne our griefs, and carried our sorrows: yet we did esteem him stricken, smitten of God, and afflicted. But he was wounded for our transgressions, he was bruised for our iniquities: the chastisement of our peace was upon him; and with his stripes we are healed. All we like sheep have gone astray; we have turned every one to his own way; and the LORD hath laid on him the iniquity of us all. He was oppressed, and he was afflicted, yet he opened not his mouth: he is brought as a lamb to the slaughter, and as a sheep before her shearers is dumb, so he openeth not his mouth. He was taken from prison and from judgment: and who shall declare his generation? for he was cut off out of the land of the living: for the transgression of my people was he stricken. And he made his grave with the wicked, and with the rich in his death; because he had done no violence, neither was any deceit in his mouth. Yet it pleased the LROD to bruise him; he hath put him to grief: when thou shalt make his soul an offering for sin, he shall see his seed, he shall prolong his days, and the pleasure of the LORD shall prosper in his hand."* This was the Messiah Daniel spoke about, the One who would be *"cut off, but not for himself."*

Still, when Jesus was called son of David, it was significant. Right from the start, Matthew, in his gospel, plainly stated that Jesus was from the line of David. *"The book of the generation of Jesus Christ, the **son of David**, the son of Abraham,"* (Matthew 1:1). Then Matthew listed the ancestors by name so there would be no doubt.

Luke 1:32 adds to this by explaining how the angel Gabriel appeared to Mary to give her the news of the coming Messiah and her part in it, and said this about Him: *"He shall be great, and shall be called the **Son of the Highest**: and the Lord God shall give unto him the throne of **his father David**."* So, not only was Messiah to come from the line of David, He was also to be God Himself.

Then to top it off, when Jesus was born, the angel of the Lord appeared to the shepherds and said in Luke 2:11, *"For unto you is born this day in the **city of David** a Saviour, which is **Christ the Lord**."* The Scripture calls Jesus, "Christ", which is *"Christos"* in Greek and means, "the anointed, the Messiah." Also, the fact that the angel called Jesus, "Saviour," indicated that though Jesus was the future King from the line of David, He was here now as Messiah ben Joseph. The angel was pointing them back to Isaiah 53.

But there's more. That word, "Lord," in Greek is *kurios* and means, "supremacy, supreme in authority." In other words, there is none higher or with more rank and power. It was no accident that Jesus, the future King of kings and Lord of lords, was born in Bethlehem, the city of David.

These two Scriptures, Luke 1:32 and Luke 2:11, encapsulate the two comings of Jesus, the one as Messiah ben Joseph, the suffering servant or Saviour, and Messiah ben David, the King.

Paul in Romans 1:3 said, *"Concerning his Son Jesus* **Christ** *(the Messiah) our Lord, which was made of the* **seed of David** *according to the flesh."* Paul later added this in 2 Timothy 2:8, *"Remember that Jesus* **Christ** *(the Messiah) of the* **seed of David** *was raised from the dead according to my gospel."*

And here's what Jesus said about Himself in Revelation 3:7, *"And to the angel of the church in Philadelphia write; These things saith he that is holy, he that is true, he that hath the* **key of David**, *he that openeth, and no man shutteth; and* **shutteth, and no man openeth**.*"* It's Jesus who holds David's key, meaning Jesus is the rightful heir to David's throne, that He has the right to be King and rule over Jerusalem, as well as over all of Israel. But it goes beyond that. As King of kings and Lord of lords, He will rule over the entire world. And going even deeper, Jesus holds the very key to the Kingdom of heaven, itself. It is only through Him that one can enter. He does indeed have the authority to *"shutteth and no man openeth."*

Further down in Revelation 5:5 the apostle John, while in heaven, wept because no one was found worthy to open the scroll with seven seals. Then this happened: *"And one of the elders saith unto me, Weep not: behold, the Lion of the tribe of Juda,* **the Root of David,** *hath prevailed to open the book, and to loose the seven seals thereof."* Again, this affirms that Jesus came from the line of David.

And finally, in Revelation 22:16 Jesus Himself leaves no doubt about this. *"I Jesus have sent mine angel to testify unto you these things in the churches.* **I am the root and the** *offspring of David, and the bright and morning star."* Could He make it any plainer?

Other people called Jesus the son of David:

In Matthew 9:27, two blind men wanted Jesus to heal them and they *"followed him crying, and saying, Thou **son of David**, have mercy on us."*

Another time, after Jesus healed a man with the withered hand and cast out a devil from another who was blind and dumb, then healed him in Matthew 12, verse 23 says, *"And all the people were amazed, and said, Is not this the **son of David**?"* By virtue of His miracles, many believed Jesus was the Messiah.

Even a Canaanite woman acknowledged Jesus as the Jewish Messiah when she said in Matthew 15:22, *"Have mercy on me, O Lord, thou **son of David**; my daughter is grievously vexed with a devil."* Remember, when people used the term, "son of David," they were claiming that person was the Messiah.

Then in Matthew 21:9, Jesus entered triumphantly into Jerusalem on a donkey when, *"the multitudes that went before, and that followed, cried, saying, Hosanna to the **son of David**: Blessed is he that cometh in the name of the Lord; Hosanna in the highest."* Mark 11:10 also described this scene and included this statement by the people, *"Blessed be the kingdom of our father **David**, that cometh in the name of the Lord: Hosanna in the highest."*

And oh, how this offended the religious rulers according to Matthew 21:15. *"And when the chief priests and scribes saw the wonderful things that he (Jesus) did, and the children crying in the temple, and saying, Hosanna to the **son of David**; they were sore displeased."* They knew exactly who the people believed Jesus was and they didn't like it.

Jesus was also called Messiah or Christ (the Anointed One).

When Mary and Joseph brought Jesus to the Temple in Jerusalem to *"present him to the Lord,"* in Luke 2:22, they encountered a man named Simeon. God had given Simeon an incredible promise. That promise is restated in verse 26, *"he should not see death, before he had seen the Lord's **Christ** (God's Anointed Messiah)."* And when Simeon saw baby Jesus, this is what he said in verses 29-30, *"Lord, now lettest thou thy servant depart in peace, according to thy word: For mine eyes have seen thy salvation."* In other words, Simeon knew Jesus was the promised Messiah, the suffering Servant, Messiah ben Joseph, Who would bring salvation to His people.

But many would not believe. Because Jesus' ministry was so often conducted in Galilee, they claimed He did not fulfill prophecy, *"Shall **Christ** come out of Galilee? Hath not the scripture said, that **Christ** (the Messiah, the anointed one) cometh of the seed of David, and out of the town of Bethlehem, where David was?"* (John 7:41-42). Obviously, they had not done their homework.

But Herod believed. That's why he asked the wise men to come back and let him know where this baby, whose star they had followed, could be found. And that's why, in panic, he consulted his priests and scribes. Matthew 2:4 says, *"And when he* (Herod) *had gathered all the chief priests and scribes of the people together, he demanded of them where* **Christ** (the Anointed One) *should be born."* Herod took this seriously and proactively wanted to cut off the Messiah, to destroy Him before He could grow up to become ruler. He, like the rest of Israel, expected Messiah ben David and had no intention of relinquishing his power. To that end, Herod was willing to slaughter the young children of an entire town. But hasn't the lust for power corrupted people down through the ages? Even today, we have people in authority who are willing to do anything to keep their power. Lord Dalberg-Acton got it right when he said power corrupts. The only One Who can handle such power, and rule in righteousness is Jesus.

It was Andrew who first told his brother, Peter, about Jesus and said in John 1:41-42, *"We have found the* **Messias**, *which is, being interpreted, the* **Christ** *and he* (Andrew) *brought him* (Peter) *to Jesus."* So, we see that Messiah and Christ (the Anointed One) are interchangeable in the New Testament.

This was confirmed by both Jesus and the Samaritan woman at the well. She said in John 4:25, *"I know that* **Messias** *cometh, which is called* **Christ***: when he is come, he will tell us all things."* To which Jesus replied in verse 26, *"I that speak unto thee am he."* So, not only do we see in these Scriptures that Christ is another name for Messiah, but that Jesus claimed to be the Messiah.

The Samaritan woman believed Him because after she left, she quickly told the townspeople, *"Come, see a man, which told me all things that ever I did: is not this the **Christ**?"* (John 4:29). Then something wonderful happened. The townspeople went out to see for themselves and came to this conclusion in verse 42: *"Now we believe, not because of thy saying: for we have heard him ourselves, and know that he is indeed the **Christ**, the Saviour of the world."*

What's remarkable here is not only did the Samaritans acknowledge that Jesus was the Messiah but that He was also Savior of the *world* not just the Saviour of the Jewish people. Unlike the Jews, they did not see Jesus as Messiah ben David, but Messiah ben Joseph.

Lazarus had died and Jesus was on his way to Bethany when He encountered Lazarus' sister, Martha. She was grief stricken and told Jesus that if He had arrived sooner her brother would not have died. He answered her in John 11:25-26, *"I am the resurrection, and the life, he that believeth in me, though he were dead, yet shall he live: And whosoever liveth and believeth in me shall never die. Believest thou this?"* To which she responded in verse 27, *"Yea, Lord: I believe that thou art the **Christ**, the Son of God, which should come into the world."*

But the religious rulers were greatly distressed that people believed Jesus was the Messiah and wanted to put an end to it. After Jesus healed the man who had been blind from birth, the priests tried to get the parents to admit their son was never blind. When the parents refused, the priests asked by what means their son received his sight. Unfortunately, the parents took the cowardly way out. John 9:21-22 gives this account. *"But by what means he now seeth, we* (the parents) *know not; or who hath opened his eyes, we know not: he is of age; ask him: he shall speak for himself. These words spake his parents, because they feared the Jews: for the Jews had agreed already, that if any man did confess that he* (Jesus) *was* **Christ***, he should be put out of the synagogue."*

Hoping to stop people from proclaiming Jesus as Messiah, the religious rulers used intimidation and threats. The Temple and synagogues were the center of Jewish life, therefore, it would be devastating to be expelled from them. It was a threat that got results.

But even demons knew who Jesus was. In Luke 4:38-40, Jesus is at Peter's house. He had already healed Peter's mother-in-law and now people poured in from all over just to receive a touch from Him. And Jesus, full of compassion and mercy, healed them all. Then in verse 41 this happened: *"And devils also came out of many, crying out, and saying, thou art* **Christ** *the Son of God."*

When Jesus asked Peter who Peter thought He was, Peter answered in Matthew 16:16, *"Thou art the* **Christ***, the Son of the living God."* Here, Peter was saying that he understood that Jesus was not only the Messiah but God Himself. And Jesus didn't contradict him. In fact, He told

Peter that only His Father in heaven could have revealed this to him.

Again, Jesus didn't deny this when He was before the high priest during his mock trial. Jesus had been grilled for hours, during which time He had remained silent, fulfilling what was said in Isaiah 53 that, *"he opened not his mouth."* Finally, the high priest had had enough and took matters into his own hands. He would handle the interrogation himself. In Matthew 26:63 he said, *"I adjure thee by the living God, that thou tell us whether thou be the* **Christ***, the Son of God."* What a surprise it must have been when, in verse 64, Jesus answered, *"Thou hast said."* This was no wishy-washy statement. Rather, it was a Jewish expression meaning. "emphatically yes" or "absolutely" or, in modern lingo, "you've got that right!" By Jesus' affirmation, He was again acknowledging that He was both the Messiah and God Himself.

Then after Jesus told them they would see Him *"sitting on the right hand of power, and coming in the clouds of heaven,"* referring to His second coming when He returns as King, the high priest ripped his clothes and pronounced the death sentence. At once these so-called holy men began abusing Jesus, spitting in His face, slapping Him, taunting Him. *"Prophesy unto us, thou* **Christ***, Who is he that smote thee?"* (Matthew 26:68). They were mocking His claim of Messiahship.

According to Luke 23:2, the accusations brought against Jesus when He stood before Pilate were these: *"And they began to accuse him* (Jesus) *saying, We found this fellow perverting the nation, and forbidding to give tribute to Caesar, saying that he himself is* **Christ** *a King."*

Even Pilate knew there were those who considered Jesus to be the Messiah. In Matthew 27:17, Pilate offered the people a choice of which prisoner they wanted released. *"Therefore when they* (the crowd of people) *were gathered together, Pilate said unto them, Whom will ye that I release unto you? Barabbas, or Jesus which is called* **Christ***?"* And again, in verse 22, Pilate repeated this phrase after the people chose Barabbas. *"Pilate saith unto them, What shall I do then with Jesus which is called* **Christ***?"* And the answer was, *"Let him be crucified."* This is exactly the reason Jesus the Christ, the Messiah, the Anointed One came the first time, to lay down His life for many, to become the sacrificial Lamb without spot or blemish so there could be a remedy for sin. How fortunate for us that He did!

But the matter didn't end there. The chief priests and scribes just couldn't help themselves. As Jesus hung on the cross, they continued heaping their scorn. Mark 15:31-32 says, *"Likewise also the chief priests mocking said among themselves with the scribes, He saved others; himself he cannot save. Let* **Christ the King of Israel** *descend now from the cross, that we may see and believe. And they that were crucified with him reviled him."* Little did they know that some of their words were prophetic. Yes, Jesus, Messiah ben Joseph, was dying a horrible death before their very eyes, but He would return as Messiah ben David, **King of Israel**.

Romans 14:10b confirms this. *"We shall all stand before the judgment seat of **Christ**."* Jesus will be our judge and He will judge the nations.

2 Corinthians 5:10 repeats this. *"For we must all appear before the judgment seat of **Christ** (Messiah) that every one may receive the things done in his body, according to that he hath done, whether it be good or bad."* Someday it won't be the meek and mild Lamb of God people will face, but Messiah ben David, the Lion of the Tribe of Judah.

Revelation 11:15 also decrees that one day Jesus, the Christ, will rule. *"And the seventh angel sounded; and there were great voices in heaven, saying, The kingdoms of this world are become the kingdoms of our Lord, and of his **Christ**; and he shall reign for ever and ever."*

After Jesus rose from the dead, John 20:31 said, regarding all that Jesus had done, *"But these are written, that ye might believe that Jesus is the **Christ** (the Messiah) the Son of God; and that believing ye might have life through his name."*

On the day of Pentecost, the world was turned upside down. Peter and the disciples had been set on fire by the Holy Spirit. No longer timid and hiding in fear, Peter openly preached to a crowd, telling them about Jesus. In Acts 2:36 he said, *"Therefore let all the house of Israel know assuredly, that God hath made that same Jesus, whom ye have crucified, both Lord and **Christ**."* That word "Lord" here is *kurios* in Greek and means, "supreme in authority." So, Peter not only proclaimed the Messiahship of Jesus but His Lordship.

Encountering Jesus Throughout the Bible

In Acts 4, after Peter healed a lame man through praying in the name of Jesus, he and John were thrown into prison. The following day they were hauled before Annas the high priest and asked by what name or power they had healed the man. That was Peter's cue. Filled with the Holy Spirit and fearless, he began speaking about Jesus. This further outraged those who were there, and they ordered Peter and John to stop talking about or teaching in that name. After the high priest threatened them, the two men were released. That's when the apostles went back and told the others, and they all began praising God. In verses 27-29 they said, *"For of a truth against thy holy child Jesus, whom thou (God) hast **anointed**, both Herod, and Pontius Pilate, with the Gentiles, and the people of Israel, were gathered together, For to do whatsoever thy hand and thy counsel determined before to be done. And now, Lord, behold their threatenings: and grant unto thy servants, that with all boldness they may speak thy word."* God had anointed Jesus. He was the "anointed one," which is just another name for Messiah. The apostles recognized that Jesus was the "anointed one," and nothing was going to keep them from broadcasting it to the world.

This is again referenced in Acts 10:38. It speaks about Jesus' baptism and, *"How God **anointed** Jesus of Nazareth with the Holy Ghost and with power* (after being baptized) *who went about doing good, and healing all that were oppressed of the devil; for God was with him."* Jesus was both God and man. As God, Jesus needed no anointing, but as man He did, and Scripture is careful to inform us that He was indeed anointed by God.

In the first chapter of Hebrews, Paul talked about Jesus being the Son of God. Verses 8-9 say, *"But unto the Son* (Jesus) *he saith,* **Thy throne, O God***,* (meaning Jesus) *is for ever and ever: a sceptre of righteousness is the sceptre of thy kingdom. Thou* (Jesus) *hast loved righteousness, and hated iniquity; therefor God, even thy God, hath* **anointed** *thee with the oil of gladness above thy fellows."* This is God the Father's promise that Jesus, the Second Person of the Trinity, as the Anointed One, will rule forever. This rule will begin after the seven-year Tribulation and continue for a thousand years. Then a new heaven and earth will be formed over which Jesus will rule and reign forever.

After His resurrection, Jesus acknowledged He had come as Messiah ben Joseph to suffer. In Luke 24:26, He said to the two men on the road to Emmaus, *"Ought not* **Christ** *(*Messiah*) to have suffered these things, and to enter into his glory?"* Then later when He appeared to his disciples in Luke 24:46 and showed them the wounds in His hands and feet He said, *"Thus it is written, and thus it behoved* **Christ** *to suffer, and to rise from the dead the third day."*

Peter, in Acts 3:18, acknowledged that, *"those things, which God before had shewed by the mouth of all his prophets, that* **Christ** *should suffer, he hath so fulfilled."* Peter finally got it. He had come a long way. From trying to stop Jesus from going to Jerusalem to be crucified, Peter now understood that Jesus had to fulfill Scripture. He finally understood that Jesus came as Messiah ben Joseph.

Encountering Jesus Throughout the Bible

This was the message the disciples preached after Jesus' resurrection. So, when Philip was directed by the Holy Spirit to seek out the Ethiopian eunuch, he obeyed and found the eunuch sitting in a chariot reading Isaiah. After Philip explained to him what the passages meant and told him about Jesus, the eunuch wanted to be baptized. In Acts 8:37 we see what happened next. *"And Philip said, If thou believest with all thine heart, thou mayest. And he answered and said, I believe that Jesus* **Christ** *(the Messiah) is the Son of God."*

According to Acts 9:22, Paul preached that Jesus was the Christ, the Messiah, in Damascus. And wasn't this the very message Paul and Silas gave the jailer after the jailer asked Paul what he needed to do to be saved? Acts 16:31 says, *"And they* (Paul and Silas) *said* (to the jailer) *Believe on the Lord Jesus* **Christ** *(The Messiah) and thou shalt be saved, and thy house."*

At a Thessalonica synagogue, Paul told the Jews, *"that* **Christ** *must needs have suffered, and risen again from the dead; and that this Jesus, whom I preach unto you, is* **Christ** *(the Messiah, the Anointed One)."* (Acts 17:3)

And John said in 1 John 5:1, *"WHOSOEVER believeth that Jesus is the* **Christ** *(Messiah, the Anointed One) is born of God."*

Fortunately, many understood this. John 7:31 says, *"And many of the people believed on him* (Jesus) *and said, When* **Christ** *cometh, will he do more miracles than these which this man hath done?"*

It was Jesus' miracles that got many to believe. Why? Because the ancient rabbis had taught that only Messiah, when He came, could do four specific miracles, all of which Jesus did and more. The four are:

Heal a person who was mute because of demon possession: Jesus did this in Matthew 9:32-33. *"As they went out, behold, they brought to him (Jesus) a dumb (mute) man possessed with a devil. And when the devil was cast out, the dumb spake: and the multitudes marveled, saying.* **It was never so seen in Israel.***"* Mark 9:17-27 also details Jesus casting out a demon from a man who couldn't speak after which the man could. Luke 11:14 talked, too, about Jesus doing this miracle. *"And he (Jesus) was casting out a devil, and it was dumb. And it came to pass, when the devil was gone out, the dumb* (the mute person) *spake; and the people wondered."*

Heal a leaper: Matthew 8:2-3 details how Jesus performed this miracle. *"And, behold, there came a leper and worshipped him, saying, Lord, if thou wilt, thou canst make me clean. And Jesus put forth his hand, and touched him, saying, I will; be thou clean. And immediately his leprosy was cleansed."* But Jesus healed other lepers, too. In Luke 17:12-19 He healed ten of them.

Heal someone blind from birth: We see Jesus do this in John 9:1-7 *"And as Jesus passed by, he saw a man which was blind from his birth. And his disciples asked him, saying, Master, who did sin, this man, or his parents, that he was born blind? Jesus answered, Neither hath this man sinned, nor his parents: but that the works of God should be made manifest in* him . . . *As long as I am in the world, I am the light of the world. When he had thus spoken, he spat on the ground, and made clay of the spittle, and he anointed the eyes of the blind man with the clay, and said unto him Go, wash in the pool of Siloam (which is by interpretation, Sent.) He went his way therefore, and washed, and came seeing."* As previously mentioned, when the Pharisees got wind of this, they interrogated both the parents and the man who was healed. When they couldn't get the parents or the man to confess he had not been blind since birth, they were enraged. And after the healed man told them in John 9:32, *"Since the world began was it not heard that any man opened the eyes of one that was born blind,"* which was a direct reference to something only the Messiah could do, the Pharisees had had it, and cast him out of the Temple.

Raise **a dead person after four days**: Why four days? Because the rabbis believed that the spirit of a person could linger for three days with the body after death and possibly reenter it, but on the fourth day there was no possibility that the dead would return to life. In John 11:39 we learn that Lazarus has been dead for four days. *"Jesus said, Take ye away the stone. Martha, the sister of him that was dead, saith unto him. Lord, by this time he stinketh; for* **he hath been dead four days**.*"* Nevertheless, Jesus called Lazarus forth from the grave and he came out.

When John the Baptist sent two of his disciples to ask Jesus if He was the Messiah, Jesus responded in Luke 7:22 by citing the "only-Messiah-can-do-miracles" He had done, thus claiming He was.

Though many believed, many others chose to be willfully ignorant and dismissed these miracles. This was especially true of the religious rulers, the ones who should have known better, causing them to miss Jesus' first coming.

But God loves Israel and has made an everlasting covenant with them. In the end, the whole nation of Israel will acknowledge Jesus as their Messiah. Then they will have the honor of becoming the head of nations as well as having their Messiah rule in their capital of Jerusalem.

"And I saw thrones, and they sat upon them, and judgment was given unto them: and I saw the souls of them that were beheaded for the witness of Jesus, and for the word of God, and which had not worshipped the beast, neither his image, neither had received his mark upon their foreheads, or in their hands; and they lived and reigned with **Christ** *a thousand years."* (Revelation 20:4)

Encountering Jesus Throughout the Bible

Shepherd

Because Moses disobeyed God by striking the rock instead of speaking to it, he was not allowed to enter the Promised Land. The reason for God's anger and this harsh punishment has already been covered in the chapter entitled, *Rock*. Moses accepted his punishment without complaint but was distressed at the prospect of leaving his people without a shepherd. This drove him to ask God in Numbers 27:16-17, *"Let the LORD, the God of the spirits of all flesh, set a man over the congregation. Which may go out before them, and which may go in before them, and which may lead them out, and which may bring them in; that the congregation of the LORD be not as sheep which have no **shepherd**."* After leading his people for so many years, Moses understood they would not survive as a nation without proper guidance.

Early on, Scripture called God's leaders "shepherds" and His people, "sheep." What God was doing was setting the stage for the Good Shepherd, the only Shepherd Who would or could lead people the way God meant for them to be lead.

Psalm 23 also touched on this. In it, King David talked about God being his Shephard, how God would protect, provide, and refresh him. The word "shepherd" here is *raah* and not surprisingly, means, "to tend flock." But what is surprising is that it also means, "to associate with as a friend, companion, keep company with." This implies intimacy, reflecting the type of relationship David desired as a sheep with his Shepherd. It's the very type of relationship we should also want with our Shepherd.

The psalmist, Asaph, acknowledged in Psalm 80:1, 3 that God was Israel's Shepherd. *"Give ear, O **Shepherd of Israel**, thou that leadest Joseph like a flock; thou that dwellest between the cherubims* (the ark of the covenant), *shine forth . . . Turn us again, O God, and cause thy face to shine; and we shall be saved."* So, it was God Who was to provide, protect, and lead Israel.

In Isaiah 40, God comforted His people, Israel, and prophesied the coming of John the Baptist. He also prophesied that Jesus would come as a Shepherd. Isaiah 40:10-11 says, *"Behold, the Lord GOD will come with strong hand, and his arm shall rule for him: behold, his reward is with him* (see Revelation 22:12 where Jesus says 'my reward is with me') *and his work before him. He shall feed his flock like a **shepherd**: he shall gather the lambs with his arm, and carry them in his bosom, and shall gently lead those that are with young."*

The prophet Jeremiah also acknowledged that God was Israel's Shepherd. *"Hear the word of the LORD, O ye nations, and declare it in the isles afar off, and say, He that scattered Israel will gather him, and keep him, as a **shepherd** doth his flock,"* (Jeremiah 31:10). Though Israel was now held captive by the Babylonians, Jeremiah declared

God's promise that He would act as their Shepherd and regather them again in their land.

In Ezekiel 34, God rebuked the leaders, the shepherds of Israel. They had failed miserably and caused Israel to sin. God listed their transgressions and said in verse 5, *"they (Israel) were scattered, because there is no **shepherd**: and they became meat to all the beasts of the field, when they were scattered."*

Isaiah 56:11 describes these corrupt shepherds. *"Yea, they are greedy dogs which can never have enough, and they are **shepherds** that cannot understand: they all look to their own way, every one for his gain, from his quarter."*

In Jeremiah 50:6, God again described these faithless shepherds. *"My people hath been lost sheep: their **shepherds** have caused them to go astray, they have turned them away on the mountains: they have gone **from mountain to hill**, they have forgotten their resting place."* Typically, in the Old Testament, God revealed Himself on mountains such as when He met with Moses on Mount Sinai. High places were close to heaven, thus the Israelites believed closer to God and where He would commune with them. Psalm 9:11 says, *"Sing praises to the LORD, which dwelleth in Zion."* God also declared He would set His throne on Mount Zion in Zechariah 8:2-3, *"Thus saith the LORD of hosts; I was jealous for Zion with great jealousy, and I was jealous for her with great fury. Thus saith the LORD; I am returned unto Zion, and will dwell in the midst of Jerusalem: and Jerusalem shall be called a city of truth; and **the mountain of the LORD** of hosts the holy mountain."*

According to Jeremiah and 2 Kings, the Canaanites worshipped their idols *"upon the high mountain, upon the hills, and under every green tree."* Jeremiah 50:6 infers that Israel followed their pattern, going from place to place to worship false gods. And it was the corrupt shepherds who caused the people to go astray. Symbolically speaking, these shepherds brought the people from the high place where they had once worshipped God to the low place of idol worship. God said in Hosea 4:13, *"They (Israel) sacrifice upon the tops of the **mountains**, and burn incense upon the **hills**, under oaks and poplars and elms, because the shadow thereof is good: therefore your daughters shall commit whoredom, and your spouses shall commit adultery."* And in Jeremiah 13:27, God said, *"I (God) have seen thine adulteries, and thy neighings, the lewdness of thy whoredom, and thine abominations on the **hills** in the fields. woe unto thee, O Jerusalem! wilt thou not be made clean? When shall it once be?"* The shepherds had led Israel into gross idolatry and sin, thus polluting the land. Israel's trust and rest were always meant to be in the God of Abraham, Isaac, and Jacob and not in pagan idols.

To these shepherds, God issued a warning in Jeremiah 23:1-2, *"Woe be unto the pastors that destroy and scatter the sheep of my pasture! saith the LORD . . . behold, I will visit upon you the evil of your doings, saith the LORD."*

Obviously, God held these corrupt shepherds accountable for Israel's fall and subsequent judgment. But because the people were so willing to follow them, God said He would allow other false shepherds to rise up. And that's exactly what happened. Israel was plagued with false prophets and kings who did not follow the Lord.

Then Zechariah 11:16-17 warned of this future evil shepherd.: *"For lo, I will rise up **a shepherd** in the land, which shall not visit those that be cut off, neither shall seek the young one, nor heal that that is broken, nor feed that that standeth still: but he shall eat the flesh of the fat, and tear their claws in pieces. Woe to the idol shepherd that leaveth the flock! The sword shall be upon his arm, and upon his right eye: his arm shall be clean dried up, and his right eye shall be utterly darkened."*

Who is this evil shepherd? I believe it's a prophesy of the final malevolent shepherd, the antichrist, who will abuse, harass and kill the Jews during the time of "Jacob's Trouble" also called the Tribulation.

Even so, God promised in Ezekiel 34:12, *"As a **shepherd** seeketh out his flock in the day that he is among his sheep that are scattered; so will I seek out my sheep, and will deliver them out of all places where they have been scattered in the cloudy and dark day."* Then in verses 22-23 God also promised this: *"Therefore will I (God) save my flock (Israel) and they shall no more be a prey; and I will judge between cattle and cattle. And I will set up one **shepherd** (Jesus) over them, and he shall feed them, even my servant David; he shall feed them, and he shall be their **shepherd**."*

In Ezekiel 37:24, God added: *"And David my servant shall be king over them; and they all shall have one **shepherd**: they* shall also walk in my judgments, and observe my statutes, and do them."

Both Ezekiel 34:23 and Ezekiel 37:24 have already been discussed in the previous chapter, so I'll just briefly touch on them now. As mentioned, Ezekiel wrote this during the Babylonian captivity long after King David's death. These Scriptures refer to Jesus, the Messiah, the **son of David**, Who will come to earth a second time to rule and reign. And God calls Jesus, His Shepherd. No shepherd would or ever could be like Jesus, the Good Shepherd.

Zechariah 12:10b is a prophecy about Jesus the suffering Messiah, *"and they (Israel) shall look upon me whom they have **pierced**, and they shall mourn for him, as one mourneth for his only son, and shall be in bitterness for him, as one that is in bitterness for his firstborn."*

Then Zechariah 13:6-7 goes on to talk about Jesus the coming Shepherd, *"And one shall say unto him (Jesus) What are these **wounds in thine hands**? Then he shall answer, Those with which I was wounded in the house of my friends. Awake, O sword, against my **shepherd**, and against the man that is my fellow, saith the LORD of hosts: smite the **shepherd**, and the sheep shall be scattered: and I will turn mine hand upon the little ones."* In Matthew 26:31, when Jesus and His disciples went to the Mount of Olives prior to Judas' betrayal, Jesus quoted Zechariah 13:7 when He said, *"I will smite the **shepherd**, and the sheep of the flock shall be scattered abroad."*

But that's not the only time in the New Testament when Jesus referred to Himself or was referenced by others as Shepherd. Here are additional ones:

Matthew 9:36 talks about how Jesus went about teaching, preaching, and healing the people because He had compassion on them. Why? *"because they fainted, and were scattered abroad, as sheep having no **shepherd**."*

Jesus always moved in compassion. Just before feeding the five thousand in Mark 6, verse 34 says, *"And Jesus, when he came out, saw much people, and was moved with compassion toward them, because they were as sheep not having a **shepherd**."*

In John 10:1-5, 11, 14, 16, Jesus made it perfectly clear that He was the Good Shepherd: *"Verily, verily, I say unto you, He that entereth not by the door into the sheepfold, but climbeth up some other way, the same is a thief and a robber. But he that entereth in by the door is the **shepherd** of the sheep. To him the porter openeth; and the sheep hear his voice: and he calleth his own sheep by name, and leadeth them out. And when he putteth forth his own sheep, he goeth before them, and the sheep follow him: for they know his voice. And a stranger will they not follow, but will flee from him: for they know not the voice of strangers . . . I am the **good shepherd**: **the good shepherd** giveth his life for the sheep . . . I am the **good shepherd**, and know my sheep, and am known of mine. . . and other sheep* (the Gentiles) *I have, which are not of this fold: them also I must bring, and they shall hear my voice; and there shall be one fold, and one **shepherd**."*

Encountering Jesus Throughout the Bible

When referring to His second coming, Jesus said in Matthew 25:31-34, *"When the Son of man shall come in his glory, and all the holy angels with him, then shall he sit upon the throne of his glory: And before him shall be gathered all nations: and he shall separate them one from another, as a **shepherd** divideth his sheep from the goats: And he shall set the sheep on his right hand, but the goats on the left. Then shall the King say unto them on his right hand, Come, ye blessed of my Father, inherit the kingdom prepared for you from the foundation of the world."* The right hand generally implied power, influence, and position, while the left hand was often associated with an inclination to evil. When the Son of man comes *"in his glory,"* what a wonderful day that will be for His sheep. But for the goats, not so much.

Jesus couldn't have made it any plainer. But notice, He is not just the shepherd, but the Good Shepherd. He's not a lackluster shepherd or one like the corrupt shepherds in Israel's past. He will not use and abuse people to satisfy His own desires. Rather, He lays down His life for them.

Hebrews 13:20 even calls Jesus a great shepherd. *"Now the God of peace, that brought again from the dead our Lord Jesus, that **great shepherd** of the sheep, through the blood of the everlasting covenant."*

As mentioned, Luke 2:8-20 tells us that the first people to whom the angel told about the birth of Jesus were lowly shepherds tending their flock in Shepherd's Field on the edge of Bethlehem. God honored these simple shepherds and in so doing implied that prophetically, Jesus was one of them, and was allowing the shepherds to be the first to reverence the Greatest Shepherd of all.

The now deceased W. Phillip Keller, a former shepherd, wrote a wonderful book, *A Shepherd Looks at Psalm 23*. In it, he describes the enormous and constant care sheep need, as well as the utter devotion of the shepherd. The parallels between a physical shepherd and his flock, and Jesus, the Good Shepherd, and us as His sheep, are stunning.

Sheep are among the most foolish of God's creatures. They simply cannot survive by themselves. If left on their own, they would return to the same overgrazed and polluted pastures, unable to find new ones upon which to feed. They would become sickly without the saltlicks and other trace minerals the shepherd provides. They would drink from polluted holes unless taken to a pure source of water. Or they would drown if not kept away from swift running streams. Their eyes need constant cleaning and medication to prevent blindness from infections caused by flies and other insects. And they need sheltering during inclement weather for they don't know enough to shelter themselves. And when a sheep becomes "cast" or ends up on its back unable to scramble to its feet, it would die unless the shepherd picked it up and rubbed its legs. In addition, sheep are utterly unable to protect themselves from predators and must rely solely on their shepherd.

It's no accident that the Bible compares us to sheep, for we are just as foolish and incapable of caring for ourselves. And it's for this reason we need The Good Shepherd. For it is the Shepherd Who keeps us from pollution by providing His Word for us to feed on. He is the living water that keeps us refreshed. He is the salve that keeps us from spiritual blindness. He is our provider, our shelter, our protector. His constant care and commitment are all encompassing. He is tender and loving, ever mindful of our weaknesses but never repulsed by them. He picks us up when we fall and carries us when we are weak. He has laid down his life for us, the sheep. He has held nothing back.

In this time of uncertainly and upheaval, isn't it wonderful that we have such a Shepherd? We need not fear, but only allow Him to lead, guide and protect us. And we, His sheep, can remain in perfect peace if we follow His leading.

*"For we were as sheep going astray; but are now returned unto the **Shepherd** and Bishop of your souls."* 1 Peter 2:25,

*"And when the **chief Shepherd** shall appear, ye shall receive a crown of glory that fadeth not away."* 1 Peter 5:4

Healer

The first time we encounter God as Healer is in Genesis 20. Abraham, fearing he would be killed by someone who wanted his wife, acted the coward by telling Abimelech, king of Gerar, that Sarah was his sister. When seeing how beautiful Sarah was, the king took her into his harem. That brought trouble to his court. The king's wife and female servants stopped bearing children. Then in a dream, God told Abimelech he was a "dead man" and that Sarah was another man's wife. He then commanded the king to restore Sarah to her husband and to ask Abraham to pray for him so he would live. Abimelech did and Genesis 20:17-18 says, *"So Abraham prayed unto God: and God **healed** Abimelech, and his wife, and his maidservants; and they bare children. For the LORD had fast closed up all the wombs of the house of Abimelech, because of Sarah Abraham's wife."*

Then in Exodus 15:26b, God came right out and said: *"I am the LORD that **healeth** thee,"* leaving no doubt Who the Healer was.

Numbers 12 tells how Aaron and Miriam spoke against Moses, criticizing him for marrying an Ethiopian woman, then questioning his authority. After all, they heard from God, too. Why should Moses call all the shots? This provoked God's anger and He put a quick end to the rebellion by making Miriam a leper. Numbers 12:13 says, *"And Moses cried unto the LORD, saying,* **Heal** *her (Miriam) now, O God, I beseech thee."* By this time, there was no doubt that God's people saw Him as Healer.

But they were seeing something else, too. They were seeing that those who did not follow God's ways had no right to expect His healing or benefits. God warned in Deuteronomy 32:39, *"See now that I (God) even I, am he, and there is no god with me: I kill, and I make alive; I wound and I* **heal***: neither is there any that can deliver out of my hand."* This was a sobering warning. It was the other side of the coin, the side that created a reverential fear among the people. Hosea 6:1 also restated this theme. So did Jeremiah 8:15: *"We (the unrighteous) looked for peace, but no good came; and for a time of* **health***, and behold trouble!"*

Because God determines the number of our days, He can cut an evil life short. He can also allow difficulties to enter a life in order to make that person rethink his course. But in His mercy, He can also heal and restore them to the right path. He is utterly amazing. He is ever ready to forgive those who repent of their wrongdoings. Isaiah 57:18 is such an example. God was speaking to the Jews upon whom had fallen His judgment. *"I (God) have seen his (the unrighteous) ways, and will* **heal** *him: I will hear hm also, and restore comforts unto him and to his mourners."* Jeremiah 3:22 also shows God's heart of compassion and says: *"Return, ye backsliding children, and I (God) will* **heal** *your backslidings."*

Jeremiah indicated that he understood this when he wrote in Jeremiah 17:14, *"**Heal** me, O LORD, and I shall be **healed**; save me, and I shall be saved: for thou art my praise."*

And in Jeremiah 30:17 God promised He would not abandon Israel but that He would, *"restore health unto thee, and I (God) will **heal** thee of thy wounds."* God takes no pleasure in inflicting wounds. But sometimes He must in order to turn rebellious and disobedient people back to Him.

In Psalm 41:4 David said, *"LORD be merciful unto me: **heal** my soul; for I have sinned against thee."* That word soul, here, is *nephesh* and means, "a breathing creature." It refers to both mind and body. So, not only does God heal our bodies, but He heals our minds. It's the complete package. He wants to heal us totally. David was confident in his Psalm 41:4 prayer because he had already experienced God's healing in Psalm 30:2, *"O LORD my God, I cried unto thee, and thou hast **healed** me."* He had come to know that God was more than able to make him whole in every way.

David, in Psalm 103:2-3, goes on to say, *"Bless the LORD, O my soul, and forget not all his benefits: Who forgiveth all thine iniquities; who **health** all thy diseases."* David also said in Psalm 147:3, *"He **health** the broken in heart, and bindeth up their wounds."* God indeed deserves to be blessed and adored. He is still forgiving iniquities and healing diseases. But He also cares about our hurting hearts, about those deep wounds of rejection, abandonment, betrayal, etcetera, and He wants to heal them, too.

David even understood that God was the healer of nations as evidenced by Psalm 67:2, *"That thy (God's) way may be known upon earth, thy saving **health** among all nations."*

David's son, Solomon, when speaking about God's wisdom and commandments said in Proverbs 3:8, *"It (Solomon's instructions on God's wisdom and commandments) shall be **health** to thy navel, and marrow to thy bones."* In Proverbs 4:22, Solomon added, *"For they (God's wisdom and commandments) are life unto those that find them, and **health** to all their flesh."*

Isaiah 58:8 confirms this. *"Then (after sinners turn to godliness) shall thy light break forth as the morning, and thine **health** shall spring forth speedily: and thy righteousness shall go before thee; the glory of the LORD shall be thy **rereward**."* That word "health" here is *arukah* and means, "restore to wholeness." God restores. He is the God of second chances. He will restore what the locust have eaten and will often even restore what our sinful life has robbed from us. He will heal our wounds, both in body and soul.

And He will rereward. What exactly does that mean? That word is *acaph* in Hebrew, and means, "to gather, receive, put all together," as well as, "destroy, consume." An oxymoron? No. It means that after we repent and return to God, He will gather and make available to us all the precious promises He has made to us, while at the same time, consuming and destroying the dross in our life to make us more like Him and change us from glory to glory.

So, God was Israel's healer. But the Jews weren't the only ones who understood that God healed. We see this in 1 Samuel chapters 4, 5, and 6. During a battle between Israel and the Philistines, the Philistines managed to capture the Ark of the Covenant. In so doing, they believed Israel's God would now stop helping Israel and aid them, instead. They took the Ark to Ashdod, one of their major cities, and placed it in the house of Dagon their chief god.

What a mistake! In the morning, the priests of Dagon found the statue of their god face down on the ground before the Ark. But they ignored the message. Instead, they dusted off the idol and put it back in its place. The following morning, they again found the statue face down on the ground, but this time its head and hands were severed and Dagan, now nothing more than a stump, lay in humiliation before the Ark. In addition to this humiliation, the Philistines began dying.

Time to get rid of the Ark and send it to another Philistine city. But sickness struck each city as the Ark was carried from Gath, Ashkelon, Gaza and Ekron. Finally, the Philistines had had enough and decided to return the Ark to Israel. But to appease the God of Israel, the Philistine priests instructed them to include a trespass offering comprised of five gold images of mice and five golden emerods (a tumor looking mass) so, that according to 1 Samuel 6:3, *"ye shall be **healed**."* They had learned the hard way that the God of Israel was greater than their gods and One they petitioned for healing.

We see that God is Healer, but do any Old Testament Scriptures point to Jesus, the Second Person of the Trinity, as Healer?

Yes.

The forty-year wandering of the Israelites in the wilderness is a study in our frail and disappointing human nature. Despite all the miracles they saw God perform, they constantly murmured and complained. One such time was when they journeyed from Hor, skirting the territory of Edom. The trip was hard, and as usual the people complained. Numbers 21:5 (Amplified) says, *"And the people spoke against God, and against Moses. Why have you brought us out of Egypt to die in the wilderness? For there is no bread, neither is there any water, and we loathe this light contemptible, unsubstantial manna."* What was God's response? Verse 6 (Amplified) tells us: *"Then the Lord sent fiery burning serpents among the people; and they bit the people, and many Israelites died."*

After the people repented, Moses prayed for them. Verses 8-9 (Amplified) tell us what happened next. *"And the Lord said to Moses, Make a fiery serpent of bronze and set it on a pole; and everyone who is bitten, when he looks at it, shall live. And Moses made a serpent of bronze and put it on a pole, and if a serpent had bitten any man, when he looked at the serpent of bronze (attentively, expectantly, with a steady and absorbing gaze), he lived."*

These are significant passages. First, let's look at the word "pole." It is *huperupsoo* in Hebrew and means, "to elevate above others, raise to highest position, highly exalted, superior." What exactly was being elevated to the "highest position"? The snake, which represented Satan? No. Jesus! It's a picture of Jesus, hanging on the cross, actually becoming sin as He took on our sins for us, and destroying the works of the devil. It's a prophetic picture of Jesus our Saviour, our deliverer, our **healer**. It was a foreshadowing of how when people look upon Jesus, in other words, accept Him and what He did for them, believe in Him, follow Him, then they, too, will live and not die.

Isaiah 53:4-12 is a prophecy of the coming Messiah who would suffer and die not only for man's sins but for man's sicknesses and diseases. Verse 5 says, *"But he* (the Messiah) *was wounded for our transgressions, he was bruised for our iniquities: the chastisement of our peace was upon him; and with his stripes we are* **healed***."* Notice, it's done. It's past tense. Jesus already did it. All we need do is believe and receive.

Psalm 107:20 gives us another clue regarding Jesus. *"He* (God) *sent his* **word***, and* **healed** *them, and delivered them from their destructions."* And Who is the Word of God? Jesus. John made that clear in John 1:1, 14 *"In the beginning was the* **Word***, and the* **Word** *was with God, and* **the Word was God** *. . . And the* **Word** *was made flesh, and dwelt among us, and we beheld his glory, the glory as of the only begotten of the Father, full of grace and truth."* So, it was Jesus, the Word, who did the healing.

Encountering Jesus Throughout the Bible

And Malachi 4:2, the last book in the Old Testament, promised this: *"But unto you that fear my (God's) name shall the Sun of righteousness arise with **healing** in his **wings**; and ye shall go forth, and grow up as calves of the stall."* The Sun of righteousness is just another title for the Messiah and, of course, the Messiah is Jesus. And as a Jew, Jesus wore *tzitzit* or tassels/fringe that could be seen. These were often referred to as "wings." The Jews knew of the prophecy of the Messiah Who would have *"healing in his wings,"* therefore it is reasonable to conclude that the widow with the issue of blood in Matthew 9:20 who wanted to touch the *"hem of his* (Jesus') *garment,"* actually wanted to touch his *tzitzit*. Indeed, that word "hem" in this verse is *kraspedon* and means, "fringe or tassel."

Again, in Matthew 14:35-36, when Jesus was in *"the land of Gennesaret"* the crowd brought all those sick to Jesus *"And besought him* (Jesus) *that they might only touch the **hem** of his garment: and as many as touched were made **perfectly whole**."* That word "hem" is *kraspedon*, the same word as in Matthew 9:20, and means, "fringe or tassel." By touching Jesus' tassels, they not only got healed, but they were acknowledging that He was the Messiah.

Speaking of wings, Jesus also referred to them. In Matthew 23:37, heartbroken over the Jews' rejection of Him and foreseeing the ensuing destruction of Jerusalem, He said: *"O Jerusalem, Jerusalem, thou that killest the prophets, and stonest them which are sent unto thee, how often would I have gathered thy children together, even as a hen gathereth her chickens under her **wings**, and ye would* *not!*" Here the word "wings" is *pterux* and literally means, "feathers or wings." Jesus was using symbolism, comparing Himself and His spiritual wings to a mother hen who wants to protect her young under her feathery wings.

The New Testament is full of stories of Jesus as Healer.

In fact, according to Luke 4:18-19, that was one of the reasons Jesus said He had come. *"The Spirit of the Lord is upon me, because he hath anointed me to preach the gospel to the poor; he hath sent me to **heal** the brokenhearted, to preach deliverance to the captives, and **recovering of sight to the blind**, to set at liberty them that are bruised, To preach the acceptable year of the Lord."*

And Jesus was true to His Word. Wherever He went, He healed people. In Matthew 8:1-3 Jesus healed a leper, then healed the Centurion's son just by speaking a word. In Luke 5:18-25 He healed a man with palsy. In Luke 8:33-35 Jesus healed the man with a legion of demons. Then a few verses down, He healed the woman with the issue of blood followed by the healing of Jairus' daughter. In Luke 9:38-42 He healed the man's son vexed by devils. In Matthew 8:14-16 He healed Peter's mother-in-law, then healed many others who came to Peter's house. In Matthew 12:15 He healed "great multitudes." Matthew 4:24 says, *"all sick people that were taken with divers diseases and torments, and those which were possessed with devils, and those which were lunatic, and those that had the palsy; and he **healed** them."* And Matthew 9:35 says, *"Jesus went about all the cities and villages, teaching in their* *synagogues, and preaching the gospel of the kingdom and* **healing** *every sickness and every disease among the people."*

The list could go on and on, but the New Testament leaves no doubt that Jesus was Healer. And people knew this and flocked to Him because of it.

Referring to Jesus, Peter said in 1 Peter 2:24, *"Who his own self bare our sins in his own body on the tree, that we, being dead to sins, should live unto righteousness: by whose stripes ye were* **healed.***"* He was tying the Old and New Testament together by quoting a portion of Isaiah 53:5.

Matthew 8:17 also says Jesus had come to fulfill Isaiah's prophecy. *"He (Jesus) took our infirmities, and bare our sicknesses."*

Jesus not only healed, He also gave power to His disciples to heal. Matthew 10:1 clearly states this. *"And when he (Jesus) had called unto him his twelve disciples, he gave them power against unclean spirits, to cast them out, and to* **heal** *all manner of sickness and all manner of disease."* Then in Matthew 10:8 Jesus told them this: *"***Heal** *the sick, cleanse the lepers, raise the dead, cast out devils: freely ye have received, freely give."* This mandate is repeated in Luke 9:2 and Luke 10:9.

After Jesus' death and resurrection, His disciples did, indeed, heal many. Their stories abound in the New Testament. In Acts 3:7 Peter healed a lame man. In Acts 5:15-16 multitudes were healed just from coming in contact with Peter's shadow. In Acts 8:5-7 Philip healed many in Samaria while, according to Acts 28, Paul healed others on the island of Melita, also called Malta.

And the wonderful thing is this: as disciples of Jesus, we, too, through the power of the Holy Spirit, can extend the love of Jesus and His healing. In fact, Jesus said in Mark 16:17-18 that, *"these signs shall follow them that believe; In my name shall they cast out devils; they shall speak with new tongues; They shall take up serpents; and if they drink any deadly thing, it shall not hurt them; **they shall lay hands on the sick, and they shall recover.**"*

And according to 2 Chronicles 7:14 we can pray and even see God heal nations. *"If my people, which are called by my name, shall humble themselves, and pray, and seek my face, and turn from their wicked ways; then will I hear from heaven, and will forgive their sin, and will **heal** their land."*

Notice, God is speaking to His people, not to unbelievers. If we want healing, not only in our lives, but in our nation, then we need to take Jesus' words seriously. He truly is our Healer and there's nothing impossible for Him.

Bridegroom

What is the relationship between a bridegroom and bride? Between a husband and wife? It is intimate, caring, exclusive and deep. And throughout the Bible we see references to this relationship, both naturally and spiritually.

Leviticus contains God's statutes given to Israel. One of them concerns the type of wife a priest should marry as well as the type of wife he should not. Leviticus 21:7 says, *"They (the priests) shall not take a wife that is a whore, or profane; neither shall they take a woman put away from her husband (divorced): for he (the priest) is holy unto his God."*

So, we see that priests were only to marry respectable women; women who had kept themselves pure for their husbands. But what does it tell us on a deeper level? Just this. That since God is also holy, in fact the very definition of holiness, then He, too, would never take a whore for a wife. And why is that important? Because the marriage relationship is the very relationship God desired with His people, and He was describing the necessary qualifications of *His* wife, Israel.

As referenced in Leviticus, God cannot abide an unfaithful wife. And like an unfaithful wife breaks a loving husband's heart, so unfaithful Israel, when she committed spiritual adultery with other gods, broke God's heart.

Early on, God made His intentions to His bride, clear. As a husband to Israel, He brought them out of Egyptian bondage as referenced in Jeremiah 31:32b, *"in the day that I (God) took them by the hand to bring them out of the land of Egypt; which my covenant they brake, although I was an* **husband** *unto them, saith the LORD."* So, Israel's adultery began early and continued in varying degrees throughout their history.

In Jeremiah 2:32, God laments, *"Can a maid forget her ornaments, or a bride her attire? yet my people have forgotten me days without number."* You can almost feel God's heartache in those words. But His accusations became even more pronounced in Jeremiah 3:20. *"Surely as a wife treacherously departeth from her husband, so have ye dealt treacherously with me, O house of Israel, saith the LORD."* And that's how God saw Israel's idolatry. It was treachery itself. It was as a faithless wife dishonoring her husband.

In Ezekiel 16, God listed Israel's treachery. He talked about how He made a special covenant with her; how He raised her up above other nations; how He provided and protected her. But despite all this, she offered her children as human sacrifices to Molech, served other gods, and played the whore. In Ezekiel 16:30-32 God said, *"How weak is thine heart, saith the Lord GOD, seeing thou doest all these things, the work of an imperious whorish woman; In that thou buildest thine eminent place in the head* *of every way, and makest thine high place in every street; and hast not been as an harlot, in that thou scornest hire; But as a **wife** that committeth adultery, which taketh strangers instead of her **husband**!"* What a sad description of how Israel had degraded herself through idolatry!

Even so, God made this promise in Isaiah 54:5-7, *"For thy Maker is thine **husband**; the LORD of hosts is his name; and thy Redeemer the Holy One of Israel; The God of the whole earth shall he be called. For the LORD hath called thee as a woman forsaken and grieved in spirit, and a **wife** of youth, when thou wast refused, saith thy God. For a small moment have I forsaken thee; but with great mercies will I gather thee."*

What a beautiful picture! Here, God is telling Israel that though they had sinned, though they had prostituted themselves by following other gods, He would, once again, have mercy on them. And not only that, He would still be their *husband*, One who would tenderly love, protect, and provide for them.

Though mercy and restoration were coming, Israel's whoredoms could not go unpunished. Inevitable judgment would fall. The story of Hosea and Gomer is a touching illustration of this, depicting God's heartbreak as well as His anger and mercy.

Hosea was a prophet during the reign of king Uzziah, Jotham, Ahaz, and Hezekiah, four kings of Judah (the two southern tribes), as well as during the reign of Jeroboam, king of Israel (the ten northern tribes). Because the land was riddled with idolatry, God, in Hosea 1:3, ordered Hosea to marry a prostitute. Hosea 1:2b says, *"And the LORD said to Hosea, Go, take unto thee a wife of whoredoms and children of whoredoms: for the land hath committed great whoredoms, departing from the LORD."* So, Hosea did, and their marriage produced three children: Jezreel, meaning, "God will sow;" in other words, judgment is coming; Lo-ruhamah, which means, "God will show no compassion or mercy;" and Lo-ammi, which means, "You are not my people."

It was meant to be an illustration of God's marriage to Israel, both the northern and southern kingdoms. Like Gomer, Israel had been a prostitute. And just as Gomer had left her husband, Hosea, after their marriage for other lovers, so had Israel. Now God was telling Israel she was *Jezreel*, that she would be judged; *Lo-ruhamah*, that she had exhausted His compassion; and *Lo-ammi*, no longer His people. What a heartbreak! The very people God had loved as a husband loves a wife, the very people He had wanted to gather to Himself and protect, had committed adultery with other gods.

Then this amazing thing happened. God instructed Hosea to buy back his wife, Gomer, who had left him and was now owned by and working for the local prostitution ring. Hosea obeyed and purchased her for an omer and a half of barley (about 64 ounces) and fifteen pieces of silver. Hosea 3:1-4, says, *"Then said the LORD unto me* (Hosea), *Go yet, love a woman beloved of her friend, yet an adulteress, according to the love of the LORD toward the children of Israel, who took to other gods, and love flagons of wine. So I* (Hosea) *bought her to me for fifteen pieces of silver, and for a homer of barley, and an half homer of barley: And I said unto her, Thou shalt abide for me many days; thou shat not play the harlot, and thou shalt not be for another man: so will I also be for thee. For the children of Israel shall abide many days without a king, and without a prince, and without a sacrifice, and without an image, and without an ephod, and without teraphim:"* This prophetically speaks of how God still loved Israel, His wife, but would, like Hosea, keep Himself from her for a time. After the Roman destruction in 70 A.D., Israel was dispersed and had no king. Their Temple was destroyed, and they had no priest (an ephod was part of the priestly garments), so all sacrifices ceased. Then followed a time when God would hold His people, Israel, at arm's length.

Then in Hosea 3:5, God added: *"Afterward shall the children of Israel return, and seek the LORD their God, and David their king: and shall fear the LORD and his goodness **in the latter days**."* It's a beautiful foreshadowing of the future, when God would once again redeem Israel during the end times.

God also stated this same promise in Jeremiah 31:31, *"Behold, the days come, saith the LORD, that I will make a new covenant with the house of Israel, and with the house of Judah."* This was a hope they could count on. God was not finished with them.

As unbelievers, before we came to Christ, we, too, like Hosea's wife, Gomer, were spiritual prostitutes. We worshipped other gods—the gods of materialism or pleasure or fame or position, or money, etcetera. But just as Hosea purchased Gomer from slavery and the prostitution ring, so Jesus purchased us from the slave markets of this world, cleaned us up and called us His own.

Oh, how faithful God is! Yes, Israel has experienced judgment for her many sins, but God has restored her as a nation and will, during the Tribulation or Jacob's Trouble, again be her husband. Isaiah 61:10-11, which speaks about Jesus and the end times, confirms this: *"I (the Messiah) will greatly rejoice in the LORD, my soul shall be joyful in my God; for he hath clothed me with the garments of salvation, he hath covered me with the robe of righteousness, as a **bridegroom** decketh himself with ornaments, and as a bride adorneth herself with her jewels. For as the earth bringeth forth her bud, and as the garden causeth the things that are sown in it to spring forth; so the Lord GOD will cause righteousness and praise to spring forth before all the nations."*

Here, the Messiah is likened to a bridegroom, who, like a typical groom of that day, was lavishly adorned along with the bride. And during the millennial reign, Jesus, our bridegroom, will reign in all His ornaments, His glory, and will indeed cause *"righteousness and praise to spring forth before all the nations."* And here's the amazing thing: we, His bride, will reign with Him! Can God be any more forgiving? Or loving? Or generous? What a wonderful future He offers those who believe in Him and follow His ways!

It is interesting to note that when Jesus was in the synagogue and quoted Isaiah 61, which speaks of both

Messiah ben Joseph and Messiah ben David, and announced His ministry, He stopped at verse 2 and didn't proclaim *"the day of vengeance of our God."* Why? Because that part of Scripture was not to be fulfilled during His first coming but is to be fulfilled during the Tribulation when the world will feel the full force of God's wrath. At the end of it, Jesus, Messiah ben David, will return with His bride, after being sequestered with her during this seven-year period, then rule as King.

Isaiah 62:5b goes on to say, *"As the **bridegroom** rejoiceth over the bride, so shall thy God rejoice over thee."* God wants to be our husband. He loves us and *wants* to protect, guide, and bless us, and keep us in His tender care. This image of God as husband truly reveals His heart of love.

For an even deeper picture we go to the Song of Solomon. It is more than the love story between King Solomon and the Shulamite woman. It is a foreshadowing of the love between Jesus, the King, and His bride, the church. The word "Shulamite" means peaceful, thus alluding to the fact that only through Jesus can we have peace with God and therefore be "peaceful."

Solomon's song is sweet, deep, passionate, and intense. In it is buried the foreshadowing of the rapture when Jesus, the bridegroom, will return for His bride, the church, and take her to the bridal chamber in heaven. It is stunningly beautiful and illustrates the tender heart of our spiritual husband. Oh, how fortunate to be so loved by our Creator, that He offers us this special relationship!

Encountering Jesus Throughout the Bible

The New Testament continues this theme of King Jesus as our bridegroom. In Matthew 9:15 (and also in Mark 2:19-20 and Luke 5:34-35) John the Baptist's disciples had come to Jesus asking why His disciples didn't fast. Jesus answered by saying, *"Can the children of the bridechamber mourn, as long as the **bridegroom** is with them? but the days will come, when the **bridegroom** shall be taken from them, and then shall they fast."* Here, Jesus called Himself the bridegroom. He would be husband to His church.

Then again in Matthew 25, Jesus likened Himself to the bridegroom in the parable of the ten virgins. The five wise virgins (born-again believers) who had oil in their lamps (symbolizing the oil of the Holy Spirit and being guided by Him) were the ones who heard their bridegroom's voice and *"went in with him to the marriage; and the door was shut"* (Matthew 25:10b), while the five foolish virgins were not allowed entrance. It is both a promise and a cautionary tale. Our bridegroom is coming back for a bride that is without spot or blemish, meaning those who are redeemed by His blood and are walking in the spirit. It will not include "religious" people who have no relationship with Him and who live like the world.

In John 3:28-29, John the Baptist, who claimed his mission was to bear witness to Jesus, said this of Him to those who were disturbed that Jesus' disciples were also baptizing, *"Ye yourselves bear me witness, that I said, I am not the Christ, but that I am sent before him. He that hath the bride is the **bridegroom**: but the **friend** of the **bridegroom**, which standeth and heareth him, rejoiceth greatly because of the **bridegroom's** voice: this my joy therefore is fulfilled."*

Here, John was claiming that Jesus was the bridegroom and that he, John, was merely the groom's friend.

The apostle Paul also spoke of Jesus as the bridegroom and the church as the bride in 2 Corinthians 11:2. *"For I (Paul) am jealous over you with godly jealousy: for I have espoused you to one **husband**, that I may present you as a chaste virgin to Christ."* Paul again touched on this in Ephesians 5 when he spoke about marriage and the role of husbands and wives. In verses 24-25 he said, *"Therefore as the church is subject unto Christ, so let the wives be to their own husbands in every thing. Husbands, love your wives, even as Christ also loved the church, and gave himself for it."* He was not only speaking of human marriage, but the very marriage between Christ and His church.

The ancient Jewish wedding is symbolic of the marriage between Jesus and the church. It's the very pattern Jesus followed. Let's take a quick look at some of the elements.

The ancient Jewish wedding has many parts, and the entire process can take over a year. First came the purchase of the bride when a bride price must be paid. Jesus purchased His bride with His blood. Then the marriage contract is drawn up. It details the obligations and responsibilities of both the groom and bride. The New Testament is our marriage contract. It lays out Jesus' responsibilities to us and ours to Him. He saves us from eternal damnation, He protects us, we hide His Word in our heart, we obey His voice, etcetera.

In the Jewish wedding, the bride must accept or reject the offer and voice this acceptance or rejection. In the same way, we, too, must accept or reject Jesus' offer of salvation and voice it. Romans 10:9 says, *"if thou shall **confess with thy mouth** the Lord Jesus, and shalt believe in thine heart that God hath raised him from the dead, thou shalt be saved."*

Then once the bride accepts the proposal, the groom offers her gifts. Ephesians 1:13b-14 tells us that after we accept Jesus we are *"sealed with the holy Spirit of promise, which is the earnest of our inheritance."* That word, "earnest" in Greek means, "a pledge given in advance as security for the rest." The Holy Spirit is given to us as a pledge. It's like an engagement ring. Then the nine gifts of the Spirit are given to us.

After the gift-giving, the bridegroom returns to his father's house to prepare the bridal chamber. In John 14:2-3 Jesus said, *"In my father's house are many mansions: if it were not so I would have told you. I go to prepare a place for you. And if I go and prepare a place for you, I will come again, and receive you unto myself; that where I am there you may be also."* Jesus, the bridegroom, has gone to prepare our bridal chamber which is in heaven. Therefore, we must return to heaven in order to complete the wedding.

It is the father who tells his son when it's time to bring his bride home. That's why Jesus said in Matthew 24:36 (Amplified) He didn't know the time of his return: *"but of that exact day and hour no one knows, not even the angels of heaven, nor the Son, but only the Father."*

While the bridegroom is away preparing, the bride must keep herself pure for him. And they are legally married even though their marriage has not been consummated. Therefore, because of its legal and binding status, the marriage, even at this stage, can only be ended by a bill of divorcement.

With that in mind, 2 Thessalonians 2:3 takes on added meaning: *"Let no man deceive you by any means: for that day* (the Tribulation) *shall not come, except there come a **falling away** first, and that man of sin* (the antichrist) *be revealed, the son of perdition."*

What is this saying? Due to intense persecution and the circulation of fake letters and/or false teaching, the Thessalonians believed the rapture had already taken place and they were left to face the Tribulation. Paul was reminding them that, no, they were NOT in the Tribulation because the great falling away had not occurred nor had the antichrist been revealed. So, from this we learn the rapture won't come until there is a departing first or falling away. The word in Greek for "falling away" is *apostasia* and has these three meanings: a defection from truth, a divorce or writing of divorcement, and to physically remove. It's a play on words indicating people leaving the Truth (Jesus) and as a consequence, God divorcing them, then physically removing those He has not divorced—in the rapture.

Further down in 2 Thessalonians 2:6-7 (Amplified) it says, *"And now you know what is restraining him* (the antichrist) *from being revealed at this time; it is so that he may* *be manifested {reveled} in his own appointed time. For the mystery of lawlessness {that hidden principle of rebellion against constituted authority} is already at work in the world, {but it is} restrained only **until he who restrains is taken out of the way.**"* The "restrainer" is, of course, the Holy Spirit residing within the body of Christ, the church. And as long as we are still in the world, we will have a restraining influence and the man of sin or antichrist will not be revealed. Remember, part of the church's function is to prevail against the gates of hell.

But it doesn't say the Holy Spirit will be taken out of the world, only out of the **way** when the church is raptured. He will still be active on earth working to bring many to Jesus during the Tribulation as well as empowering the two witnesses and the 144,000 Jewish evangelists.

Think about how amazing the rapture will be! We, His bride, will be taken out of this dark and evil world, given our glorified body, and joined with Jesus forever.

In the Jewish wedding, grooms typically came suddenly and at night. And when the groom came, he'd take his bride immediately to the bridal chamber. So, too, will the rapture come, suddenly and without warning, and we will be taken immediately into heaven. In the Jewish wedding, the bride and groom were sequestered together in the bridal chamber for seven days. It's a symbolic picture for how, in the same way, during the seven terrible years of the Tribulation, we, the raptured bride, will be sheltering safely in the heavenly bridal chamber.

Remembering the parable of the ten virgins and the three meanings of *apostasia*—a defection from truth, a divorce or a writing of divorcement, and to physically remove—provides a sobering reminder that Jesus will divorce those who have defected from the truth and only take those who have not, to the bridal chamber.

Then came the marriage supper. When Jesus celebrated the Passover with His disciples and raised the cup and offered it to them, He was not only declaring Himself to be the sacrificial Passover Lamb, and offering His blood, but He was referring to the marriage supper in heaven. Matthew 26:29 says, *"But I (Jesus) say unto you, I will not drink henceforth of this fruit of the vine, until that day when I drink it new with you in my Father's kingdom."* He was offering the cup to His bride, His followers, the same way a Jewish bridegroom offered a cup of wine to his bride to seal their marriage agreement, and the apostles understood this. And as in a Jewish wedding where the bride and groom don't drink together again until the marriage feast, so Jesus was telling His disciples that He would not drink again until He could do so with them in the marriage supper of the Lamb.

After seven days, the bridegroom would bring out his bride and they would both join the guests for a marriage feast. Revelation 19:9 says, *"And he saith unto me. Write, Blessed are they which are called unto the marriage supper of the Lamb."* By Revelation 19:9 the Tribulation is over. The bride of Christ is ready to leave the bridal chamber with her bridegroom and participate in the feast.

As previously mentioned, the rapture is the fulfillment of the promise, buried in the Song of Solomon, between the King (Jesus) and His bride (the church). One day, born-again believers will hear the trumpet and the command to *"come up hither"* and will be taken up to heaven by their bridegroom.

In Revelation 22:16 Jesus said, *"I Jesus have sent mine angel to testify unto you these things in the churches. I am the root and the offspring of David, and the bright and morning star,"* to which John then wrote in verse 17, *"And the Spirit and the **bride** say, Come. And let him that heareth say, Come. And let him that is athirst come. And whosoever will, let him take the water of life freely."*

And this should be the prayer of the bride, *"Come quickly Lord Jesus!"*

Priest

The first time we encounter a priest in Scripture is in Genesis 14:18-20. First mentions are significant. The First Mention Principle or Law of First Mention assigns the word first mentioned its most precise and full meaning and provides both a foundation and key for later mentions. Therefore, it's important we look closely at these Genesis verses.

In chapter 14, four kings have waged war with five other kings, and in the process Abraham's nephew, Lot, and his property, became spoils of war. When Abraham learned of this, he took 318 of his servants, armed them, then headed for the territory of Dan where the captives were being held. He and his servants defeated the enemy, freed the prisoners, and recovered the spoils.

After the battle, Abraham returned to the valley of Shaveh where Melchizedek met him. Genesis 14:18-20 says, *"And Melchizedek king of **Salem** brought forth **bread and wine**: and he was the **priest** of the most high God. And he blessed him (Abraham) and said, Blessed be Abram of the most high God, possessor of heaven and earth: And blessed be the most high God, which hath delivered thine enemies into thy hand. And he (Abraham) gave him tithes of all."*

Encountering Jesus Throughout the Bible

Who was this mysterious Melchizedek? As previously mentioned, the Bible calls him king of Salem, which refers to Jerusalem but also means "peaceful" making him King of Peace. In addition, the name, Melchizedek, literally means King of Righteousness. He was also the priest of the most high God. This priest carried bread and wine, then blessed Abraham after which Abraham offered him, *"tithes of all."*

The Bible never wastes words. It never gives details without a reason. So, why does it mention the titles, the bread and wine, and the tithes?

First, let's look at Salem. Psalm 76:1-2 says, *"In Judah is God known: his name is great in Israel. In **Salem** also is his tabernacle, and his dwelling place in Zion."* God has claimed Salem/Jerusalem as His dwelling place. It is where His first two Temples were built and where He will physically sit as King and Ruler for a thousand years in a new Temple.

Also, titles are important. Consider the only one worthy of being called King of Peace, King of Righteousness, King of Salem/Jerusalem and the only one worthy of our tithes. Only One fills that bill, and that One is Jesus. Thus, Melchizedek was the preincarnate Christ. We need to understand that Melchizedek is a title, not a name, indicating the bearer of that title is both a king and priest, just as Jesus is both a king and priest.

The only other time Melchizedek is mentioned in the Old Testament is in Psalm 110:4. This Psalm is a Messianic prophecy. It says, *"The LORD hath sworn, and will not repent, Thou* (Messiah) *art a priest **for ever** after the order of Melchizedek."* We've already seen that Jesus is the Messiah. And here, Melchizedek is tied to Jesus. And the order of Melchizedek, a king-priest-order, is clearly superior to the order of Aaron, a priest-only-order, and will be the order that lasts throughout all eternity.

Does that mean Abraham literally encountered Jesus when He appeared to him as Melchizedek the priest?

Yes.

However, some scholars believe Melchizedek was a Canaanite king or perhaps Shem, the son of Noah. Let's look at these possibilities:

First, regarding the matter of Melchizedek being a Canaanite king:

Canaanites were idol worshippers; therefore, Abraham would never acknowledge one as King of Righteousness or King of Peace or give the priest of a false god, tithes, because tithes belonged to the true God, the maker of heaven and earth. Malachi 3:8-10 says, *"Will a man rob God? Yet ye have robbed me* (God). *But ye say, Wherein have we robbed thee? In tithes and offerings. Ye are cursed with a curse: for ye have robbed me, even this whole nation. Bring ye all the tithes into the storehouse, that there may be meat in mine house, and prove me now herewith, saith the LORD of hosts, if I will not open you the windows of heaven, and pour you out a blessing, that there shall not be room enough to receive it."*

Indeed, right after Abraham's encounter with Melchizedek, the king of Sodom offered him spoils recovered in his victory. Abraham refused. Why? Genesis 14:22 tells us. *"And Abram said to the king of Sodom, I have lift up mine hand unto the LORD, the most high God, the possessor of heaven and earth, That I will not take from a thread even to a shoelatchet, and that I will not take any thing that is thine, lest thou shouldest say, I have made Abram rich."* Abraham had just given Melchizedek tithes and reconfirmed his covenant with God through the bread and wine. It was his God who would provide for him, and that's what Abraham was telling the king of Sodom.

Therefore, it is reasonable to conclude that Abraham knew this Melchizedek to be his God's high priest, as well as the King of Peace and Righteousness, and thus appropriately gave Him tithes.

As mentioned, bread and wine were symbols of a covenant. God had already made a covenant with Abraham and his seed. Therefore, Abraham would never make a different covenant with an idol worshipper. Rather, Melchizedek's offering of bread and wine was the foreshadowing of a future covenant involving Jesus (Abraham's seed); a covenant that would again feature bread and wine.

Sylvia Bambola

Regarding whether or not Melchizedek was Shem:

For this answer, we need to go to Hebrews 7:1-4 where it talks about Melchizedek's encounter with Abraham. *"For this **Melchisedec**, king of Salem, priest of the most high God, who met Abraham returning from the slaughter of the kings, and blessed him; To whom also Abraham gave a tenth part of all; first being by interpretation King of righteousness, and after that also King of Salem, which is, King of peace;* ***Without father, without mother, without descent, having neither beginning of days nor end of life; but made like unto the Son of God; abideth a priest continually.*** *Now consider how great this man was, unto whom even the patriarch Abraham gave the tenth of the spoils."*

Here it clearly states that this King of Salem, this King of Righteousness, this priest after the order of Melchizedek who met Abraham had no earthly lineage nor beginning of days nor end. That could never apply to Shem. Everyone knew who his father and mother were and when his days began. And it's documented that Shem died when he was six hundred years old. But at the time of the Genesis 14:18-20 meeting between Melchizedek and Abraham, Shem was still alive and was well known by both Abraham and his son, Isaac. In fact, after Sarah died, Jasher 24:17 claims Abraham *"went to the house of Shem and Eber* (Shem's son), *to learn the ways of the Lord and His instructions, and Abraham remained there three years."* Why? Because according to Jasher, at that time Shem had a religious school that taught the precepts of God.

Encountering Jesus Throughout the Bible

The New Testament clearly talks about Jesus being in the order of Melchizedek. Hebrews 5:5-6 says, *"So also Christ glorified not himself to be made an high priest; but he that said unto him, Thou art my Son, to day have I begotten thee. As he saith also in another place, Thou art a priest for ever after the order of **Melchisedec**."*

In the above Scripture, the spelling of Melchisedec is slightly different than in the Old Testament but it's still the same word with the same meaning. Jesus was after the order of Melchizedek. That word "order" is *taxis* in Greek and means, "ordained, appoint, determine, to arrange in orderly manner, official dignity." This implies that Jesus was ordained and appointed to a king-priest order where He is King of Righteous and Peace, as well as the priest of the most high God. From this we understand that God the Father ordained Jesus as a priest. It was the heavenly ordination of the heavenly priesthood.

Hebrews 5:10 goes on to say that Jesus is not only a priest but a **high priest**. *"Called of God an **high priest** after the order of Melchisedec."* And Hebrews 6:19-20 (Amplified) tells us that, *"we have this {hope} as a sure and steadfast anchor of the soul {it cannot slip and it cannot break down under whoever steps out upon it—a hope} that reaches farther and enters into {the very certainty of the Presence} within the veil, Where Jesus has entered in for us {in advance}, a Forerunner having become a **High Priest** forever after the order {with the rank} of Melchizedek."*

Hebrews 7:3 also stated that Melchizedek, the priest, was *"made like unto the Son of God."* Those two words "made like" are exactly the same word in Greek, *"aphomoioo,"* and is used nowhere else in the New Testament. So, in the original Greek, *aphomoioo* is repeated when describing the priest and the Son of God. What does that word mean? It means to assimilate. And Webster defines "assimilate" this way: "to make similar, to take up and make part of itself or oneself, absorb and incorporate, to be like, to be absorbed and incorporated." The repetition of the word, *aphomoioo*, depicts the binary aspects of Jesus as both God and man. Melchizedek resembled the Son of God, the Second Person of the Trinity, because He **was** the Son of God. And as the priest after the order of Melchizedek in the New Testament, Jesus, the Son of God, the Second Person of the Trinity, was absorbed and incorporated into the form of man, while Melchizedek in the Old Testament was the preincarnate Jesus. Both similar because they were one and the same.

Hebrews 7:11, 13-15, 21 (Amplified) explains it perfectly. *"Now if perfection {a perfect fellowship between God and the worshiper} had been attainable by the Levitical priesthood—for under it the people were given the Law—why was it further necessary that there should arise another and different kind of Priest, one after the order of **Melchizedek**, rather than one appointed after the order and rank of Aaron? . . . For the One of Whom these things are said belonged {not to the priestly line but} to another tribe, no member of which has officiated at the altar. For it is obvious that our Lord sprang from the tribe of Judah, and Moses mentioned nothing about priests in connection with that tribe. And this becomes more plainly* *evident when another Priest arises Who bears the likeness of Melchizedek. . .. For those who formerly became priests received their office without its being confirmed by the taking of an oath by God, but this One was designated and addressed and saluted with an oath, The Lord has sworn and will not regret it or change His mind, You (Jesus) are a Priest forever according to the order of Melchizedek."* Remember, Melchizedek refers to a king-priest line. Note again that it was God the Father, Himself, Who confirmed Jesus as a priest after the Melchizedek order.

Hebrews 7:27 (Amplified) goes on to say, *"He (Jesus) has no day by day necessity, as {do each of these other} high priests, to offer sacrifice first of all for his own {personal} sins and then for those of the people, because He {met all the requirements} once for all when He brought Himself {as a sacrifice} which he offered up."*

The order of Melchizedek existed long before the establishment of the Aaronic priesthood. This tells us that Jesus, as High Priest, through His blood, has paid the price for sin, once and for all. And this enables us to enter the heavenly Holy of Holies, the place symbolized by the earthly Holy of Holies where only the Jewish high priest could enter once a year with a blood sacrifice for the atonement of Israel.

Hebrews 4:14 says, *"Seeing then that we have a great **high priest**, that is passed into the heavens, Jesus the Son of God, let us hold fast our profession."* Hebrews 8:1b says, *"We have such an **high priest** (Jesus), who is set on the right hand of the throne of the Majesty in the heavens."* And Hebrews 9:11

says, *"But Christ being come an* **high priest** *of good things to come, by a greater and more perfect tabernacle, not made with hands, that is to say, not of this building."* And 1 John 2:1 calls Jesus our "advocate" with the Father.

Jesus clearly was the preexisting Melchizedekian High Priest of God, a priesthood superior to the Aaronic priesthood. And according to Hebrews 7:24-28, He continues as our High Priest today.

As previously mentioned, John 20:1-12 tells us how Mary Magdalene went to the empty tomb and saw the two angels, one at each end of the blood-covered slab, symbolizing the mercy seat on the ark of the covenant.

Then when Mary saw Jesus, He told her, *"**Touch me not**; for I am not yet ascended to my Father: but go to my brethren, and say unto them, I ascend unto my Father and your Father; and to my God and your God."* Yet, a few verses later (John 20:27) Jesus told Thomas to **touch Him**. What happened in between?

Jesus, as High Priest after the Order of Melchisedec, had to ascend to His Father and perform his high priestly function by pouring His blood on the heavenly Mercy Seat. The Jewish Temple, ark of the covenant, altar of incense, menorah, etcetera, were all replicas of what exists in heaven. And Jesus was duplicating what the Jewish high priest did every year when he entered the Holy of Holies and poured the blood of sacrifice over the mercy seat for the atonement of Israel's sins, except Jesus poured His blood over the heavenly Mercy Seat, not just for Israel, but for the whole world, for "whosoever will" come to Him. And it was a sacrifice that would never have to be repeated.

Under Levitical law, a high priest couldn't touch or be touched by anything unclean prior to offering sacrifices to God. One can only assume it applies to the Order of Melchisedec as well. That's why Mary couldn't touch Him.

But there's more. Isaiah 61 talks about the Messiah. It's the very Scripture Jesus quoted when He stood up in the synagogue and announced His ministry. Isaiah 61:6 goes on to talk about a time when Israel will be exalted but it also applies to believers. It says, *"But ye shall be named the* **Priests** *of the LORD: men shall call you the Ministers of our God: ye shall eat the riches of the Gentiles* (unbelievers)*, and in their glory shall ye boast yourselves."* Prophetically, it speaks of a time when believers, both Jew and non-Jew, will officiate as priests of God.

1 Peter 2:5 also touched on this, *"Ye* (believers) *also, as lively stones, are built up a spiritual house, an holy* **priesthood***, to offer up spiritual sacrifices, acceptable to God by Jesus Christ."* Then 1 Peter 2:9 added, *"But ye* (believers in Christ) *are a chosen generation, a royal* **priesthood***, an holy nation, a peculiar people; that ye should shew forth the praises of him who hath called you out of darkness into his marvellous light."*

Revelation 1:5-6 continued this theme, *"And from Jesus Christ, who is the faithful witness, and the first begotten of the* *dead, and the prince of the kings of the earth. Unto him that loved us and washed us from our sins in his own blood. And hath made us **kings and priests** unto God, and his Father; to him be glory and dominion for ever and ever. Amen."* Jesus not only washed us with His blood, but that washing then transformed us into kings and priests. How amazing!

Even the Old Testament foresaw this. Imbedded in the law of the leper is an amazing message that's worth digressing in order to examine it.

In ancient times, leprosy was one of the most dreaded diseases. It was contagious and disfiguring, affecting the skin, nerves, and mucous membranes. Lepers were shunned and forced to live apart from the rest of society. They were required to cover their mouth and cry, "unclean, unclean" whenever any healthy person approached as detailed in Leviticus 13:45, *"And the leper in whom the plague is, **his clothes shall be rent, and his head bare,** and **he shall put a covering upon his upper lip, and shall cry, Unclean, unclean."***

Leprosy is an illustration of sin. Uncovering a head and renting clothes were signs of mourning the dead. Covering the upper lip mirrored the tradition of Jewish burial when the jaw was tied up by a cloth. And a dead body was "unclean." In essence, the leper was considered dead by the community, therefore he had to cry "unclean." It is a picture of the sinner who is dead in his sins.

A leper may not manifest symptoms for years, then break out in the telltale sores. Like leprosy, secret sin can be hidden from others for years. Then it manifests, starting out small like a patch of raised skin or blemish, before spreading. The corruption becomes gradually visible, just like sin.

Leprosy first affects the skin, then the flesh, then the bones. Sin, like leprosy becomes progressively more corrosive, eating away at our life. And like leprosy, sin disfigures a life. It keeps a person from being all God wants him/her to be. And like leprosy, sin causes separation from God and others.

The illustration of leprosy shows how terrible sin is; how it affects the lives of not only those who sin but their families. When a person had leprosy, it changed the dynamics of that entire family just like sin can change the dynamics of a family. And like leprosy, sin can be contagious. Hanging out with the wrong crowd or filling one's mind with wrong books, TV programs, movies, music, etcetera, can open one up to sin.

When we really see how terrible leprosy was, how it could mar and disfigure a life, how it isolated and separated a person, then we begin to understand how God views sin.

But then came Jesus and changed everything. He became the remedy as stated by the following Scriptures:

Romans 6:23 *"For the wages of sin is death; but the gift of God is eternal life through Jesus Christ our Lord."*

John 1:29b *"Behold the Lamb of God, which taketh away the sin of the world."*

2 Corinthians 5:21 *"For he had made him (Jesus) to be sin for us, who knew no sin; that we might be made the righteousness of God in him."*

Romans 6:6 *"Knowing this, that our old man is crucified with him (Jesus), that the body of sin might be destroyed, that henceforth we should not serve sin."*

But how did Jesus react when He encountered a physical leper? And does it translate to us as spiritual lepers? Matthew 8:2-3 tells us. A leper approached Jesus saying, *"Lord, if thou wilt, thou canst make me clean."* Jesus' reaction was astonishing considering how leprosy was viewed at that time. The first thing He did was **touch** him. He touched the untouchable for that's what lepers were. Then He said, *"I will; be thou clean."*

What an amazing God! This illustrates His tender heart, His kindness, His love, His mercy. He could have easily healed the leper with a word. He did just that only a few verses later in Matthew 8:5-13 when He healed the centurion's servant.

Jesus wants to cleanse us, too, and He's not afraid to put His finger into our puss-filled sores. He's not afraid to touch the dirty, the defiled places within us. He's not afraid to look upon our poor spiritual deformity. The wonderful thing is this: God sees us for who we really are but loves us anyway. And He loves us not because we're good, but because *He* is good.

Because the wages of sin is death, we can understand why, we, like lepers of old, were considered dead before coming to Jesus. And just as the lepers in ancient Israel had to cry "unclean," so we, too, have to declare we are "unclean" before being cleansed by Jesus' blood. We must make the declaration that we are a sinner and turn to Jesus and accept what He has already done for us. Then, something wonderful happens. Because Jesus took our sins upon Himself and because our old man is crucified with Him, we no longer serve sin. We are free and made new. Romans 6:4 tells us *"Therefore we are buried with him by baptism into death; that like as Christ was raised up from the dead by the glory of the Father, even so we also should walk in newness of life."* So, we are no longer outcasts, no longer putrid and disfigured with the sores and lesions of sin, and no longer shunned by God.

But it gets better—now we even hold an exalted position as priests who can come before God, the Creator of the Universe, any time we wish. And we see a foreshadowing of this in how lepers were cleansed in the Old Testament after they were healed of leprosy.

Here's the protocol: Leviticus 14:2 says, *"This shall be the law of the leper in the day of his cleansing."* Verses 3-32 go on to detail what must be done: A leper had to be inspected by the priest outside the camp and declared healed. The leper then gave the priest sacrifices to be offered on his behalf, the blood of which the priest sprinkled on the leper seven times and declared him clean. Then the cleansed leper had to shave all his hair, then wash himself and his clothes. Only then could he enter the camp, where he stayed in a tent for seven days. On the seventh day he again shaved his hair, washed his clothes and body, and put on clean garments, symbolizing the start of a new life. In this same way we are clothed with Jesus' garment of righteousness after we accept Him and are cleansed, then begin a new life.

What follows next symbolizes the priesthood consecration of believers in Jesus. On the eighth day, the cleansed leper brought animals for sacrifice, along with flour and oil for a wave offering, and gave them to the priest. The priest then presented the cleansed leper and all these offerings to the Lord at the **door of the tabernacle of the congregation.** After the sacrifices were made, the priest took some of the blood and put it on the **tip of the cleansed leper's right ear, the thumb of his right hand, the big toe of his right foot.** Following that, the priest also anointed these same areas with oil. Then the rest of the oil was poured over his head.

Why is all that significant? Because it mirrors the preparation and consecration of Aaron and his sons for the priesthood. It was at the **door of the tabernacle of the congregation** that Moses washed Aaron and his sons. They then put on new priestly garments (Exodus 29:7-21), after which Moses sacrificed animals on their behalf, then anointing oil was poured over their heads. The blood of the sacrifice was applied to the **tip of their right ear, the thumb of their right hand, and the big toe of their right foot.** Then oil and blood were sprinkled on their priestly garments. In addition, their consecration lasted seven days. At no other time was blood applied to a person's right ear, thumb, and toe except when consecrating a priest or cleansing a leper. This is unique to only those two groups.

The one big difference I find interesting is that the Levitical priests' right ear, thumb and toe were not anointed with oil as were the cleansed lepers. The priests and cleansed lepers both had oil poured over their heads, but only lepers had their ear, thumb and toe anointed with oil. Since oil speaks of the Holy Spirit, I believe it suggests the empowerment of the Holy Spirit promised to believers in Jesus. By listening (the ear) to and being guided by the Holy Spirit, we will be empowered to do (the thumb/hand) the work He wants us to do and go (the toe/foot) wherever He wants us to go.

We have already seen in 1 Peter 2:5 and in 1 Peter 2:9 that we are priests. But not just priests, but holy and royal priests. As holy priests we are to keep ourselves clean and consecrated to God. As royal priests, we are priests of a king, the very King of Kings and Lord of Lords. That word, "royal" also indicates power and the foundation of power. So, we, too, have power, and that foundation of power is Jesus.

But what exactly is the office of our priesthood? What are we to do as priests? Romans 12:1 tells us. We are to bring our God and King, sacrifices. *"I beseech you therefore brethren, by the mercies of God, that ye present your bodies a living sacrifice, holy, acceptable unto God, which is your reasonable service."*

So, first we present our bodies to God, which means all that we are, our flesh, our thoughts, our emotions, our dreams and desires, everything, and offer them to Him.

Hebrews 13:15 says *"By him therefore let us offer the sacrifice of praise to God continually, that is, the fruit of our lips giving thanks to his name."* Then after we've presented our bodies, we continually praise Him no matter what. That means no complaining, no fussing, no faultfinding.

What a great privilege! God has taken us spiritual lepers, with all our wounds and imperfections, and elevated us to a holy and royal priesthood through which we can come before Him, our High Priest after the order of Melchizedek, anytime we want!

Encountering Jesus Throughout the Bible

Prince of Peace

The Old Testament associated God with peace. Psalm 29:11 says, *"The LORD will give strength unto his people; the LORD will bless his people with **peace**."* That word here for "peace" is *shalom* and means, "well, happy, health, prosperity, welfare, rest, safety." These are the things God promised His people. It's a *shalom* only He can give. In fact, one of the Hebrew names for God is Jehovah-Shalom, the One Who gives peace.

In the previous chapter we saw that Jesus was the priest after the order of Melchizedek as well as King of Salem or **King of Peace** by translation (Genesis 14:18). This was also confirmed in Hebrews 7:1-4. So, right from the beginning, Jesus was linked to peace, even the King of Peace, the One Who has the authority and power to bestow it.

Isaiah 9 prophetically refers to the Messiah, which we already know is Jesus. Verse 6 says, *"For unto us a child is born, unto us a son is given: and the government shall be upon his shoulder: and his name shall be called Wonderful, Counsellor, The mighty God, The everlasting Father, **The Prince of Peace**."* This is a marvelous Scripture revealing amazing aspects of Messiah. He is in control. He is God. He is wonderful. He is Counsellor. He is eternal. And He is the Prince of Peace.

Unpacking the words "Prince" and "Peace" is also revealing. That word "Prince" in the Hebrew is *sar* and means, "head person, keeper, lord, having dominion," while that word "Peace" in Hebrew is the same word, *shalom*, as in Psalm 29:11. But on page 930, the *Theological Wordbook of the Old Testament* goes even further and defines *shalom* this way: "entering into a state of wholeness and unity, a restored relationship." It can also mean "anointed," which is what Messiah means, "the anointed One," bringing it full circle. The "anointed One" is both Messiah and Prince of Peace.

What a beautiful description of Jesus. He is head. He has dominion. He is the keeper and author of peace. And when He became the sin offering, He restored "wholeness and unity" to those who believed in Him. It is the very "wholeness and unity" Adam and Eve once had with God before the fall. How incredible is that!

Because Jesus is called King of kings and Lord of lords in Revelation 19:16, why would He also be referred to as "prince," a title which usually refers to the son of the king but a seemingly lesser position? Because this title of prince is especially relevant in conjunction with Jesus' role as Messiah. We must remember that as Messiah, Jesus, the **Son of God**, left His exalted position in heaven, took on flesh, and made Himself subordinate to God the Father, the King of the universe. Jesus made this clear in John 5:19 when He said, *"Verily, verily, I say unto you, The* **Son** *can do nothing of himself, but what he seeth the* **Father** *do: for what things soever he doeth, these also doeth the Son likewise."*

Actually, the New Testament calls Jesus a "Prince" several times. Revelation 1:5 calls Him the *"Prince of the kings of the earth,"* Acts 3:15 calls Him the *"Prince of life,"* while Acts 5:31 calls Him a *"Prince and a Saviour,"* linking together the dual aspects of Jesus as both Messiah ben David, the ruler, and Messiah ben Joseph, the suffering servant.

How is God's peace obtained?

Psalm 119:165 tells us, *"Great **peace** have they which love thy law; and nothing shall offend them."* Isaiah 26:3 adds this, *"Thou (God) wilt keep him in perfect **peace**, whose mind is stayed on thee: because he trusteth in thee."* Isaiah 32:17 says, *"And the work of righteousness shall be **peace**; and the effect of righteousness quietness and assurance for ever."* Isaiah 48:18 says, *"O that thou hadst hearkened to my commandments! then had thy **peace** been as a river, and thy righteousness as the waves of the sea."*

In the Old Testament, only those who followed God's commandments and trusted Him had any hope of peace. And that becomes even more important when we read God's warning in Isaiah 48:22: *"There is **no peace**, saith the LORD, unto the wicked."* So, the wicked have "no peace."

But following and trusting God was not as easy as it sounds. His laws were many, complex, and easy to violate. That meant numerous blood sacrifices were required to pay for offenses and sins. It seemed hopeless. Who could live up to the holiness of God? Who could ever walk perfectly in His ways? As it turns out, **no one**!

Then came the prophecy in Isaiah 53:5 regarding the Messiah. *"But he* (Messiah Jesus) *was wounded for our transgressions, he was bruised for our iniquities: the chastisement of our **peace** was upon him; and with his stripes we are healed."*

Hope was on the way. The Messiah would come and through His death, restore peace between God and man. Isaiah 54:13 goes on to promise that, *"All thy children shall be taught of the LORD; and great shall be the **peace** of thy children."* And Isaiah 55:12 adds this promise for future believers in Messiah: *"For ye shall go out with joy, and be led forth with **peace**: the mountains and the hills shall beak forth before you into singing, and all the trees of the field shall clap their hands."* God, through the prophet Isaiah, promised a remedy for sin, a remedy for us and our children. No longer would we be separated and cringing in fear before a Holy God, but Messiah would restore us and enable us to enter through the veil (His body and blood) into His presence in the very Holy of Holies.

The New Testament also acknowledged that peace comes from God.

Romans 1:7, Galatians 1:3, Ephesians 1:2, Philippians 1:2, Colossians 1:2, 1 Thessalonians 1:1, 2 Thessalonians 1:2, 1 Timothy 1:2, 2 Timothy 1:2, Titus 1:4, and Philemon 3 all pray that their readers have, *"peace from God."* And the New Testament is specific on how to obtain this peace.

Zacharias, a righteous priest *"of the course of Abia,"* was visited by the angel Gabriel while burning incense in the

Temple. His wife, Elizabeth, was barren and because they were old, all hope of having children was gone. So, when Gabriel told Zacharias that Elizabeth was going to have a son, Zacharias didn't believe him. This proved costly. Zacharias would not be able to utter a word until after the birth of his son, who was to be called, John. When that day came, and John the Baptist was born, Zacharias once again could speak and prophesied in Luke 1:79 saying that the Messiah, the Savior, would *"give light to them that sit in darkness and in the shadow of death, to guide our feet into the way of **peace**."* It was to be the Messiah, the very Prince of Peace, Who would guide people into peace.

We've already learned that another angelic appearance occurred in Bethlehem on the night Jesus was born. This time it was to local shepherds. The angel told them of this wonderous event in Luke 2:11, 14, *"For unto you is born this day in the city of David a Saviour, which is Christ* (Messiah) *the Lord. . . .Glory to God in the highest, and on earth **peace**, good will toward men."*

The angel was announcing the arrival of the Prince of Peace. And it would be this Prince that would bring peace to the earth. Not the kind of peace everyone was looking for, the kind when there would be no more wars. That kind of peace He will bring when He comes the second time. But His first coming would bring a more important peace, that of healing the rift between God and man.

Encountering Jesus Throughout the Bible

Then in Luke 19:37-38 we see Jesus riding into Jerusalem on a donkey amid a throng of rejoicing people. *"And when he (Jesus) was come nigh, even now at the descent of the mount of Olives, the whole multitude of the disciples began to rejoice and praise God with a loud voice for all the mighty works that they had seen; Saying, Blessed be the King that cometh in the name of the Lord: **peace** in heaven, and glory in the highest."*

The disciples also believed Jesus had come as king and would rid Israel of the Romans, their cruel taskmasters. At this stage, they didn't understand that He would come twice, this first time as the suffering servant. Nevertheless, these Scriptures are prophetic, pointing to when Jesus, the King, would come after the Tribulation, destroying the antichrist and his army, then bringing peace from the sword on earth, as well as peace in heaven.

One must understand that Satan's fall had brought discord to both the heavenly and earthly realms. Therefore, both heaven and earth had to be reconciled. Romans 16:20 alludes to the earthly realm, *"And the God of **peace** shall bruise Satan under your* (the believers in Jesus) *feet shortly,"* while Colossians 1:20 mentions them both: *"And, having made **peace** through the blood of his* (Jesus) *cross, by him to reconcile all things unto himself; by him, I say, whether they be **things in earth, or things in heaven**."*

I covered the reason it was necessary for both a heavenly and earthly reconciliation, due to Satan's as well as man's rebellion, in my book, *The Coming Deception*. It's too long to repeat the material here, but suffice it to say, Jesus, the Prince of Peace, brought peace to both the heavenly and earthly realms.

After Jesus rose from the dead, He appeared to His disciples in Luke 24:36. The first thing He said was, "***Peace be unto you.***" He knew they were frightened, confused, and distraught. These were again His first words when He appeared to His disciples the second time to confront doubting Thomas in John 20:26, "***Peace be unto you.***" It was the kind of peace Philippians 4:7 talks about, the peace that *"passeth all understanding,"* the kind that keeps *"your hearts and minds through Christ Jesus."* It's the kind of peace that can keep one calm through the worst storm or trial; the kind of peace that comes only through Jesus, the Prince of Peace.

Jesus told His disciples that the Holy Spirit, the Comforter, would come after He returned to heaven. In John 14:27 He said, "***Peace** I leave with you, my **peace** I give unto you: not as the world giveth, give I unto you. Let not your heart be troubled, neither let it be afraid."* Jesus promised believers He would not leave them without a helper, His Holy Spirit, and that included leaving them with His peace. Therefore, believers need not be afraid or troubled. If they abide in Him, they can have perfect peace no matter the circumstances. Remember Isaiah 26:3, *"Thou* (God) *will keep him in perfect peace whose mind is stayed on thee because he trusted in thee."*

Encountering Jesus Throughout the Bible

In Acts 10 we find Peter preaching to Cornelius and his household. Though Cornelius was a centurion and Gentile, God had instructed Peter to go to his house and share the gospel. This had taken Peter by surprise. Could God really want him to enter the home of an unclean Gentile? Because God had given Peter a vision illustrating that what He now called clean was not to be considered unclean, Peter obeyed. *"Of a truth I perceive that God is no respecter of persons: But in every nation he that feareth him, and worketh righteousness, is accepted with him. The word which God sent unto the children of Israel, preaching **peace** by Jesus Christ: (he is Lord of all),"* Acts 10:34-36.

So, this peace with God through Jesus was to be for everyone who believed and "worked righteousness." In other words, those who believe and obey the gospel. Romans 5:1 confirms this: *"Therefore being justified by faith, we have **peace** with God through our Lord Jesus Christ."*

And Jesus does indeed give us His peace via the Holy Spirit. Galatians 5:22 tells us that peace is the fruit of the Holy Spirit. And Romans 14:17 says, *"For the kingdom of God is not meat and drink; but righteousness, and **peace**, and joy in the Holy Ghost."*

Ephesians 2:13-14 says, *"But now in Christ Jesus ye who sometimes were far off are made nigh by the blood of Christ. For he* (Jesus) *is our **peace**, who hath made both one, and hath broken down the middle wall of partition between us* (Jew and Gentile)."

Jesus is peace Himself, even over the elements as evidenced in Mark 4:39 when He rebuked the wind that was tossing around His boat and causing it to fill with water, *"**Peace** be still, and the wind ceased, and there was great calm."*

And because He is peace Himself, His absence will create a lack of it. Daniel 8:11 and 8:25 foretells of the time when the antichrist will magnify *"himself even to the **prince** of the host* (Jesus as captain of the heavenly hosts)*"* and *"stand up against the **Prince** of princes* (Jesus).*"* It's referring to the Tribulation when the antichrist will defy Jesus and declare himself god in Jerusalem. The sad thing is that when this happens, the world will experience a lack of peace in a big way. In Revelation chapter 6, when Jesus opens the seals during the beginning of the Tribulation, the first thing to be taken from the earth is peace (Revelation 6:4). The discord will come through various judgments as well as the antichrist, but it's Jesus, the Prince of Peace, who authorizes it. It will be a time of great darkness and conflict, the worst the world has ever experienced; a time when the earth will be judged, and Satan exposed for the evil entity he is.

What a terrible thing to be without the peace of God! Nothing the antichrist or anyone else does during the Tribulation can or will bring peace to the earth or calm the raging elements of nature. Fortunately, before this happens, believers will be raptured and taken to heaven. However, those who come into the saving knowledge of Jesus during the Tribulation will also experience God's peace but will not escape the fury of Satan via his puppet, the antichrist.

Daniel 9:25 goes on to give additional prophecies regarding end-time events and mentions *"the Messiah the Prince."* That word "Prince" is *nagiyd* and means "commander, occupying the front." It's referring to Jesus as Messiah ben Joseph when He occupied the front lines, facing off with the devil to achieve eternal victory for us through His death. But Jesus will come again as Messiah ben David and again face off with Satan, chain him for a thousand years, toss both his men—the antichrist and false prophet—into the lake of fire, then claim His own kingship and authority over the earth. What a wonderful time that will be!

"Now the Lord of peace himself give you peace always by all means." 2 Thessalonians 3:16

King

Old Testament Scriptures acknowledge that Israel considered God to be not only their King, but King of the world and universe. Below are a few of them:

First, as King of Israel:

Jacob was nearing the end of his life. Before he died, he wanted to bless his twelve sons. But along with his blessings came prophesies. In Genesis 49:9-10 Jacob called Judah the *"lion's welp,"* and prophesied that, *"The **sceptre** shall not depart from Judah, nor a **lawgiver** from between his feet, until **Shiloh** comes; and unto him shall the gathering of the people be."*

This is profound. A scepter implies authority to rule. Jacob was prophesying that a lawgiver, a future ruler would come from the tribe of Judah, as would the Messiah, for "Shiloh" means Messiah. So early on, the Jews began watching for their promised king, the one who would rule and reign over them. In the meantime, God would be their King.

At first, Israel had no problem with this. After all, they were God's chosen people according to Deuteronomy 7:7-8: *"The LORD did not set his love upon you* (Israel*), nor **choose** you because ye were more in number than any people;*

for ye were the fewest of all people: But because the LORD loved you, and because he would keep the oath which he had sworn unto your fathers, hath the LORD brought you out with a mighty hand, and redeemed you out of the house of bondmen, from the house of Pharaoh king of Egypt."

God's very presence, in the form of a cloud and fire, led Israel safely in the wilderness for forty years. All this contributed to Israel's awareness that He was their ruler, their King. The following Scriptures illustrate this:

Psalm 24:7-10, *"Lift up your heads, O ye gates; and be ye lift up, ye everlasting doors; and the **King** of glory shall come in. Who is this **King** of glory? The LORD strong and mighty, the LORD mighty in battle. Lift up your heads, O ye gates; even lift them up, ye everlasting doors; and the **King** of glory shall come in. Who is this **King** of glory? The LORD of hosts, he is the **King** of glory."*

Psalm 89:18, *"For the LORD is our defence; and the Holy One of Israel is our **king**."*

Israel in Psalm 149:2, acknowledged that God was not only their King but their Creator. *"Let Israel rejoice in him (God) that made him (Israel); let the children of Zion be joyful in their **King**."*

Next, as King of the world and universe:

Israel understood that God's authority didn't end with them. He was also King of the world and universe.

Psalm 103:19, *"The LORD hath prepared his **throne** in the heavens; and his **kingdom ruleth over all**."* The phrase "over all" means the known and unknown world as well as the heavens where God is enthroned.

1 Chronicles 29:11, *"Thine, O LORD, is the greatness, and the power, and the glory, and the victory, and the majesty: for all that is in the **heaven and in the earth is thine**; thine is the **kingdom**, O LORD, and **thou art exalted as head above all**."*

Psalm 47:2,6-8 *"For the LORD most high is terrible; he is a great **King** over all the earth. . . .. Sing praises to God, sing praises: sing praises unto our **King**, sing praises. For God is the **King of all the earth**: sing ye praises with understanding. **God reigneth over the heathen**: God sitteth upon the throne of his holiness."*

Jeremiah 10:7, 10, *"Who would not fear thee (God), O **King of nations**? for to thee doth it appertain: forasmuch as among all the wise men of the nations, and in all their kingdoms, there is none like unto thee. . . .. But the LORD is the true God, he is the living God, and an everlasting **king**: at his wrath the earth shall tremble, and the nations shall not be able to abide his indignation."*

Psalm 22:28, *"For the **kingdom** is the LORD'S: and he is the governor among the **nations**."* A governor is just another name for ruler. Israel clearly understood and believed that God's rule extended far beyond their nation.

Even when Israel was ruled by earthly kings, some of them, like David, personally acknowledged God as the true King. The following verses make David's feelings clear:

Psalm 10:16, *"The LORD is **King** for ever and ever."*

Psalm 29:10b, *"The LORD sitteth **King** for ever."*

In Psalm 95:3, *"the LORD is a great God, and a great **King** above all gods."*

Psalm 5:2, *"Hearken unto the voice of my cry, my **King**, and my God: for unto thee will I pray."*

Psalm 145:1, *"I (David) will extol thee, my God, O **king**; and I will bless thy name for ever and ever."*

David was so overwhelmed by God's goodness and glory, and so sure others would be too, he said this in Psalm145:11, *"They (the righteous) shall speak of the glory of thy **kingdom**, and talk of thy power."* Though God had His own glorious heavenly kingdom, there was no doubt in David's mind that God was also King over the kingdoms of the world, including his.

Hezekiah, in 2 Kings 19:15, also declared that God alone was God over *"all the kingdoms of the earth."*

Sylvia Bambola

Individuals acknowledged God as King:

When Isaiah saw God on His throne, he saw himself for what he was, a sinner, and saw God as utterly pure and holy. He said in Isaiah 6:5, *"Woe is me! for I am undone; because I am a man of unclean lips, and I dwell in the midst of a people of unclean lips: for mine eyes have seen the **King**, the LORD of hosts."* What an awesome sight that must have been! And how humbling! The great and powerful are nothing in the light of the majesty, glory, and holiness of God.

Even Nebuchadnezzar, the pagan king of Babylon, had his moments. In 598 B.C. he captured Jerusalem and brought many prisoners to his city. Daniel was one of them. At that time, the Babylonian kingdom was very powerful. But when King Nebuchadnezzar's pride became too great, God decided to whittle him down to size by decreeing that Nebuchadnezzar would, for seven years, become beast-like, eating grass, and living in the open fields. At the end of that time, Nebuchadnezzar's sanity was restored, and he said this in Daniel 4:37, *"Now I Nebuchadnezzar praise and extol and honour the **King of heaven**, all whose works are truth, and his ways judgment: and those that walk in pride he is able to abase."* What a lesson to learn the hard way!

Temple musicians also acknowledged God as their King. This can be found in Psalms 44:4, 68:24 and 84:3 as well as in Psalm 74:12 when Maschil of Asaph said, *"For God is my **King** of old, working salvation in the midst of the earth."*

Then there was Gideon, who was notable in his declaration that God was King. Here's what happened:

The Midianites had been a thorn in Israel's side for years, invading their land, plundering their food and goods. Finally, God called Gideon to put an end to it. It's an interesting story revealing numerous spiritual truths. It culminates in Midian's defeat at the hands of Gideon and his army. After this great victory, the people wanted Gideon and his son to rule over them.

The promise of power can be heady and difficult to refuse. But it's also dangerous. 1800's English Lord Acton said it best, "Power tends to corrupt, and absolute power corrupts absolutely."

Was it difficult for Gideon to subdue his natural pride and ego? Perhaps. But in the end, he refused to allow his countrymen to thrust him into a position that he understood only God should occupy, and said this amazing thing in Judges 8:23, *"I will not rule over you, neither shall my son rule over you: the* **LORD** *shall* **rule** *over you."*

God Himself acknowledges that He is King:

In Isaiah 41:21, God chastised His people for worshipping idols, *"Produce your cause* (give a reason why you have chosen to worship idols)*, saith the LORD; bring forth your strong reasons, saith the* **King** *of Jacob* (Israel)." God is making His position clear. **He** is King over Israel, and as King, He has the right to demand loyalty and obedience from His subjects or the reason why they weren't forthcoming.

Again, in Isaiah 43:15, God makes His position clear. *"I am the LORD, your Holy One, the creator of Israel, your **King**."*

God's kingdom is an everlasting kingdom.

Psalm 45:6, *"Thy throne, O God, is for **ever and ever**: the sceptre of thy **kingdom** is a right sceptre."*

Daniel 4:3, *"How great are his* (God's) *signs! and how mighty are his wonders! his **kingdom** is an **everlasting kingdom**, and his dominion is from generation to generation."*

Psalm 93:2, *"Thy* (God's) ***throne** is established of old: thou art from **everlasting**."*

Psalm 145:11-13, *"They* (the righteous) *shall speak of the glory of thy **kingdom**, and talk of thy power; To make known to the sons of men his* (God's) *mighty acts, and the glorious majesty of his **kingdom**. Thy **kingdom** is an **everlasting kingdom**, and thy dominion endureth throughout all generations."*

God's kingship is not a new development. Long before He was Israel's King and even before the earth was created, He ruled over a vast heavenly empire.

Though many kings in Israel understood they were merely representing God to their people, and that their rule was temporary while God's was everlasting, the fact remained Israel was never meant to have an earthly king.

Before seeing what went wrong, let's examine a few things.

First, we need to define "kingdom." It's a specific territory or realm headed and ruled by a king and by the king's laws. It is NOT a democracy. Rather, the king is the absolute ruler.

Even so, a king has certain responsibilities to those he governs. Among them are properly maintaining the kingdom by providing structures like roads and bridges. He and his surrogates must also maintain and enforce laws that protect his people. And when those laws are violated, he must see that justice is carried out. And finally, a king must protect his kingdom from invaders, and if required, fend them off in battle, which necessitates having a sufficient army. In this way, he keeps the borders of his kingdom from being breached and overrun by hostiles.

But what about his subjects? Do they have any responsibility? Yes. It can be summed up in one word: obedience.

There are three kingdoms. I list them in order of power: the Kingdom of God, the Kingdom of Satan, and the Kingdom of Self.

How do we know that Satan has a kingdom? Because during Jesus' temptation in the wilderness Matthew 4:8-9 says that Satan showed Jesus, *"all the **kingdoms** of the world...and saith unto him, All these things will I give thee, if thou wilt fall down and worship me."* Note that Jesus didn't dispute Satan's claim. He didn't say, "these kingdoms aren't yours." Rather, Jesus said, *"It is written, thou shalt not tempt the Lord thy God."* Indeed, the Bible calls Satan "prince of this world" or "god of the world." His kingdom is corrupt and evil, but very real.

This explains why our world is so wicked and chaotic. Its systems are ruled by Satan. But this will not last forever. One day, when Jesus returns, Satan will lose his kingdom. But for now, it's thriving.

And finally, there is the Kingdom of Self. We need to understand that God's kingdom is more powerful than Satan's, but Satan's kingdom is more powerful than Self's. That's why Satan wants us to reign as King Self because that's the only kingdom he can defeat.

Why do you think Satan tempted Eve with the promise of *"ye shall be as gods?"* He was telling her, "Eat the fruit. Be like God. Do it your way. Make yourself king!"

The sad thing was that Adam and Eve were already like God. They had been made in His image and likeness, and Satan knew it. From their creation until their fall, they had been clothed in God's glory and that's why they didn't even know they were naked.

We need to understand that if "self" is king it is not under the provision and protection of God's kingdom and becomes easy prey for Satan's takeover. Remember, it is the only kingdom Satan can conquer. God gave us free will. And we can choose whether we want God as King, Satan as King, or Self as King. But if we choose Self, Satan will eventually overthrow our kingdom.

James 4:7 says, *"submit yourselves therefore to God. Resist the devil, and he will flee from you."* Submission to God indicates He is King.

And Joshua 24:15 says, *"choose you this day whom ye will serve."* He was telling the Israelites that they were free to serve other gods (which represents not only Satan's kingdom, but Self's) if that's what they wanted. They had the right to choose, just as we have the right to choose. The biggest obstacle to the Kingdom of God is not the Kingdom of Satan, but the Kingdom of Self.

Now, we go to Israel and her first king, Saul.

King Saul is a type of King Self. As mentioned, prior to Saul, Israel had no earthly king. God was King and ruled over them through the prophets and judges.

1 Samuel 8: 4-7 details how this all changed. *"Then all the elders of Israel gathered themselves together, and came to Samuel* (the prophet) *unto Ramah, And said unto him, Behold, thou art old, and thy sons walk not in thy ways: now make us a king to judge us* **like all the nations***. But the thing displeased Samuel, when they said, Give us a king to judge us.*

And Samuel prayed unto the LORD. And the LORD said unto Samuel, Hearken unto the voice of the people in all that they say unto thee: ***for they have not rejected thee, but they have rejected me, that I should not reign over them.***"

First, notice they wanted to be like other nations when God clearly didn't want that. They were to be His people, set apart in covenant relationship with Him. Deuteronomy 7:6: *"For thou (Israel) art an holy people unto the LORD thy God: the LORD thy God hath chosen thee to be a special people unto himself, above all people that are upon the face of the earth."* Even so, God gave Israel the same free will He gave Adam and Eve, the same free will He gives us, and allowed them to have Saul as king.

Then notice the broken heart of God. His people had rejected Him when all He wanted to do was care for them—to provide for and to protect them—as their King. He also knew the suffering that was in store for Israel because of their decision, a decision which would have far reaching and dire consequences.

This request of the people showed there was already a spiritual decline in Israel. Leaders always reflect what's going on in a society. If you want to know the condition of a society, look at the caliber of its leaders. The people of Israel had already been reigning privately in their own lives, and this desire to be like all the other nations, to have a human king over them instead of God, was just a manifestation of that condition.

It only took Saul two years into his reign before he blundered. What happened? He and his men were gathered in Gilgal, preparing to face the Philistines. The prophet Samuel was supposed to come before the battle to offer sacrifices. When he didn't, many Israelites panicked. Some deserted. Fearing his whole army was going to abandon him, Saul took matters into his own hands and offered a burnt sacrifice to God, something only priests were permitted to do.

When Samuel finally arrived, he said to Saul in 1 Samuel 13: 13-14, *"thou has done foolishly* (by offering the animal sacrifices)*: thou hast not kept the commandment of the LORD thy God, which he commanded thee: for now would the LORD have established thy kingdom upon Israel for ever. But now thy kingdom shall not continue."* God, through Samuel, was telling Saul his kingdom was going to be cut off, that he would be the last in his bloodline to wear the crown.

Saul's next blunder came soon after. In I Samuel 15:3, God commanded Saul to utterly destroy Amalek *"Now go and smite Amalek, and utterly destroy all that they have, and spare them not; but slay both man and woman, infant, and suckling, ox, and sheep, camel and ass."*

Again, Saul disobeyed. In addition to keeping Agag, the Amalek king, alive, he also kept alive the best animals out of fear his soldiers would resent not sharing the spoils of war, a common practice at that time. When Samuel rebuked him, Saul lied and said he had planned to use the animals as a sacrifice to God. Samuel responded in 1 Samuel 15:22, *"Behold, to obey is better than sacrifice."* Then Samuel killed king Agag.

Why is obedience better than sacrifice? Because obedience is the relationship, the interaction between a subject and his king. Whoever we obey is the king. If we obey God's Word, He is King. If we obey our own dictates and desires, then Self is King.

God was not king over Israel or Saul, but Self was. Because Saul disobeyed God, his rightful King, he lost God's favor. After that, Saul's reign continued to go downhill. We see him years later, once again preparing to face the Philistines in battle. We find him worried and anxious because he is unable to hear from God. 1 Samuel 28:6 says, *"And when Saul enquired of the LORD, the LORD answered him not, neither by dreams, nor by U'rim, nor by prophets."* As "King Self" he was on his own, with only his counsel to lean on, and that terrified him.

What was he to do? Left to his own devices, Saul made the worst decision possible. He disguised himself and sought guidance from the witch of Endor. He asked her to conjure up the spirit of Samuel (1 Samuel 28:7-20). Verse 15 says, *"And Samuel said to Saul, Why hast thou disquieted me, to bring me up? And Saul answered, I'm sore distressed; for the Philistines make war against me, and **God is departed from me**, and answereth me no more, either by prophets, nor by dreams: therefore I have called thee, that thou mayest make known unto me what I shall do."*

What a pathetic picture of King Self! From ruling as God's representative, with God's anointing, guidance and help, Saul was now alone and heading for his final degradation by consulting a witch, a practice forbidden by God. Because Saul ruled as King Self, Satan had been tormenting him for years. 1 Samuel 16:14 says, *"But the Spirit of the LORD departed from Saul, and an evil spirit from the LORD troubled him."* While 1 Samuel 16:23 adds, *"And it came to pass, when the evil spirit from God was upon Saul, that David took an harp, and played with his hand: so Saul was refreshed, and was well, and the evil spirit departed from him."*

How miserable Saul must have been! As King Self he had opened himself up to the wiles of the devil and had reaped years of despair and sorrow. Now, with Saul's last act of foolishness, Satan was able to complete the takeover of King Self. And true to form, Satan, the destroyer, did just that. Saul died in the ensuing battle.

God wants to be King over every aspect of our lives. When we accept Jesus as our Savior, it's the first step in setting up God's kingdom within us. After that, we need to make Him Lord. When we do, we make God part of both the big and little things in our lives. That means He is King over our attitudes, our desires, our ambitions, our money, our family, our relationships, our time, our **everything**.

God must be King over all. Remember, a king is the absolute ruler over a kingdom or territory. Jesus said in John 14:30 *"Hereafter I will not talk much with you: for the prince of this world cometh, and hath nothing in me."* Jesus was 100% man. When the temperature dropped, He was cold. When he went too long without food, He was hungry. He also had emotions that could prick His heart and make Him weep. And even though He was also 100% God, He surrendered kingship of His life to God the Father. He continually made statements like: *"I do only what the Father tells me to do. I do nothing without the Father,"* etcetera.

Because Jesus was totally submitted to the Father and obeyed the Father in everything, He could say that Satan had nothing in Him. All His fleshly and soulish (mind) territory were under submission. That's why Jesus tells us to seek first the kingdom of God, and that the kingdom of God in within us, etcetera. That's why the apostle Paul could say everything was dung (manure) compared to Jesus. God was King over his life.

So, if being King Self guarantees us being conquered by King Satan, obviously the smart thing would be to make God King over our lives. And as a King Who loves us, God has precious promises He wants us to inherit. He wants only the best for us; to enable us to stand in times of trouble and live the full life He has planned.

Now, encountering Jesus as King in the Old Testament.

In Genesis 14:18-20 we saw the preincarnate Jesus as the priest after the order of Melchisedec and King of Righteousness and King of Peace offering Abraham bread and wine. We also saw His typology in the Song of Solomon as both King and Bridegroom. But are there other places in the Old Testament that depict Jesus as King either directly or through symbolism or prophesy?

Yes, many.

In 1 Chronicles 17:14, God promised David that his seed would have an eternal throne. This promise is speaking of Jesus, Messiah ben David, whose kingdom will never end. *"But I (God) will settle him in mine house and in my kingdom for ever: and his* **throne** *shall be established for evermore."*

Isaiah 9:6 foretells the birth of Jesus and describes Him this way: *"For unto us a child is born, unto us a son is given: and the* **government** *shall be upon his shoulder: and his name shall be called Wonderful, Counsellor, The mighty God, The everlasting Father, The Prince of Peace."* It's a comprehensive description which has already been discussed, but for our study now, note the phrase, *"the government shall be upon his shoulder."* It indicates God is ruler. Jesus will carry the government of all the earth. It will be solely in His control.

Zechariah 9:9 prophetically speaks of Jesus. *"Rejoice greatly, O daughter of Zion; shout, O daughter of Jerusalem: behold, thy* **King** *cometh unto thee: he is just, and having salvation; lowly, and riding upon an ass, and upon a colt the foal of an ass."*

This prophecy was fulfilled by Jesus when he entered Jerusalem on a donkey. Jesus knew the end was near. Soon He would fulfill His role as the "Lamb of God" and sacrifice His life for all. But before He did, something interesting happened. In Luke 19:30-40 He told his disciples to get a certain donkey with its colt, and then He rode that donkey into Jerusalem. The crowd went wild. People waved palm branches and spread them, as well as their cloaks, on the ground before Him. Palm branches symbolized victory, and waving them was meant to honor kings. By waving their branches and lining the road with them, the people were expressing not only their joy, but their belief that goodness and victory would finally come through this new King. *"Hosanna,"* they shouted. *"Blessed be the **King** that cometh in the name of the Lord: peace in heaven, and glory in the highest"* (Luke 19:38). *"Blessed be the kingdom of our father David, that cometh in the name of the Lord,"* they said in Mark 11:10. They were acknowledging that Jesus was Messiah ben David, the King of Israel. In addition, by riding a donkey into Jerusalem and accepting the people's praises, Jesus, too, acknowledged He was King.

Soon after, Jesus was indeed crowned King—with a crown of thorns. Matthew 27:28-29, *"And they* (the Roman soldiers) *striped him* (Jesus*), and put on him a scarlet robe. And when they had plated a crown of thorns, they put it upon his head, and a reed in his right hand: and they bowed the knee before him, and mocked him, saying, **Hail King of the Jews."***

Notice, in addition to having a crown, Jesus was draped with a scarlet robe. John 19:5 called it a "purple robe," representing the color of the royal robe of a king. I want to stop here and drill down a bit on Jesus' scarlet robe as described in Matthew 27:28. That word scarlet is *kokkinos* in Greek and is an unusual word. It means crimson or red. It's the color of blood. But it also means a kernel of seed, corn, grain. John 7:42 reminds us that Jesus came from the **seed** of David. And in John 12:24 (Amplified), Jesus said, *"I assure you, most solemnly I tell you, Unless a* **grain** *(a seed) of wheat* **falls into the earth and dies**, *it remains (just one grain; it never becomes more but lives) by itself alone. But if it dies, it produces many others and yields a rich harvest."* Hidden in that word, scarlet, is the picture of Jesus, the Son of God, as the Seed, "falling to the earth," shedding his blood and dying for us so that God the Father could have many sons and daughters. Jesus made it possible for a great harvest of believers to share His kingdom forever.

Now, back to Jesus being crowned king. The soldiers crowned Him with thorns, draped Him in a royal-colored robe, gave Him a reed scepter, all to mock Him. They had no idea of the significance of what they were doing. But God did.

It was the month of Nisan. The first of Nisan was considered the New Year for Kings, the day when the calculation of a king's reign began. And Jesus was crowned on Passover, the 15th of Nisan, the very day Israel's kings were coronated. Coincidence? Absolutely not. Jesus, appearing before Pilate and the leaders of Israel as crowned and robed, then presented to the people, fulfilled every requirement of a legal coronation. Unbeknown to them, the soldiers, Pilate, and the elders of Israel were performing an official act.

At His public presentation as King, Pilate even said in John 19:14b, *"Behold your King."* And in John 19:19, Pilate had "JESUS OF NAZARETH THE KING OF THE JEWS" inscribed on a plaque which was nailed to the cross.

And it wasn't unusual for a king to ride a donkey, either. Solomon did it in 1 Kings 1:33 when he rode a mule to Gihon to be anointed by the prophet, Nathan, as king over Israel. It was a sign of humility but also a sign of peace. Kings rode donkeys when coming in peace, and they rode war horses when going into battle.

Israel longed for the prophesied Davidic King to bring peace and righteousness to their land. They were not looking for, nor were they interested in, Messiah ben Joseph, the Suffering Servant. Though Jesus was indeed their King, He first came to suffer, and most of Israel didn't understand that. Even so, John 12:15 says, *"Fear not, daughter of Sion: behold thy **King** cometh, sitting on an ass's colt,"* indicating that though now wasn't the right time for Jesus' Kingdom to be realized, the One sitting on the donkey was indeed their true King and they could hope and rejoice in His future reign.

So, here we see a picture of Jesus, the King of kings, entering Jerusalem in peace; humble and meek and ready to die for each of us. What a picture of the heart and character of God! But there's another side. When Jesus returns, He'll not be riding a donkey. Revelation 19:11-16 tells us that He will be riding a white horse, a war horse, and His vestures will be dipped in blood, *"and on His thigh a name written, KING OF KINGS AND LORD*

OF LORDS." He will not be a King of Peace, but a King coming to do battle with the unsaved of the world. What a contrast to King Jesus in Matthew.

It is a cautionary tale. Let us submit ourselves to our meek, gentle King now, for if we don't, we will eventually be forced to submit to the King whose vesture is dipped in blood.

Psalm 2 talks about the reign of Jesus and how the kings of the earth will try to thwart His rule, but God has the last laugh. Verse 6 says, *"Yet **have** I set my **king** upon my holy hill of Zion."* Notice the word "have." It is past tense, meaning it is done, it is settled in the spiritual realm and when the time is right, nothing can stop it from manifesting in the physical realm.

Then there is Psalm 45 which is all about Jesus' kingdom. Verses 1, 11, and 14 say, *"My heart is inditing a good matter: I speak of the things which I have made touching the **king*** (Jesus): *my tongue is the pen of a ready writer. . . . So shall the **king*** (Jesus) *greatly desire thy beauty* (the beauty of believers): *for he is thy Lord; and worship thou him. . . . She* (the church, the bride of Christ) *shall be brought unto the **king** in raiment of needlework: the virgins her companions that follow her shall be brought unto thee."*

This is talking about the time when Jesus will officiate as both God and King, for not only is He to rule but to be worshipped. He loves his believers and considers them beautiful because they are clothed in His righteousness. And when the rapture occurs, His church, His bride, will be brought to Him and then He will take her to the bridal chamber in heaven. It is a glorious passage, full of promise for those who love Jesus and follow Him.

And Psalm 48:2 goes on to tell us where Jesus will rule. *"Beautiful for situation, the joy of the whole earth, is mount Zion, on the sides of the north, the city of the great **King**."* Jesus, the great King, will rule from Jerusalem, fulfilling the promise God made to David concerning an everlasting throne and kingdom. God keeps His promises. All of them.

Jeremiah 23:5-6 continues the theme of Jesus coming from the line of David. *"Behold, the days come, saith the LORD, that I will raise unto David a righteous Branch, and a **King** shall reign and prosper, and shall execute judgment and justice in the earth. In his days, Judah shall be saved, and Israel shall dwell safely: and this is his name whereby he shall be called, THE LORD OUR RIGHTEOUSNESS."* It is repeated in Jeremiah 33:15. Both Scriptures specifically refer to the end times when Jesus will sit on the throne.

Isaiah 11:1-5 supports this and gives more details. *"And there shall come forth a rod out of the **stem of Jesse** (David's father) and a **Branch** (Jesus is the Branch) shall grow out of his roots: And the spirit of the LORD shall rest upon him, the spirit of wisdom and understanding, the spirit of counsel and might, the spirit of knowledge and of the fear of the LORD. And shall make him of quick understanding in the fear of the LORD; and he shall not judge after the sight of his eyes, neither reprove after the hearing of his ears: But with righteousness shall he judge the poor, and reprove with equity for the meek of* *the earth: and **he shall smite the earth with the rod of his mouth**, and with the breath of his lips shall he slay the wicked."*

Zechariah 3:8b also mentions the "branch." In it, God is speaking about the Messiah and says, *"I will bring forth my servant the **BRANCH**."* God again affirms this in Zechariah 6:12-13.

Notice, it continues the theme that the Messiah and King will come from the line of David. Also notice that Isaiah 11:5 mentions how this king will smite the earth with the rod of his mouth. Revelation 1:16 and 2:16 alluded to this when referring to the *"sword of his (Jesus') mouth,"* and also Revelation 19:15-16 which says, *"And **out of his** (Jesus') **mouth goeth a sharp sword**, that with it he should smite the nations: and he shall rule them with a **rod of iron**: and he treadeth the winepress of the fierceness and wrath of Almighty God. And he hath on his vesture and on his thigh a name written, KING OF KINGS, AND LORD OF LORDS."*

And here's a warning in Isaiah 60:12: *"For the nation and kingdom that will not serve thee (Jesus) shall perish; yea those nations shall be utterly wasted."*

Scripture explains Scripture. There will come a time when the bill is due. And it will be terrifying for those who don't know the Lord and have fought against Him. That's why it's so important to come to Jesus now, while there is still time.

As previously mentioned, Psalm 2:12 refers to this by saying, *"Kiss the Son, lest he be angry, and ye **perish from the way**, when his wrath is kindled but a little. Blessed are all they that put their trust in him."* And just to recap, that word, "kiss" is *nashaq* and means, "to attach, to fasten together." It refers to the custom of kissing a kings' foot to show respect, homage, and obedience. By kissing the foot of a king one fastened or attached himself to that king's rule. The action suggested that person would be a willing and obedient subject. In the same way, we are to attach ourselves to Jesus, acknowledging that He is our king and ruler before we *"perish from the way."*

It's interesting to note that in Luke 7:37-38, when the woman with the alabaster jar came and anointed Jesus' feet, she also kissed them. That word "kissed" means, "kiss earnestly," but it also means, "that which is joined." It's impossible to know if she was kissing Jesus as King. But it is possible to understand that through her actions, she was joining or attaching herself to Him.

And for those who do attach themselves to Jesus, a wonderful future awaits. Daniel 7:18 says, *"But the **saints** of the most High shall take the kingdom, and possess the kingdom for ever, even for ever and ever."* And Daniel 7:27 says, *"And the kingdom and dominion, and the greatness of the kingdom under the whole heaven, shall be given to the people of the **saints** of the most High, whose kingdom is an everlasting kingdom, and all dominions shall serve and obey him* (King Jesus).*"*

Encountering Jesus Throughout the Bible

It couldn't be clearer. Only the saints of God, both Jew and Gentile who have accepted Jesus and follow Him, will inherit the kingdom. Oh, how sad for those left out and consigned to hell for all eternity when God made it so easy to be reconciled to Him through Jesus!

Isaiah 44:6 says, *"Thus saith the LORD the **King** of Israel, and his **redeemer** the LORD of hosts* (Jesus); ***I am the first, and I am the last***; *and beside me there is no God."*

Jesus, the LORD of hosts, is not only redeemer King, but as previously stated in Revelation 1:17 and 22:13, Jesus called Himself the "first and the last."

Jeremiah 48:15 also identifies the Lord of host to be king. *"Moab is spoiled, and gone up out of her cities, and his chosen young men are gone down to the slaughter, saith the **King**, whose **name is the LORD of hosts**."* This exact phrase, *"the King, whose name is the LORD of hosts,"* is repeated in Jeremiah 51:57. Jesus is both the King and Lord of hosts. Here He has decreed Moab's coming fate.

Joseph is a type of Jesus as ruler. Hated by his brothers and sold into slavery, Joseph was destined to rule over Egypt, symbolic of the world. He became second in command under Pharaoh. Like Joseph, Jesus was hated by His Jewish brethren and sold for thirty pieces of silver by one of His own disciples. But also, like Pharaoh who put Joseph in command, God the Father, one day, will hand over earth's rule to Jesus. Also, like Joseph, who took a Gentile bride, so Jesus, after being rejected by His brethren, took a Gentile bride. And when Joseph's brothers came to him and repented, Joseph forgave them and took care of them. In the same way, Jesus will forgive His brethren, the Jews, and care for them.

And last to be mentioned is the scepter in the Book of Esther. Kings carried scepters. It was a symbol of their royal authority. We've already seen that Jacob's prophecy to Judah in Genesis 49:10 declared that *"the **scepter** shall not depart from Judah."* Numbers 24:17 goes on to say, *"there shall come a Star out of Jacob, and a **Sceptre** shall rise out of Israel."* The *"Star out of Jacob"* refers to Jesus and the *"Sceptre"* indicates He will be ruler. In the above two Scriptures that word "sceptre" is *shebet* and means not only a mark of authority, but a rod and staff. And we have already seen Scriptures referring to Jesus carrying both a staff as our Shepherd and a rod as our King.

Psalm 45:6 says, *"Thy throne, O God, is for ever and ever: the **sceptre** of thy kingdom is a right **sceptre**."*

And Hebrews 1:8, speaking about Jesus, says, *"But unto the Son he* (God) *saith, Thy throne, O God, is for ever and ever: a **sceptre** of righteousness is the **sceptre** of thy kingdom."*

Ok, but what does all this have to do with the Book of Esther and Jesus? Let's find out.

Queen Esther of Persia was a secret Jewess who became queen by winning King Ahasuerus' beauty contest. Haman, the viceroy to the king and arch enemy of the Jews, hatched a plot to destroy the Jews living in the vast Persian Empire which stretched from Africa to India to form 127 provinces. Through his scheming, Haman was able to get King Ahasuerus to sign a decree allowing this.

Esther's relative, Mordecai, discovered Haman's plot and told Esther, hoping she would approach the king for a remedy. This was a problem. Once a Persian king issued a decree, it could not be revoked. Plus, according to Esther 4:11, it was risky. *"All the king's servants, and the people of the king's provinces, do know, that whosoever, whether man or woman, shall come unto the king into the **inner court**, who is not called, there is one **law of his to put him to death, except such to whom the king shall hold out the golden sceptre, that he may live.**"* If Esther came before the king without being called and he didn't hold out his scepter to her, she would die.

Esther, knowing this, prayed and fasted before appearing before Ahasuerus. Then this happened in Esther 5:2, *"when the king saw Esther the queen standing in the court, that she obtained **favour** in his sight: and the king held out to Esther the golden sceptre that was in his hand. So Esther drew near, and touched the top of the sceptre."*

Esther lived, the plot was revealed to the king, the remedy given, Mordecai was elevated, Haman and his sons were hanged on the very gallows he had built for Mordecai, and the Jews were not destroyed. This event is remembered and celebrated today during the Jewish festival of Purim.

But here's the nugget relevant to our study. God, the King of Heaven, made a decree that *"the wages of sin"* was death, a decree that could not be revoked. Therefore, anyone who sinned would die. But God came up with a partial remedy, the shedding of innocent blood as a covering for sin which was in effect until His perfect remedy was realized, the death of Jesus on the cross.

King Jesus also has a scepter, a rod and staff, which will not only comfort but bring judgment. And no one is allowed into the inner court, the very Holy of Holies, into heaven itself, without that person obtaining favor from God. And Jesus will not extend His scepter to unbelievers at the great White Throne Judgment thus denying them this needed favor.

But how does one obtain this favor? By believing and accepting Jesus and becoming His bride. Then Jesus lovingly extends His scepter to His bride who can approach Him in safety. How gracious our King is! How merciful! He desires none to perish. He desires to extend His scepter to "whosoever will" come to Him.

Encountering Jesus as King in the New Testament.

Although I've already covered some of the New Testament when discussing the Old because the Scriptures applied or dovetailed, there is still much to see in the New Testament regarding Jesus as King.

First, when the angel Gabriel appeared to Mary and told her she was going to have a son, he went on to name and describe Him in Luke 1:31-32, *"And, behold, thou (Mary) shalt conceive in thy womb, and bring forth a son, and shalt* *call his name JESUS. He shall be great, and shall be called the Son of the Highest: and the Lord God shall give unto him the **throne of his father David**.*" So, before Jesus arrived on earth, He was declared King.

Then, Jesus was born in Bethlehem, the City of David, again foreshadowing Jesus' arrival as the future King of Israel. It's a fulfilment of the prophecy in Micah 5:2 which tells us where this future Messiah, this future King, will be born. *"But thou, Bethlehem Ephratah, though thou be little among the thousands of Judah, yet out of thee shall he come forth unto me that is to be **ruler** of Israel; whose goings forth have been from of old, from everlasting."*

As mentioned, Jesus came from the tribe of Judah. Revelation 5:5 also confirms this when describing the apostle John weeping in heaven because no one was found worthy to open the seven-seal scroll, *"And one of the elders saith unto me* (John), *Weep not: behold the **Lion of the tribe of Juda, the Root of David**, hath prevailed to open the book, and to loose the seven seals thereof."* Remember, according to Jacob's prophecy in Genesis 49:10, the eternal ruler was to come from the tribe of Judah.

And after Jesus was born, He was visited by magi. Mathew 2:1-2 says, *"Now when Jesus was born in Bethlehem of Judea in the days of Herod the king, behold, there came **wise men** from the east to Jerusalem, Saying, Where is he that is born **King of the Jews**? For we have seen his star in the east, and are come to **worship** him."*

Who were these wise men, these magi? And why was their coming to Bethlehem significant? Tradition tells us there were three of them who followed a star to Bethlehem, then presented Jesus with gifts. For the most part it's correct, except the Bible doesn't tell us the number. I suspect the tradition of "three" came about because the Bible mentions three gifts they brought: gold, frankincense, and myrrh; all costly and all prophetic.

So, were these just "smart" men who happened to be looking up at the sky one day and observed something unusual and decided to investigate? No and no. The magi were elite members of a governing class in Persia (modern-day Iran). They were powerful, educated, and extremely wealthy. They knew astronomy and prophecy, even Bible prophecy. They were from a special caste called *Magoi*, from whence the name magi comes, with no connection to magic. But because of their knowledge of astronomy and prophecy, they were considered a mystical priesthood probably with occult powers. They worshipped the elements: fire, water, earth, and air, rather than multiple gods which was more typical of that time. They had great political power that continued throughout several successive empires: Babylon, Medo-Persian, Greek, and Parthian. The *Megistanes*, comprising their upper council, were the kingmakers of the ancient world. Their decisions, even in matters of state, were considered final and binding. No one became king without their approval.

It was during the Babylonian era that the magi became acquainted with the prophet Daniel, a Jewish captive who served more than 70 years in their court and who was greatly respected. Obviously, during this time the magi were exposed to Jewish Scriptures and the writings of the Jewish prophets, including Daniel's, which spoke of a coming Messiah and King, because not long afterward, the magi's religious manifestations began to heavily reflect aspects of Judaism. Since they were well acquainted with Daniel's prophecy of the birth of a Messiah and great King, they continually studied the stars looking for signs of His coming. And when they saw it, they traveled countless miles to lay their treasures before this "promised one" and declare Him "king."

Matthew 2:3 says that Herod and all Jerusalem were "troubled" by their arrival. And no wonder. These were not just three nicely dressed men all alone on camels. Rather, the delegation of the *Magistanes* could have included up to a hundred magi, a large servant staff, and a vast army to protect them. They would have traveled in grandeur and style, necessitating numerous conveyances to carry it all. The sight of this great caravan would have inspired not only awe but fear. There was no way Herod dared lay a finger on them.

These wisemen from the east, these kingmakers, came in great pomp and ceremony to declare Jesus, KING. And their spiritual insight was sufficient that when they saw Jesus, in his humble home as a toddler, they weren't fooled. They still recognized Him for who He was, then gave Him gifts. Matthew 2:11, *"And when they* (the magi)

*were come into the house, they saw the young child with Mary his mother, and fell down, and **worshipped** him: and when they had opened their treasures, they presented unto him gifts; **gold, and frankincense, and myrrh**.*"
Note the order the gifts are listed. First gold, which represents royalty, then frankincense which was used in sacrificial cleansing, and finally, myrrh, a spice used to anoint a body for burial. The gifts say Jesus is King, but they also say He would become a sacrifice and die.

Since Jesus was born in Bethlehem, the place where the lambs for the Temple sacrifice were bred and raised, did the magi understand that Jesus, though He was a King, would be the sacrificial Lamb of God before ruling His kingdom? I don't know. But they did understand and acknowledge that here was a great king, and their presence was a declaration of that fact. And according to their power and authority, this declaration, in the natural, was final and binding. In the Medo-Persian Empire no one became a king unless the magi elected and crowned him, and Herod and all Jerusalem would have known this. Also notice, the magi **worshipped** Jesus.

We know Jesus didn't need the magi to make Him King. He already was/is/will be. But isn't it just like God to confirm His plan and purpose? To use the natural to confirm the spiritual? It was a sign to us, a sign to help us understand who Jesus really is. That is just part of God's goodness and mercy.

Encountering Jesus Throughout the Bible

In Matthew 3:2, John the Baptist declared that, *"the kingdom of heaven is at hand."* The kingdom of heaven was at hand because the Messiah and Israel's King had come. And John's job was to prepare the way for Him.

Jesus also declared that the *"**kingdom** of heaven is at hand"* in Matthew 4:17. And according to Matthew 4:23, *"Jesus went about all Galilee, teaching in their synagogues, and preaching the **gospel of the kingdom**, and healing all manner of sickness and all manner of disease among the people."* Then in the Lord's prayer, Jesus said, in Matthew 6:10, *"Thy **kingdom** come,"* referring to the kingdom of heaven. God has a kingdom, and He wants it to be manifested on earth. Someday, Jesus will return and set up God's kingdom here. But in the meantime, believers in Jesus can experience God's kingdom within them. Jesus said in Luke 17:21b, *"the **kingdom** of God is within you."* It is a kingdom of joy, peace, love, and a bright hope.

In Matthew 6:33, Jesus counsels us to "seek" the kingdom of God, desire it, make it our priority. If we do, what will happen? *"All these things* (the things we need and sometimes the things we want) *shall be added unto you."* How marvelous! We don't need to strive and strain, we just need to put God first, be obedient to His Word and allow His Holy Spirit to change and direct us. That should be a comfort to everyone.

Jesus shared the mysteries of the kingdom of heaven through eight parables in Matthew 13. That number is relevant for eight is the number of new beginnings. And that's exactly what Jesus did for us. He gave us a new beginning, a new opportunity to have peace with God, to have a relationship with Him, the very kind Adam and Eve had before the Fall. I encourage you to read the chapter yourself. I will only list them here:

parable of the sower
parable of the tares and wheat
parable of the grain of mustard seed
parable of leaven
parable of treasure in a field
parable of a merchant seeking pearls
parable of the fishing net
parable of the householder

Jesus is a gracious King.

After Peter proclaimed Jesus to be the Messiah and Son of God, Jesus promised him He would give him, *"the keys of the **kingdom** of heaven."* Matthew 16:19 says, *"I will give unto thee* (Peter and the church) *the **keys of the kingdom of heaven**: and whatsoever thou shalt bind on earth shall be bound in heaven: and whatsoever thou shalt loose on earth shall be loosed in heaven."* This is talking about the authority of every believer, not just Peter. When we take authority in Jesus' name, not even the gates of hell can prevail against us.

When Pilate asked Jesus if He was the king of the Jews, Jesus said He was but then added in John 18:36, *"My **kingdom** is not of this world."* What does that mean. We have already read how the kingdom was at hand, how it was within us, and that Jesus would give His followers the keys to it. But by Jesus' statement in John 18:36, we understand that King Jesus has yet to physically set up His earthly kingdom. That will come after the Tribulation. In the meantime, those who follow Him can experience His kingdom within them through the Holy Spirit, through His fruit and gifts. Romans 14:17 says, *"For the **kingdom** of God is not meat and drink; but righteousness, and peace, and joy in the Holy Ghost."*

Hebrews 12:28 says, *"Wherefore we receiving a **kingdom** which cannot be moved, let us have grace, whereby we may serve God acceptably with reverence and godly fear."*

And James 2:5 says, *"Hath not God chosen the poor of this world rich in faith, and heirs of the **kingdom** which he hath promised to them that love him?"* We don't have to be anyone of note. We don't have to be rich or famous or one of the elites to have a place in God's kingdom. How wonderful is that?

Jesus also said in Luke 22:29, *"I appoint unto you* (His disciples) *a **kingdom**, as my Father hath appointed unto me."* Yes, we, believers in Jesus, will rule and reign with Him and He will give us something exciting to do.

In Matthew 16:28, Jesus prophesied that at least one of His disciples would *"not taste of death, till they see the Son of man coming in his **kingdom**."* How is that possible when all the original disciples have died, and the millennial kingdom has yet to come? Certainly, this prophecy wasn't fulfilled. Yes, it was. After a door was opened and the apostle John was translated to heaven in Revelation

4:1, he was shown a series of future events. One of them was the glorious return of Jesus as King of kings and Lord of lords, to earth. John was the disciple that didn't die until he saw Jesus coming in His kingdom.

Here's what John saw and heard in Revelation 11:15, *"And the seventh angel sounded; and there were great voices in heaven, saying, The kingdoms of this world are become the **kingdoms** of our Lord, and of his Christ; and he shall reign for ever and ever,"* and again this in Revelation 12:10. *"And I (John) heard a loud voice saying in heaven, Now is come salvation, and strength, and the **kingdom** of our God, and the power of his Christ: for the accuser of our brethren (Satan) is cast down, which accused them before our God day and night."* This is a future event. Someday, God will say "ENOUGH," and put an end to Satan's shenanigans and wicked kingdom. And at the end of the Tribulation, Jesus will set up His own wonderful kingdom on earth.

Jesus in Matthew 5:35 calls Jerusalem, *"the city of the great **King**."* It is the site of Jesus' throne in the future millennial kingdom.

In Matthew 27:11 Jesus acknowledged He is the King of the Jews. *"And Jesus stood before the governor: and the governor asked him, saying, Art thou the **King of the Jews**? And Jesus said unto him, **Thou sayest**."*

Others who acknowledged Jesus as King:

Going back to Mary's visitation by the angel Gabriel, he not only described who Jesus was, but also described His kingdom in Luke 1:33b, *"of his **kingdom** there shall be no end."* This is an everlasting kingdom. It will supplant all other kingdoms. No other kingdom will ever emerge again. This is final. It is finished. It is settled.

Nathanael, the apostle, called Jesus, Son of God and King of Israel in John 1:49.

In 1 Timothy 1:17 Paul said this about Jesus, *"Now unto the **King** eternal, immortal, invisible, the only wise God, be honour and glory for ever and ever. Amen."*

Then in 1 Timothy 6:14-15, Paul counsels Timothy to keep the gospel pure *"until the appearing of our Lord Jesus Christ: Which in his times he shall shew, who is the blessed and only Potentate, the **King of kings**, and Lord of lords."*

John, when he was in heaven saw those who had died for Jesus during the Tribulation and said in Revelation 15:3, *"And they* (the martyrs) *sing the song of Moses the servant of God, and the song of the Lamb, saying, Great and marvellous are thy works, Lord God Almighty; just and true are thy ways, thou **King** of saints."* These martyred saints were singing to Jesus, their King.

Revelation 17:14 talks about Jesus overcoming the antichrist and other evil world rulers. *"These* (the antichrist and rulers) *shall make war with the Lamb, and the Lamb shall overcome them: for he is Lord of lords, and **King of kings**: and they that are with him are called, the chosen, and faithful."*

When Jesus returns to rule and reign, Revelation 19:16 says, *"And he (Jesus) hath on his vesture and on his thigh a name written, KING OF KINGS, AND LORD OF LORDS."* And according to Revelation 19:11 Jesus will be riding a white horse. Remember, kings ride horses when going into battle. How different from when Jesus rode into Jerusalem on a donkey, lowly and meek, and willing to be sacrificed. The next time Jesus comes, He will come as a warring king, ready to destroy His enemies and take control of His kingdom.

So, what should our reaction be to our King?

These Scriptures tell us:

Psalm 97:1, *"The LORD reigneth; let the earth **rejoice**; let the multitude of isles **be glad** thereof."*

Psalm 98:6, *"With trumpets and sound of cornet **make a joyful noise** before the LORD, the King."*

Psalm 99:1-3 *"The LORD reigneth; **let the people tremble**: he sitteth between the cherubims; **let the earth be moved**. The LORD is great in Zion; and he is high above all the people. Let them **praise** thy great and terrible name; for it is holy."*

Jeremiah 10:7, *"Who would not **fear** thee, O King of nations? For to thee doth it appertain; forasmuch as among all the wise men of the nations, and in all their kingdoms, there is none like unto thee."*

The above clearly indicates our rightful response to the King of all creation. It should be joyful, worshipful, reverential-fear-inspiring, awe-inspiring, and full of praise. May that be our response to the promise of His coming.

Judge

God was acknowledged as judge over Israel.

God's laws supersede all other laws. He was the lawgiver from the beginning. His heavenly kingdom is ruled by His laws. And when He created Adam and Eve, He imposed one law to be followed in the Garden and we know what happened with that. But it is a lesson. Disobeying God's laws come with consequences. For Adam and Eve, it meant expulsion from paradise and separation from God. And it still means expulsion and separation for mankind without the application of a remedy. As lawgiver, God gave His commandments and statutes to Moses. And when they were disobeyed, Israel understood that God would apply the appropriate judgment.

Daniel 7:10 describes a vision of a heavenly court where God presides as judge and books are consulted. *"A fiery stream issued and came forth from before him* (God's throne)*: thousand thousands ministered unto him, and ten thousand times ten thousand stood before him: the **judgment was set, and the books were opened.**"*

In Leviticus 18:4-5, 26 and 19:37, God affirmed that the laws Moses gave the people were **His** laws. *"Ye shall do*

***my judgments**, and keep **mine ordinances**, to walk therein: I am the LORD your God."*

Numbers 36:13 clarified this further. **"These are the commandments and the judgments, which the LORD commanded** *by the hand of Moses unto the children of Israel in the plains of Moab by Jordan near Jericho."*

Psalm 82:1 says, *"God standeth in the congregation of the mighty; he **judgeth** among the gods."* There is no judge higher than the God of Abraham, Isaac, and Jacob. No matter how powerful a person or supernatural entity, God is judge over them. He is the final authority.

Moses exhorted his people to follow God's commandments and gave the reason in Deuteronomy 4:1, 5. *"Now therefore harken, O Israel, unto the statutes and unto the judgments, which I teach you, for to do them, **that ye may live, and go in and possess the land** which the LORD God of your fathers giveth you. . .. Behold I* (Moses) *have taught you statues and judgments, even as the LORD my God commanded me, that ye should do so in the land whither ye go to possess it."* Moses was telling Israel that if they obeyed God's commands, they would not only live but inherit the promises God had given them, which included possessing the land of Canaan. Moses repeated this in Deuteronomy 4:8, 14, 45; Deuteronomy 5:1; 6:1, 20; 7:11-12; and 8:11.

On his deathbed, David admonished his son, Solomon, in 1 Kings 2:3 to keep God's commandments so that Solomon would *"prosper in all."* God, Himself, in 1 Kings

6:12-13 confirmed this to Solomon. *"Concerning this house* (the Temple) *which thou* (Solomon) *art in building, if thou wilt walk in my statutes, and execute my judgments, and keep all my commandments to walk in them; then will I* (God) *perform my word with thee, which I spake unto David thy father: And I will dwell among the children of Israel, and will not forsake my people Israel."* God's promise was that obedience to His laws would bring success and prosperity to both Solomon and the nation. Conversely, disobedience meant failure and disaster, as seen when Israel came under the rule of evil kings.

In Ezekiel 7:27, God prophesied judgment on sinful Israel, which included captivity. *"The king shall mourn, and the prince shall be clothed with desolation, and the hands of the people of the land shall be troubled: I will do unto them after their way, and according to their deserts will I **judge** them; and they shall know that I am the LORD."* Notice that God's judgment would fall on both the high and low, from the king down to the people. And His judgement would be in direct proportion to their evil deeds.

Ezekiel 16:38 goes into more detail about Israel's judgment. *"And I* (God) *will **judge** thee* (Israel), *as women that break wedlock and shed blood are judged; and I will give thee blood in fury and jealousy."* The phrase, *"as women that break wedlock"* indicates that God considered Israel's sins, adultery. They had broken their covenant with God, which He viewed as a marriage covenant, and become as harlots in His eyes. They had also shed innocent blood by sacrificing their children to Molech, and these acts would arouse His fury.

Nothing has changed. Those who follow other gods such as the gods of money, pleasure, etcetera, and shed innocent blood, will ultimately experience God's fury.

God's judgment is a constant theme in Ezekiel, Isaiah, and Jeremiah. While too numerous to mention, Ezekiel 18:30, 21:30, and 33:20 are good examples. And Isaiah 30:18b says, *"the LORD is a God of **judgment**."* And Jeremiah 11:20 says God, *"**judgest** righteously,"* as does Psalm 96:10, 13 and Psalm 98:9. While Isaiah 33:22 couldn't make it any plainer: *"For the LORD is our **judge**, the LORD is our **lawgiver**, the LORD is our king; he will save us."*

God was acknowledged as judge over individuals.

David called upon God to judge between him and king Saul in 1 Samuel 24:12. *"The LORD **judge** between me (David) and thee (Saul), and the LORD avenge me of thee: but mine hand shall not be upon thee."* That word "judge" is *shaphat* and means, "to judge, pronounce sentence, avenge, to decide a case." Saul repeatedly tried to kill David after David was anointed by God to be king. In the above verse, David was saying God would settle this case between them; that God would avenge him and therefore he would not take matters into his own hands. He would not seize the throne by killing Saul. And in God's proper time, David did indeed reign over Israel.

David was truly a man after God's own heart. His Psalms reflect both a deeply spiritual nature and the understanding of the ways of God. And in the matter of

God being judge, it was no different. In Psalm 7:8 David said, *"The LORD shall **judge** the people: **judge** me, O LORD, according to my righteousness, and according to mine integrity that is in me."* In this verse both *diyn* and *shaphat* are used. *Diyn* means, "to judge, minister judgement, sovereign, controller, owner." And as mentioned, *shaphat* means, "to avenge, to decide a case." David was asking God to be the sovereign judge of his people, Israel, as well as to judge, avenge and decide his own cases. He was also asking God to judge what was in his heart and if he was doing the right thing. David again made this plain when he asked God in Psalm 26:1, 35:24 and 43:1, to "judge" him.

Then Solomon, in Ecclesiastes 3:17 said, *"God shall **judge** the righteous and the wicked: for there is a time there for every purpose and for every work."*

People who hate God and continually do evil are mistaken if they believe they will escape consequences. David said in Psalm 7:11, *"God **judgeth** the righteous, and God is angry with the wicked every day."* A day will come when their evil deeds will be judged, just as surely as the day will come when the righteous will get their rewards. Psalm 58:11 tells us there is a *"reward for the righteous"* because God, *"**judgeth** in the earth."* Imagine that!

Solomon, when dedicating the Temple, acknowledged God as judge in 1 Kings 8:31-32, *"If any man trespass against his neighbour, and an oath be laid upon him to cause him to swear, and the oath come before thine altar in this house* (the Temple): *Then hear thou* (God) *in heaven, and do, and judge thy servants, condemning the wicked, to bring his way upon his head; and justifying the righteous, to give him according to his righteousness."* Like his father, David, Solomon knew God was not only judge of Israel but of individuals, both righteous and unrighteous.

Now, let's look at Job. Hard times were upon him. He had lost his family, his flocks, his health and had to listen to his friends' criticism. But in Job 9:15, he acknowledged God as judge. *"Whom, though I were righteous, yet would I not answer, but I would make supplication to **my judge**."*

And God's judgments are superior to man's judgments. Psalm 19:9b says, *"the **judgments** of the LORD are true and righteous altogether."* And Psalm 119:52 says, *"I remembered thy **judgments** of old, O LORD; and have **comforted** myself."*

Why do God's laws and judgments bring comfort? Because they change not. They are constant. You always know where you stand. Something isn't legal or permissible one day and not the next, unlike human law which can be changeable and inconsistent. Today, abortion isn't legal, tomorrow it is. Today marriage is between one man and one woman, tomorrow it isn't, etcetera.

God was acknowledged as judge over the Gentile nations.

God's laws and judgements went beyond Israel. In Genesis 15, God promised Abraham that his descendants would be as numerous as the stars and that they would inherit the Promised Land of Canaan. God also prophesied of the time when Abraham's descendants would be slaves in Egypt for 400 years. Then He promised this in verse 14, *"And also that **nation** (Egypt), whom they* (Abraham's descendants) *shall serve, will I **judge**: and afterward shall they* (the Israelites) *come out with great substance."* This is speaking of the Exodus and that God would judge those who had abused Abraham's descendants. And Egypt was indeed judged, and Israel left their servitude with great wealth just as God predicted.

But let's dig deeper and look at that word "judge" in Genesis 15:14. It is *diyn* and as previously mentioned, means "to judge, minister judgement, sovereign, controller, owner." The implication is obvious. God is not only judge, but sovereign, the absolute last word. He dictates what the laws are and how He wants them followed. Nothing can circumvent them. No earthly court. Not even if they call themselves the Supreme Court.

Even when interacting with other nations, the Israelites expected God to judge between them and those nations. When Ammon accused Israel of stealing part of their land and wanted to go to war to regain it, Israel's spokesman, Jephthah, denied the theft and reminded the king that after Israel left the captivity of Egypt and while on their way to the Promised Land, they had asked both the king of Ammon and Moab to allow Israel to peacefully cross their territory. But the then Ammonite king, Sihon, refused and fought against Israel. After

Israel won, they took possession of a portion of Sihon's land, which, Jephthah reminded the current king, was common practice in war and something that Ammon also did when they won wars. Then Jephthah said this in Judges 11:27, *"Wherefore I have not sinned against thee, but thou doest me wrong to war against me;* **the LORD the Judge be judge this day** *between the children of Israel and the children of Ammon."*

Here, *shaphat* is again used for "judge." As mentioned, it means "to judge, pronounce sentence, avenge, to decide a case." Jephthah was saying (I paraphrase) "I, Jephthah, speaking for the nation of Israel, have done nothing wrong. But if you insist on warring against me, then God will be the judge. God will pronounce sentence. He will decide the case and avenge Israel."

Despite this warning, the king of Ammon fought Israel. And God did indeed judge. Jephthah conquered twenty Ammonite cities, and Judges 11:33b says, *"Thus the children of Ammon were subdued before the children of Israel."*

1 Samuel 2:10 emphasized this belief that God would be their judge among the nations. They believed their enemies were the Lord's enemies. *"The adversaries of the LORD shall be broken to pieces; out of heaven shall he* (God) *thunder upon them: the LORD shall* **judge** *the ends of the earth; and* **he shall give strength unto his king, and exalt the horn of his anointed.***"* This was meant for Samuel's time but was also prophetic and pointed to the future. Though Israel had many kings, God's true king would

be Jesus, Messiah ben David. He is the King who would have God's strength and be God's true anointed.

In Jeremiah 9:23-24 God said, *"Thus saith the LORD, Let not the **wise man** glory in his wisdom, neither let the **mighty man** glory in his might, let not the **rich man** glory in his riches: But let him that glorieth glory in this, that he understandeth and knoweth me, that I am the LORD which exercise lovingkindness, **judgment**, and righteousness, **in the earth**: for in these things I delight, saith the LORD."* God wanted His people to trust Him, to allow Him to lead them and show them how to live, to show them what pleased Him just as He wants this for all of us. His judgements are superior to man's wisdom, man's power, and man's riches.

In 1 Chronicles 16, David praised and thanked God for His wonderous works and extoled Him as ruler over the earth. In verse 33, he said, *"Then shall the trees of the wood sing out at the presence of the LORD, because he cometh to **judge the earth**."*

Asaph, in Psalm 50:6 said, *"And the heavens shall declare his (God's) righteousness: for God is **judge** himself."* Asaph also said in Psalm 82:8, *"Arise, O God, **judge the earth**: for thou shalt inherit all nations."*

Psalm 67:4 says, *"O let the nations be glad and sing for joy: for thou (God) shalt **judge** the people righteously, **and govern the nations upon earth**."* Often times, earthly justice isn't justice at all. But there will come a day when the righteous judge will sit on the bench and all accounts will come due.

Even Nebuchadnezzar learned the hard way that God was judge over all the earth. When he became prideful, God dealt with him. For seven years he lost his mind and lived like a wild beast. This has been covered, but just to recap, at the end of the seven years, Nebuchadnezzar came to his senses and said in Daniel 4:37, *"Now I Nebuchadnezzar praise and extol and honour the King of heaven, all whose works are truth, and his ways **judgment**: and those that walk in pride he is able to abase."*

God is the ultimate judge. Psalm 119:160 says, *"Thy (God's) word is true from the beginning: and every one of thy righteous **judgments endureth for ever**."* God's Word and judgments will never change. They will stand long after all earthy judges have vanished.

God assigns earthly judges.

Though God judges individuals and nations, He has called for earthly judges to judge on His behalf until the millennial kingdom is established. Leviticus 19:15 describes how they should operate. *"Ye shall do no unrighteousness in **judgment**: thou shalt not respect the person of the poor, nor honour the person of the mighty: but in righteousness shalt thou **judge** thy neighbour."*

Deuteronomy 1:17 continues this theme. Moses reminded his people of God's criteria for proper judgment. *"Ye shall not respect person in judgment; but ye shall hear the small as well as the great: ye shall not be afraid of the face of man;* **for the judgment is God's.**" As judges representing God, they were told they were under God's authority and needed to judge as He would, without prejudice.

King Jehoshaphat of Judah also cautioned earthly judges in 2 Chronicles 19:5-6, "*And he* (Jehoshaphat) *set **judges** in the land throughout all the fenced cities of Judah, city by city. And said to the **judges**, Take heed what ye do: for ye **judge** not for men, but for the LORD, who is with you in the **judgment**.*"

Earthly judges, like God, were to be impartial. They were not to consider someone's condition of poverty or someone's elevated status. Unfortunately, this was and is even now, not always the case. The powerful often escape punishment while the poor rarely do.

In Deuteronomy 1:17, after Moses appointed judges to help him govern the people, he reminded them of what not to do. "*Ye shall not respect persons in **judgment**; but ye shall hear the small as well as the great; ye shall not be afraid of the face of man; for the **judgment** is God's: and the cause that is too hard for you, bring it unto me, and I will hear it.*"

Today our judicial system still follows this pattern, going from lower courts to higher courts and reaching all the way to the Supreme Court. And they are still supposed to function without partiality or fear of man. And Deuteronomy 16:19 adds this: judges are not to take bribes.

Encountering Jesus Throughout the Bible

Regarding Jesus as judge in the Old Testament:

We have seen how God was judge over Israel, over the individual and over all the nations of the earth. We also know that God the Father and Jesus are one (John 10:30) and that to see Jesus is to see the Father (John 14:9). But does the Old Testament specifically allude to Jesus as judge?

Yes.

In Psalm 9:7-8, David said, *"But the LORD shall endure for ever: he hath prepared his **throne for judgment**. And he shall **judge the world** in righteousness, he shall minister **judgment** to the people in uprightness."* This is alluding to Jesus, the righteous judge, who will preside over both the Bema Judgment—the judgment of the saints in heaven after the rapture—and White Throne Judgment—the judgment of unbelievers after the earthly one-thousand-year reign of Jesus.

And in Psalm 10:16-18, David said, *"The LORD is **King** for ever and ever: the heathen are perished out of his land. LORD, thou hast heard the desire of the humble: thou wilt prepare their heart, thou wilt cause thine ear to hear: To **judge** the fatherless and the oppressed, that the man of the earth may no more oppress."* We've already seen that the King is Jesus. It is He who will judge all mankind and this Scripture foresees a time when the *"heathen are perished out of the land,"* a time when Jesus returns as King and Judge, a time when men will no longer oppress one another.

Jeremiah 23:5 is another prophecy about Jesus the coming judge. *"Behold, the days come, saith the LORD, that I will raise unto David a righteous Branch, and a King shall reign and prosper, and shall execute **judgment** and **justice** in the earth."* We have already seen that Jesus is the Branch, the King of kings (Messiah ben David), and now this affirmation that He is the Judge of all the earth. This is repeated in Jeremiah 33:15.

Speaking of Messiah ben David, Isaiah 2:4 said this about His millennial rule, *"And he* (Messiah, Jesus) *shall **judge** among the nations, and shall rebuke many people: and they shall beat their swords into plowshares, and their spears into pruninghooks: nation shall not lift up sword against nation, neither shall they learn war any more."*

Then there's Isaiah 11:1-4 which is all about Jesus. Some of it has been covered before but note the reference to "judge." *"And there shall come forth a rod* (Jesus) *out of the stem of Jesse, and a Branch* (Jesus) *shall grow out of his roots: And the spirit of the LORD shall rest upon him, the spirit of wisdom and understanding, the spirit of counsel and might, the spirit of knowledge and of the fear of the LORD; And shall make him of quick understanding in the fear of the LORD: and he shall not judge after the sight of his eyes, neither reprove after the hearing of his ears: But with righteousness shall he **judge** the poor, and reprove with equity for the meek of the earth: and he shall smite the earth with the rod of his mouth, and with the breath of his lips shall he slay the wicked."* This is no ordinary judge. He will not be fooled by appearances or clever words. He will see the heart. The deeds of those who stand before Him will be laid bare and unable to be justified.

Isaiah 42:1-4 goes even further and prophesies this about Jesus. *"BEHOLD my servant (Jesus), whom I uphold; mine elect, in whom my soul delighteth; I have put my spirit upon him: he shall bring forth **judgment** to the Gentiles. He shall not cry, nor lift up, nor cause his voice to be heard in the street. A bruised reed shall he not break, and the smoking flax shall he not quench: he shall bring forth **judgment** unto truth. He shall not fail nor be discourage, till he have set **judgment** in the earth: and the isles shall wait for his law."*

Isaiah 9:6-7 clearly speaks of the time when Messiah Jesus will come and rule over planet earth. *"For unto us a child is born, unto us a son is given: and the **government** shall be upon his shoulder: and his name shall be called Wonderful, Counsellor, The mighty God, The everlasting Father, The Prince of Peace. Of the increase of his **government** and peace there shall be no end, upon the throne of David, and upon his kingdom, to order it, and to establish it with **judgment** and with **justice** from henceforth even for ever. The zeal of the LORD of hosts will perform this."* No matter how hard the powers of darkness or evil earthly rulers may try to stop it, one day Jesus **will** return and govern everything.

Isaiah 28:15-18 speaks of the last days when Israel will make a covenant of death with the antichrist, and prophesies of the rule and judgment of Jesus. *"Because ye (Israel) have said, We have made a **covenant with death, and with hell** are we at agreement; when the **overflowing scourge** shall pass through, it shall not come unto us: for we* *have made lies our refuge, and under falsehood have we hid ourselves: Therefore thus saith the Lord GOD, Behold I lay in Zion for a foundation a stone, a tried stone, a precious **corner stone**, a sure foundation: he that believeth shall not make haste. **Judgment** also will I lay to the line, and righteousness to the plummet: and the **hail** shall sweep away the refuge of lies, and the water shall overflow the hiding place. And your covenant with death shall be disannulled, and your agreement with hell shall not stand: when the overflowing scourge shall pass through, then ye shall be trodden down by it."*

There's a lot here. As mentioned, in the last days Israel will make a covenant with antichrist, which many will believe to be their Messiah, and will believe he and his evil regime will protect them. But instead of protecting them he will turn on Israel, persecuting and killing many Jews. But God will preserve a remnant and hide them. Where? Many believe it will be in the cliff city of Petra, Jordan, about 150 miles south of Jerusalem.

We already know the corner stone is Jesus. And when He returns, He will destroy the antichrist and his army. But let's dig deeper into some of the other words in the above Scripture.

First, it says that Israel will make this evil covenant because of an "overflowing scourge." What is that exactly? That word "overflowing" is *shataph* and means "to gush, inundate, wash, rinse, engulf." And "scourge" is *shayit* and means "to push forth, to lash, an oar, to row, rowing." So, something pushes Israel forward, as though they were in a boat being rowed by circumstances and they believe their only recourse is to enter into this covenant. But they do so knowing it's a sham, based on a lie. To their dismay, the covenant will not last, and will, in fact, be their undoing. God will judge them for making it, and hail (*barad* in Hebrew) will expose the lies. In the Bible, twenty-two out of the twenty-nine times that hail or *barad* is mentioned it is associated with a plague or a destructive force that comes as a judgment. So, things are not going to go well for Israel. God will take a dim view of this evil covenant, and judge them. Why? Because it shows that Israel, the nation in covenant with God, was counting on the hand of man to save them rather than God. And because they had made a covenant with Satan.

The good news is that while God allows judgment to fall on Israel, He will not only protect their remnant but prepare Israel to become the head of nations.

Joel 3:12 says, *"Let the heathen be wakened, and come up to the valley of Jehoshaphat: for there will I* (Jesus) *sit to **judge** all the heathen round about."* Jehoshaphat means "Yahweh shall judge." This is referring to the battle of Armageddon. It speaks of a time when Jesus will return to judge the nations. And what a terrible time that will be. The Bible says that blood will come up to the horses' bridles!

Micah 4:3 continues the prophecy by saying, *"And he* (Jesus) *shall **judge** among many people, and rebuke strong nations afar off; and they shall beat their swords into plowshares, and their spears into pruninghooks: nation shall* *not lift up a sword against nation, neither shall they learn war any more."* Image! No more wars!

Isaiah 16:5 also prophesied about Jesus. *"And in mercy shall the throne* (the millennial kingdom) *be established: and he* (Jesus) *shall sit upon it in truth in the tabernacle of David, **judging**, and seeking **judgment**, and hasting righteousness."*

Deuteronomy 32:4, speaking of Jesus, the Rock, says, *"He is the Rock, his work is perfect: for all his ways are **judgment**: a God of truth and without iniquity, just and right is he."* Jesus is the perfect judge.

Regarding Jesus as judge in the New Testament:

There are so many references or inferences to Jesus as judge in the New Testament it would take longer than this study to cover them, but we will look at a few.

At first glance it appears that Jesus made contradictory statements regarding His role as judge. In John 5:30, He called Himself a just judge. *"I can of mine own self do nothing: as I hear, **I judge: and my judgment is just**; because I seek not mine own will, but the will of the Father which hath sent me."* And in John 8:26 Jesus said He had *"many things to say and to **judge** of you* (the Jews),*"* thus again establishing Himself as a judge. Yet in John 8:15-16 Jesus said, *"Ye judge after the flesh; **I judge no man**. And yet if I judge, **my judgment is true**: for I am not alone, but I and the Father that sent me."*

What's going on? Is He a just judge or does He judge no one?

In both Scriptures the word "judge" is the same word, "*krino*" and "judgment" is the same word, "*krisis*." *Krino* means, "to distinguish, to decide, condemn, punish, avenge." While *krisis* means, "tribunal, justice, Divine law, accusations, condemnation, damnation." In both Scriptures, Jesus asserts that His judgments are just and true. Yet how does that line up with Jesus saying in John 8:15 that He judges no man?

To understand what's going on, we need to read these Scriptures in context. Prior to Jesus saying He didn't judge anyone, He said, in John 5:22, that *"the Father judgeth no man, but **hath committed all judgment unto the Son**,"* making Jesus the judge of all. Verse 27 adds that the reason the Father made Jesus judge over man was because Jesus became the Son of man. He became one of us even while remaining 100% God. Then in verse 28, Jesus tells us **when** He will act as judge. *"Marvel not at this: for the hour is coming, in the which all that are in the graves shall hear his* (Jesus') *voice."* So, when will Jesus assume His judgeship? It will be during the resurrection after the graves are opened. In other words, Jesus will act as judge after this present age is over. At that time, believers, both living and dead, will be raptured. Then, during the Tribulation He will judge the world. When He returns, He will judge the nations. And finally, He will judge unbelievers at the end of His millennial reign.

Now, we turn again to John 8:15 where Jesus said He judged no man. The scribes and Pharisees had just brought Him a woman caught in adultery. Why wasn't the man there? But I digress. The woman was brought to Jesus in hopes of trapping Him and making Him repudiate the law of Moses. Instead of mentioning the law, Jesus simply said, (I paraphrase), "whoever is without sin should throw the first stone." After that, the people departed, one by one, leaving only the woman and Jesus behind.

When their plan to trap Jesus failed, the Pharisees tried a new tactic by accusing Him of being boastful. Jesus responded by telling them, *"Ye Judge after the flesh; I judge no man. And yet if I judge, my judgment is true: for I am not alone, but I and the Father that sent me."* He was saying that currently He was not the appointed judge, implying that it was not time for Him to act as judge. That would come later, as previously mentioned. He was also saying that if He were to judge, it would be a righteous judgment because He sees the heart and worked in conjunction with God the Father.

In John 8:26, when Jesus said He had *"many things to say and to **judge** of you (the Jews),"* He was preaching in the Temple. Remember, *krino* not only means "condemn, punish, avenge," it also means "to distinguish, to decide." Jesus was in teaching mode and wanted to help them "distinguish and decide" if what they believed was of God, thus preparing them to "distinguish and decide" the validity of the New Covenant.

Jesus also said in John 12:31, *"Now is the **judgment** of this world: now shall the prince of this world be cast out,"* He was talking about the judgement that would soon come when

God the Father would pour out His wrath on Jesus, the sacrificial Lamb. Jesus was saying that God's judgment for sins was at hand, and He, Jesus, would bear the full brunt of it. And not only would Jesus' sacrifice pay for our sins, it would also be the undoing of Satan.

While in John 9:39, Jesus said, *"For **judgment** I am come into this world, that they which see not might see; and that they which see might be made blind."*

What exactly was Jesus saying here? First off, as previously mentioned, the judgment was to come upon Jesus, as the Lamb of God. He was about to take upon Himself the judgment of God the Father for the sins of the world and it would be a harsh judgment. Next, regarding the blind seeing and the seeing being blind, Jesus had just finished healing a blind man. Because the healing took place on the Sabbath, the Pharisees became unhinged and declared He couldn't possibly be of God. The windup was that the blind man saw and accepted Jesus as Messiah, which says that not only his physical but also his spiritual eyes were opened. Not so with the religious crowd. They had physical sight but were spiritually blind. And because they rejected Jesus, they remained spiritually blind.

Romans 5:18 tells us why it was necessary for Jesus to take God's judgment for our sins upon Himself. *"Therefore as by the offence of one* (Adam) ***judgment*** *came upon all men to condemnation; even so by the righteousness of one* (Jesus) *the free gift came upon all men unto justification of life."* Praise God for that!

In John 12:47, Jesus makes this clear when He said, *"if any man hear my words, and believe not, I judge him not: for **I came** not to judge the world but **to save the world**."* Again, Jesus was saying His first coming was only for the purpose of salvation. His officiating as judge will come later.

So, when we see Scriptures that sound confusing or inconsistent, we need to view them in their full context. God never contradicts Himself.

Others who acknowledged Jesus as judge in the New Testament:

When the apostle Peter preached to Cornelius, the centurion, he said in Acts10:42, *"And he (Jesus) commanded us to preach unto the people, and to testify that it is he which was ordained of God to be the **Judge** of quick and dead."* Here, Peter confirmed that it was God the Father, Himself, Who ordained Jesus to be judge. That word "quick" is *zao* in Greek and means life. So, Jesus is judge of both the living and the dead.

In Romans 2:16 Paul said, *"In the day* (at the Great White Throne Judgment) *when God shall **judge** the secrets of men by Jesus Christ according to my gospel."* Paul was indicating that there is an appointed day when Jesus will act as judge and nothing will fool Him. There will be no secrets, nothing hidden. All will be exposed.

Encountering Jesus Throughout the Bible

Paul continued this theme in 1 Corinthians 4:5, *"Therefore judge nothing before the time, until the Lord come, who both will bring to light the hidden things of darkness, and will make manifest the counsels of the hearts: and then shall every man have praise of God."* It will be a scary time for those who don't know God. All their thoughts, words, and deeds will be exposed.

In Acts 17:31, Paul reiterated this when preaching to the Greeks on Mars hill *"Because he (God) hath appointed a day, in the which he will **judge the world** in righteousness **by that man whom he hath ordained**; whereof he hath given assurance unto all men, in that he that **raised him from the dead**."* Obviously, the man God ordained as judge and Who will judge at the appointed time, was Jesus, the Son of man, who was raised from the dead.

Then in 2 Timothy 4:1 Paul said, *"I charge thee (Timothy) therefore before God, and the Lord Jesus Christ, who shall judge the quick and the dead **at his appearing and his kingdom**."* Another confirmation that there is a set time when Jesus will judge all mankind. Note, it mentions there will be two periods of judgments: one **at His appearing** when the church is raptured and refers to the Bema judgment or judgment of believers; the next referring to the time Jesus will prepare to claim **His kingdom**, which includes His opening of the seals in heaven, then the judgment of nations, and finally the White Throne Judgment when all unbelievers will be judged.

Revelation 19:11 says, *"And I (John) saw heaven opened, and behold a white horse; and he (Jesus) that sat upon him was* *called Faithful and True, and in righteousness he doth **judge** and make war."* The apostle John saw into the future when Jesus would return to earth as King and Judge.

Jude 14b-15 quotes Enoch who wrote about the end times and it says this, *"Behold, the Lord cometh with ten thousands of his saints, To execute **judgment upon all**, and to convince all that are **ungodly** among them of all their **ungodly** deeds which they have **ungodly** committed, and of all their hard speeches which **ungodly** sinners have spoken against him (God)."*

Notice the word "ungodly" is used four times. Anything repeated that often should get our attention. In addition, four is the number of earth or earthly things such as the four corners of the earth, the four points of the compass, the four seasons, the four winds, etcetera. This passage is speaking to sinners, to those who refuse to accept Jesus as their Savior, and instead, embrace the evil world and the carnality it offers. This Scripture indicates that the rapture has already occurred. The saints, the believers, have been sequestered in heaven throughout the Tribulation, and at its conclusion, they return with Jesus to rule and reign.

The current role of the saints:

Though Scripture tells us we, the saints, will someday judge alongside Jesus, what is our role now? For the answer, we must turn to Scripture. Let's look at some verses.

In Matthew 7:1-2 Jesus said, *"Judge not, that ye be not judged. For with what judgment ye judge, ye shall be judged: and with what measure ye mete, it shall be measured to you again."* Jesus repeated this in Luke 6:37. *"Judge not, and ye shall not be judged: condemn not, and ye shall not be condemned: forgive, and ye shall be forgiven."* Romans 2:1-3, 14:4 and James 4:12 also continue this theme of not judging others.

Does this mean we are not to make critical assessments about people and situations? Of course not. Otherwise, how could we proceed wisely in this life? But we are not to judge using our own judgment but are to be aided by the Holy Spirit as explained in 1 Corinthians 2:14-16. *"But the natural man receiveth not the things of the Spirit of God: for they are foolishness unto him: neither can he know them, because they are spiritually discerned. But he that is spiritual **judgeth** all things, yet he himself is **judged** of no man. For who hath known the mind of the Lord, that he may instruct him? But we have the mind of Christ."*

So, we can judge and assess people and situations because we are guided by the Holy Spirit and have the mind of Christ. We are to measure their rightness or wrongness by the Word of God. That is the only way to make proper assessments. But we must always rely on the Holy Spirit for we, in the natural, see only the outward while God sees the heart (1 Samuel 16:7).

Even so, we must always be aware of our own shortcomings and prejudices that could and sometimes do, cloud the issue. That's why Jesus said in Matthew 7:4-

5, *"how wilt thou say to thy brother, Let me pull out the mote* (a small speck) *out of thine eye; and behold, a beam is in thine own eye? Thou hypocrite, first cast out the beam out of thine own eye; and then shalt thou see clearly to cast out the mote out of thy brother's eye."*

We should also view those who have fallen into sin with compassion the way Jesus did. And we should also remind ourselves of the martyr, John Bradford's, quote, "There but for the grace of God go I." Without God, there is no sin we are incapable of committing given the right circumstances.

In addition, according to 1 Corinthians 11:31 we must judge ourselves. Again, we do this by comparing our behavior with the Word of God. If it doesn't line up, we need to change. But we do not compare ourselves to others and do not allow others to judge us by their carnal standards or allow them to conform us to their ways or the ways of the world through pressure, intimidation, or shaming. We are to be God-pleasers not people-pleasers.

The future role of the saints.

Eventually, when we are in Jesus' kingdom and have received our glorified bodies, we will officiate as judges. Paul mentioned this after some believers in Corinth brought lawsuits against other believers, lawsuits that were presented before heathen judges. Paul said in 1 Corinthians 6:1-3, *"Dare any of you, having a matter against another, go to law before the unjust, and not before the saints? Do ye not know that* **the saints shall judge the world?** *and* *if the world shall be judged by you, are ye unworthy to judge the smallest matters? Know ye not **that we shall judge angels**? how much more things that pertain to this life?"* Paul was horrified by their behavior. He was telling the Corinthian church (and I paraphrase) "How dare you ask unbelievers to judge matters concerning believers! Wake up! Some day you are going to partner with Jesus, the just judge, in judging the world as well as angels, therefore you should be more than able to judge these petty matters that arise among yourselves."

Revelation 20:4 talks about the saints sitting in judgment. *"And I* (John) *saw thrones, and they* (the saints) *sat upon them, **and judgment was given unto them**."*

Even the Old Testament in Daniel 7:22 claims the saints will judge. In chapter 7, Daniel is speaking of the end times and how the antichrist will make war with the saints, *"Until the Ancient of day come, and **judgment was given to the saints of the most High**; and the time came that the saints possessed the kingdom."* At the end of the age, Jesus will return, and we will possess His kingdom as joint heirs.

Now, let's look at the four judgments that will occur.

2 Corinthians 5:10 says, *"**For we must all appear before the judgment seat of Christ**; that every one may receive the things done in his body, according to that he hath done, whether it be good or bad."* Notice the word "all." That means every human being that every lived, that lives now, or will live in the future will have his/her own court

appearance before Jesus Christ, the judge of all the earth. There are no exceptions. But judgment will happen in four distinct phases: 1) the judgment of believers at the Bema which will begin after the rapture. 2) the judgment of the earth. 3) the judgment of the nations after the battle of Armageddon. And 4) the Great White Throne Judgment of non-believers after Jesus' one-thousand-year reign.

Judgment of the believers:

This takes place after the rapture. Each believer will go before the "Judgment Seat" of Jesus, found in Romans 14:10 and 2 Corinthians 5:10. In Greek that word "seat" is *bema*, and thus it is referred to as the Bema. It is the official seat of Jesus the Judge in heaven. But 1 John 4:17 tells us that we can be bold and unafraid. Why? Because we are in Christ. We have nothing to fear. Our salvation is assured.

So, why must believers appear before Jesus when we are already saved by grace? Why must our works be judged? Paul explained it in 1 Corinthians 3:13-15. *"Every man's work shall be made manifest: for the day shall declare it, because it shall be revealed by fire; and the fire shall try every man's work of what sort it is. If any man's work abide which he hath built thereupon,* **he shall receive a reward***. If any man's work shall be burned, he shall suffer loss: but he himself shall be saved; yet so as by fire."*

Paul is obviously speaking to believers since the passage makes it clear that salvation is not on the line but only the rewards for the works one has done for God. Our works will be tried, and if our motivation is wanting, if we have not obeyed the Lord and instead followed our own inclinations rather than the Holy Spirit's, if we have done a work, even a seemingly good work, out of self-interest, then it will be viewed as "wood, hay and stubble" and burned.

At times I've collected my share of "wood, hay and stubble," while other times I've narrowly escaped doing so. One example was during the season when God specifically impressed upon me to concentrate on three things: His Word, prayer, and writing. At that time, a friend was going through a difficulty and asked me to work with her at a local mission for the summer. After praying, I felt the Lord's permission, so I did. But at the end of the summer, I began begging God to let me stay. I think He got tired of my whining and pleading because He finally came back with a one-word question: *"WHY?"*

I thought long and hard, then came to the realization that my desire to remain working at the mission was birthed out of the good feelings it gave me about myself. I felt like a "real" Christian, and didn't my actions prove it! Sadly, lacking was God Himself. My work was not an act of obedience. Neither was it for His glory but for mine. Fortunately, I corrected my course. If I hadn't, my seemingly good effort would have been nothing more than a bit of stubble.

The Bible tells us that God Himself has prepared the specific good works that He wants each of us to do

(Ephesians 2:10) and that He gives us the will and the ability to do *His* will (Philippians 2:13). Our job is to yield ourselves. And here's the part that blows my mind. After Jesus gives us the will and ability to do His will, after He provides all the grace necessary to do the things He's asked us to do, after He's given us the provision, the ability, the courage, the talents, after He's given us everything required to succeed in our assignment, He rewards us with crowns for actually doing it! Imagine!

Yes, Jesus is planning a big award ceremony and will give us crowns based on our works. So, depending upon what we did for Jesus and the purity of our motives, God will determine what rewards we get, thus the purpose for the Bema judgment. Here's what 2 Timothy 4:8 says. *"Henceforth there is laid up for me a **crown** of righteousness, which the Lord, the righteous judge, shall give me at that day: and not to me only, but unto all them also that love his appearing."*

These will be like the crowns that John saw the elders tossing at Jesus' feet when worshipping in Revelation 4:4, 10, *"And around about the throne were four and twenty seats: and upon the seats I (John) saw four and twenty elders sitting, clothed in white raiment; and they had on their heads **crowns** of gold . . . The four and twenty elders fall down before him that sat on the throne, and worship him that livethth for ever and ever, and cast their **crowns** before the throne."*

And just like these elders, we, too, will cast our crowns before Jesus. Why? Because we know that it was only through His grace and power that we were able to earn them!

Who is like our God?

Judgment of the earth:

This begins when Jesus opens the seven-seal scroll and kicks off the seven-year Tribulation in preparation of claiming what is rightfully His, and cleansing and preparing the earth for His millennial reign. It will be a time of trouble, the likes of which the world has never seen. Characterized by wars, famines, pestilence, heightened demonic activity, the cruel antichrist, and devastating natural disasters, it will kill billions of people. Those who don't die will wish they did. Though the church has been evacuated via the rapture, there will be many who come to Jesus during this time. Yes, Jesus will be with them via His Holy Spirit, but life will be hard. Remember, rain (a good thing) falls on both the just and unjust (Matthew 5:45). But that can also be said of calamity. In addition, God has already decreed that the antichrist will be given power to hunt down and kill believers. We don't know what the future brings or how long or short the time will be before the Tribulation begins. So why wait? NOW is the time to come to Jesus. He is calling your name.

Judgment of the nations:

If Scripture tells us that *"Righteousness exalteth a nation,"* (Proverbs 14:34) and *"Blessed is the nation whose God is the*

LORD," (Psalms 33:12), does that mean the opposite is also true? Does that mean nations that follow unrighteousness and whose god is not the LORD are cursed and brought low? I think so. Can we not point to the world collapsing around us as ample proof?

The Bible tells us these nations will be judged. One of the things they must answer for is how they treated the nation of Israel. Isaiah 34:1-8 is sobering text that speaks about the last days and how the *"indignation of the LORD is upon all nations and his fury upon all their armies."* It goes on to tell us what is going to happen to them. Then the reason for this indignation and fury is revealed in verse 8: *"For it is the day of the LORD's vengeance, and the year of recompences for the controversy of Zion."* That word "controversy" in Hebrew means, "contest, contention, strife," and the nations God is talking about are the Gentile nations. Isaiah 29: 6-8 also explains what will happen to those nations *"that fight against mount Zion."* The Scriptures in both Isaiah 29 and 34 speak of destruction, slaughter, land soaked with blood, stinking carcasses, storms, earthquakes, tempests, huger, and thirst. It is a terrifying picture!

But if that's not plain enough, Zechariah 12:9 says it all in one paragraph, *"And it shall come to pass in that day, that I will seek to destroy all the nations that come against Jerusalem."* That day is the battle of Armageddon when Jesus returns on a white horse.

These are troubling words when you consider how many nations are currently against Israel. It is a cautionary tale of what will happen to them. It should drive us to our knees and cause us to diligently pray for our own nation, as well as the nation of Israel.

Judgment and thrones have already been set as mentioned in Psalm 122:5. *"For there are set thrones of judgment, the thrones of the house of David."* It is done. And it proceeds from the line of David, meaning Jesus, and nothing can change it.

Judgment of Unbelievers:

This is the fourth and last of the judgments, and the one that makes me weep because it doesn't have to be since God made a remedy. Revelation 20:11-12 tells us this judgment will occur after Jesus' one-thousand-year reign on earth and after Satan is released from the bottomless pit and allowed to deceive the world one last time before he's cast into the lake of fire for all eternity. *"And I (John) saw a **great white throne**, and him that sat on it, from whose face the earth and the heaven fled away; and there was found no place for them. And I saw the dead, small and great, stand before God; and the books were opened: and another book was opened, which is the **book of life**: and the dead were judged out of those things which were written in the books, according to their works."*

From previous Scriptures, we know that believers have already been judged, even the believers who died during the Tribulation and who did not worship the beast or take his number (Revelation 20:4). Thus, those at this judgment are unbelievers only. No one will escape. The great as well as the lowly will have their day in court when, according to Revelation 20:13, the dead will be summoned. *"And the sea gave up the dead which were in it; and death and hell delivered up the dead which were in them; and they were judged every man according to his works."*

We must understand that every deed, every thought, every word of every person has been recorded in books kept in heaven. During this Great White Throne Judgment those books will be opened, and each person will come before the Great Judge and give an account. Ecclesiastes 12:14 says, *"For God shall bring every work into judgment, with every secret thing, whether it be good, or whether it be evil."* Nothing will escape Him. All those things people have done in secret, thinking no one would ever find out, will come to light. And those found guilty will be cast into the lake of fire for all eternity.

But found guilty of what? Revelation 20:15 tells us; *"whosoever was not found written in the book of life was cast into the lake of fire."* And that's the thing that sends them into eternal torment—*not being found written in the book of life.*

If that's so, how does one get in? Philippians 4:3 talks about those who are followers of Christ and His gospel and *"whose names are in the **book of life**."* And again, in Luke 10:20 after the disciples bragged about how *"even the devils were subject to them,"* Jesus said this: *"rejoice not, that the spirits are subject unto you; but rather rejoice, because your names are written in heaven* (the book of life)*."* Revelation 21:27 calls it the *"Lamb's book of life."* And there's only one way in. Through Jesus. Those who have rejected Jesus will not be written in that book, and at the White Throne Judgment it will be too late for them to change their minds.

And those who think they will have more than one life and therefore more than one chance to get into heaven should pay heed to Hebrews 9:27, *"it is appointed unto men once to die, but after this the **judgment**."* No, we will not be reincarnated thousands of times until we get it right and become spiritually evolved. We only have one shot at it, one life. Then judgement.

2 Peter 2:4-9 is sobering: *"For if God spared not the angels that sinned, but cast them down to hell, and delivered them into chains of darkness, to be reserved unto judgment; And spared not the old world, but saved Noah the eighth person, a preacher of righteousness, bringing in the flood upon the world of the ungodly; And turning the cities of Sodom and Gomorrah into ashes condemned them with an overthrow, making them an ensample unto those that after should live ungodly; And delivered just Lot, vexed with the filthy conversation of the wicked: (For that righteous man dwelling among them, in seeing and hearing, vexed his righteous soul from day to day with their unlawful deeds;) The Lord knoweth how to deliver the godly out of temptations, and **to reserve the unjust unto the day of judgment to be punished**."*

What this is saying is that if God didn't spare the fallen angels or Noah's world or Sodom and Gomorrah from His judgement, why would anyone think he/she would be spared judgment for their sins? No one will be spared. All will face their day in court.

Psalm 9:16-17, *"The LORD is known by the **judgment** which he executeth: the wicked is snared in the work of his own hands.* ***The wicked shall be turned into hell***, *and all the nations that forget God."* Strong words. But notice that the wicked are undone by their works and go to hell not because God wants them there. Their deeds and rejection of God put them in hell. God desires all to spend eternity with Him in heaven.

Psalm 37:28-31, *"For the LORD loveth judgment, and forsaketh not his saints; they are preserved for ever:* ***but the seed of the wicked shall be cut off****. The righteous shall inherit the land, and dwell therein for ever. The mouth of the righteous speaketh wisdom, and his tongue talketh of judgment. The law of his God is in his heart; none of his steps shall slide."*

The righteous, those who believe in Jesus, will inherit the land. Not so the sinners, the rejecters of Christ. Their lot is eternal damnation. It's the law of reciprocity, the law of sowing and reaping. What these people have sown throughout their life they will now reap (Galatians 6:7).

The difference between them and believers is not that believers have never sinned. It's that believers have obtained forgiveness for their sins because they accepted Jesus as their Savior. Their sins have been confessed and are covered by His blood. Jesus paid for their sins, so believers don't have too. Because non-believers have rejected Jesus, their sins have not been paid for by His blood so they must pay for these sins themselves.

In Revelation 1:17, when the apostle John was in heaven and saw Jesus in all His glory it says this: *"And when I (John) saw him (Jesus), I feel at his feet as dead. And he laid his right hand upon me, saying unto me, Fear not: I am the first and the last."* What a picture! The sight of Jesus glorified was so overpowering that John literally fell to the ground. And oh, how sweet Jesus was! He immediately told John not to fear. Why? Because John was one of His. Those who belong to Jesus will not have to fear when coming face to face with Him.

And that's the tragedy. It's the easiest thing in the world to avoid the White Throne Judgment. God made it so simple according to Acts 16:31, *"Believe on the Lord Jesus Christ and thou shalt be saved."* And the alternative? Hebrews 10:31 says it well, *"It is a fearful thing to fall into the hands of the living God."*

Conclusion:

As seen, Jesus can be found throughout the Bible. Both the Old and New Testament provide evidence of His marvelous character and attributes. His love for us is so deep it's difficult to comprehend. He laid it all down at the cross so we wouldn't have to experience God's wrath and judgment. He desires that none should perish but that everyone be with Him for all eternity. His loving arms are extended to "whosoever will" come, but they will not be extended forever. Now is the time to make this important decision. When Jesus returns as King and Judge, it will be too late. And that return could be sooner than we think.

If you have never asked Jesus to come into your life and wish to do so now, pray this prayer with a sincere heart and welcome Him in.

Sinner's Prayer:

Father God, I come before you in the name of Jesus. I acknowledge that I am a sinner and can't save myself. Forgive me for my sins and for trying to live a life without Jesus. I accept Him now as my Savior. I believe He is Your only begotten Son, that He came to earth in the form of man and died for my sins, that He was buried and rose from the dead on the third day and will come again to rule as King and Judge over the earth. I also want to make Jesus Lord over my life and to serve him all the days of my life. Amen.

If you have prayed this prayer, angels are rejoicing in heaven! The next step is to find a solid Bible-believing church and get connected. Then begin reading this wonderful book we call the Bible.

Love and Blessings,

Sylvia Bambola
sylviabambola45@gmail.com

www.ingramcontent.com/pod-product-compliance
Lightning Source LLC
Chambersburg PA
CBHW060820050426
42453CB00008B/519